Beware the Winner's Curse

Beware the Winner's Curse

• • • • • • •

Victories That Can
Sink You and Your Company

G. Anandalingam and Henry C. Lucas, Jr.

OXFORD
UNIVERSITY PRESS

2004

OXFORD
UNIVERSITY PRESS

Oxford   New York
Auckland   Bangkok   Buenos Aires   Cape Town   Chennai
Dar es Salaam   Delhi   Hong Kong   Istanbul   Karachi   Kolkata
Kuala Lumpur   Madrid   Melbourne   Mexico City   Mumbai   Nairobi
São Paulo   Shanghai   Taipei   Tokyo   Toronto

Copyright © 2004 by Oxford University Press, Inc.

Published by Oxford University Press, Inc.
198 Madison Avenue, New York, New York 10016

www. oup.com

Library of Congress Cataloging-in-Publication Data
Anandalingam, G.
Beware the winner's curse : victories that can sink you and your company /
G. Anandalingam and Henry C. Lucas, Jr.
    p. cm.
Includes bibliographical references and index.
ISBN 0-19-517740-1
1. Consolidation and merger of corporations—Psychological aspects.
I. Lucas, Henry C.   II. Title.
HD2746.5.A53 2004
658.1'62—dc22   2004002987

9 8 7 6 5 4 3 2 1

Printed in the United States of America
on acid-free paper

To our wives,
Deepa and Ellen

• • • Preface

This book grew out of our research and consulting experience in a number of industries that were subject to the Winner's Curse. The plight of telecommunications companies, especially in Europe, that bid in wireless spectrum auctions during the 1990s is well documented. In the zeal to win these licenses, the telecoms overestimated the potential for acquiring customers, paid billions of dollars, and were saddled with an enormous amount of debt in a moribund market. These disastrous spectrum auctions had an impact well beyond the balance sheets of the winning telecom bidders. The winners took on so much debt that they could not afford to build the infrastructure needed for services that use the new spectrum. The failure to build new networks meant that telecom equipment suppliers did not sell networking products, which caused them to lose money and lay off employees. And these events in the United States and Europe affected the global economy as well.

Economists who analyzed some of the Department of the Interior's early oil lease auctions in the Gulf of Mexico first coined the term *Winner's Curse* when they realized that oil companies that won the bidding for oil tracts had the highest estimate of the value of the oil among the bidders, and they could well have paid too much. Given that the winning oil company's owners had to have been the most optimistic, there was a very good chance that they bid more (sometimes *much* more) than the lease was worth. Hence a company that overvalues a good (or service) or over-bids (regardless of its estimation of the good's or service's value) has the potential to experience the Winner's Curse.

As we thought more about the Winner's Curse, it occurred to us that a few extensions to the economist's definition would create a framework for understanding a whole series of disasters in business. This new frame-work helps explain how companies like Tyco, MCI-WorldCom, Bank One, and others overpaid for acquisitions and how shareholders suffered as a result. It can elucidate the disasters that happened during the rush to acquire new technologies and illuminate the reasons that companies that were pioneers in the dot-com era fell by the wayside. Our framework also explains a number of disasters in the entertainment and sports busi-nesses. There are numerous examples in sports where a team offers a lucrative contract to a star player who just had a great season only to find that the player never performs that well again.

Our expanded view of the Winner's Curse can explain why being a winner in any industry makes you a target for all other companies in the industry. When you are the number one team in the country, your oppo-nents play above their potential in an effort to knock off number one. If a company is the unchallenged winner in the marketplace for a long period of time, it becomes complacent and misses threats to its ranking. Between people trying to knock you out of the winner's circle and the threat of complacency, being the long-time winner doesn't look all that great.

We have a number of objectives in writing this book:

1. to help the reader avoid being a victim of the Winner's Curse;
2. to develop the concept of the Winner's Curse into a framework for viewing managerial decisions;
3. to present a number of stories of firms that have experienced the Curse so that we can learn from their mistakes; and
4. to advocate some approaches to decision making that should reduce the chances of encountering the Winner's Curse.

In the first chapter we explore the factors that can lead to the Curse. These fall into two categories: psychological and personal factors and market factors. There are many forces that encourage a decision maker to overvalue an asset and experience the Winner's Curse as a result. The second chapter presents the classic case of the Winner's Curse, the wireless spectrum auctions that devastated the telecommunications industry. While the winning companies had to tighten their belts and lay off people in order to get their finances in order, the national governments of a number of European countries were blessed because revenue from the auctions provided them with an average of 4% of their annual budgets for the year.

Part II of the book looks at how the psychological and market factors in our model promote the Winner's Curse. We begin in chapter 3 by reviewing mergers and acquisitions. Managers in an acquiring firm have to assign a value to an acquisition target and formulate an offer. It is easy to dramatically overvalue a target and to later pay the consequences. In this chapter we see acquiring firms experiencing huge declines in their stock prices, then turning around and selling recent acquisitions for a fraction of what they paid for the target as little as a year before.

The first examples in the book all come from business; chapter 4 takes a look at some other familiar settings where the Winner's Curse can wreak havoc. It is particularly prevalent in the sports arena where teams offer huge contracts to coaches and players based on one or two good seasons. The former star proceeds to turn in a mediocre to substandard performance on the new team.

Chapter 5 shows how the Curse affected firms like Lucent and Nortel as they scrambled to get into the next generation of communications technology. During the heady 1990s, when everyone was excited about technology, it was easy to make multimillion-dollar decisions based on the optimism of technological potential rather than rigorous due diligence. In many cases, the leading equipment vendors ended up winning technology-based companies only to find that the promised products never materialized or there was not a market for these innovations.

In chapter 6 we turn the lens of the Winner's Curse to the dot-com fiasco of the late 1990s and early twenty-first century. We see how the promoters of these companies thought that winning market share quickly was sufficient to thwart competition and emerge as profitable entities. Stock analysts and investment bankers tremendously overvalued the business models for dot-coms. Many of the companies that won financial backing and were first out of the gate ended up expending their resources to develop markets for later entrants. Most of these pioneering companies ended up dying, generating large losses for those who held their shares.

Chapter 7 introduces us to the problems of the long-term winner in the financial services industry. The NASDAQ online securities market was a pioneer and leader in the industry. As the growth of the Internet led to the creation of electronic markets, called ECNs, NASDAQ made only minor improvements in its system. The result was the need to invest more than $100 million in a new system to try and catch up. It is not clear if this investment has come soon enough to stop the erosion in NASDAQ's market share of stock trades. This chapter also describes the New York Stock Exchange's efforts to protect its business model, which includes a physical trading floor and stock specialists.

Chapter 8 examines damaging complacency in the computer industry. We explore the history of two winners that sell computer products, IBM and DEC. IBM let the profits of its mainframe business create a complacency that almost sank the company. Fortunately, a new CEO was able to reorient IBM, and it has survived as a leader in the industry. Investors in DEC were not as fortunate; the founder-chairman was set on a strategy that stressed minicomputers and ignored PCs, which eventually cost him his job. Compaq bought an ailing DEC, and the company has pretty much disappeared since Compaq's merger with Hewlett Packard.

Part III of the book is focused on avoiding the Winner's Curse. In chapter 9 we summarize the evidence we have presented and argue that it demonstrates the prevalence of and danger from our expanded model of the Curse. We also suggest that winning is not everything, that there are times when you should walk away from a deal.

Chapter 10 examines the general factors that encourage the Curse and discusses ways to minimize them. Some of our suggestions require major changes in the behavior of CEOs and members of boards of directors. This chapter also presents some powerful techniques for analyzing decisions that should help reduce the risk of encountering the Winner's Curse, including a systems approach to decision making, scenario analysis, and game theory.

We need to make clear at the outset that this is not a book on economics, psychology, or economic psychology, which has become a hot area of research. Our overall objective is to offer an expanded model of the Winner's Curse as a way to view a series of disasters primarily in business. Armed with knowledge and insights from this analysis, managers should be in a position to make better decisions and to minimize the chances that they will encounter the Winner's Curse.

We would like to acknowledge a number of people whose comments and suggestions on the various drafts of this book really helped to create the final product. We are particularly grateful to Kirsten Sandberg and Hubert Vaz-Nayak for taking the time to read the book carefully and critique it. The chapters on technology were tightened considerably by the suggestions made by "Ari" Arjavalingam. We thank Ritu Agarwal, Corey Angst, Mike Ball, Joe Bonocore, Anil Gupta, W. A. Mahadeva, and M. J. Xavier for comments and questions that helped refine our thinking. Anand acknowledges the research done by a number of students in his class on "Telecommunications Technology and Competitive Strategy" at both the Smith School of Business, University of Maryland, and the Wharton School, University of Pennsylvania.

• • • Contents

1 • • • The Winner's Curse

1 • Origin of the Winner's Curse

"I have $50,000 from the woman in the blue dress," the auctioneer at Sotheby's announced. "Do I hear $60,000?" A short man in a dark blazer nodded to the auctioneer. Mary Ashcroft, the woman in the blue dress, felt the tension rising in the room. "I have $60,000. Is there another bid?" Mary raised her pen, and the auctioneer announced, "$70,000. Do we have $80?" A woman in front raised her hand, and the bid went to $80,000. Mary nodded again, and the auctioneer announced that bidding for the painting had hit $90,000. The man in the blazer raised his hand to indicate $100,000. Mary was getting more anxious because she had agreed on a maximum bid of $100,000 for the painting; she had almost no time to decide whether to stick to that number and drop out or to go above the maximum price she had chosen.

Mary thought to herself, *If I go over $100,000, we might not get the money out of the painting. But I think this artist is about to take off.* Making a split-second decision, Mary raised her hand just as the auctioneer was about to accept the $100,000 bid. "I have $110,000 from the woman in blue," he said. The man in back nodded again, and the price went to $120,000. Mary sighed and raised her hand, and, fortunately for her, at that point the man in the dark blazer stopped bidding; he had reached his limit.

Mary bought the painting for $130,000 spending 30% more than the limit she and her partner, Martin Lockridge, had set before the auction. *Well*, she thought,

> *I've got a little explaining to do to my partner. Martin will understand. After all, it isn't the first time I've done this. It's so hard in the middle of a bidding contest to decide to drop out, especially when I really think the painting would be good for us and the gallery. I know we're supposed to be professionals and know how to value art, but the truth is that a painting is worth what someone is willing to pay for it. I've only had four real disasters where I bid a lot more than we were able to eventually get for the piece, and I'm sure this isn't one of those times.*

She continued to rationalize her bid:

> *Business hasn't been all that good lately; the critics were not too complimentary about our last show. All of those executives getting in trouble and their companies going bankrupt has affected our customers. They're pulling back and not buying as much art. I can't get over what some of the big companies paid for firms they bought and how they had to sell them later at a big loss. It's a good thing that can't happen to us.*

Mary settled up with the cashier, collected her painting, and caught a cab downtown to their gallery to show it to Martin and explain why she had bid over their limit again.

What happened to Mary is not unique. The auction format is designed to create the maximum pressure on buyers to bid for whatever is being sold, whether a precious artwork, an item from someone's attic on eBay, or a government license to operate a wireless communications system. Mary, from her comments, was caught up in the bidding psychology that characterizes the auction environment. She relished the competition and, ultimately, winning the item she wanted. Mary was cheerful and optimistic that even if she overpaid, the gallery would recoup the money invested in the painting when it sells, or through indirect benefits that will come from owning it. She exhibited a sense of invulnerability, recalling that there have only been a few disasters from her overbidding in the past. The major uncertainty here was how Martin would react. Would he agree with Mary's logic, or would he be upset that she bid more than the value they had estimated and agreed upon for the painting before the auction?

Did you ever have a bad day?

Consider how the people involved in the following disasters felt when the magnitude of the problem became clear:

- Tyco bought CIT Financial in 2001 for $9.5 billion and spun it off in 2002 in an initial public offering (IPO) for $4.6 billion, taking a $2.4 billion charge against earnings. Telecom companies paid more than $35 billion in the United Kingdom and nearly $46 billion in Germany for wireless spectrum and found themselves struggling under high debt loads, unable to build the new wireless systems.
- First Union Bank bought the Money Store for $2.1 billion and a few years later closed the business and took a $2.9 billion charge.
- Bristol-Meyers Squibb invested more than $1 billion in ImClone in order to jointly market a drug the latter firm was developing for cancer, called Erbitux. Delays in Food and Drug Administration (FDA) approval and an insider trading scandal at ImClone resulted in BMS writing off $735 million of its investment in 2002.
- After his success with *The Deer Hunter*, studios courted Michael Cimino to make his next movie with them, and United Artists won. Cimino ended up making *Heaven's Gate*, a very expensive movie with no box office appeal that ended up sinking the studio.
- Lucent Technologies paid $4.5 billion in June 2000 to acquire Chromatis and its seemingly revolutionary, but unproven, technology to build optical networks that reached the end user. The promised products never materialized, and Lucent had to close down the business.

What do all of these events have in common with Mary Ashcroft's experience at Sotheby's? In each case, the companies involved competed with other companies to win a deal. However, in the excitement of the competition, and perhaps for other psychological and financial reasons, they ended up paying much more than they had originally valued the purchase. These executives and companies won the bid, but the victory turned out to be short-lived, and the winner was "cursed" from overpaying. The company ended up worse off than if it had walked away from the opportunity.

This book highlights the Winner's Curse in many different industries. In recent years, especially during the last decade of the twentieth century, business decisions were made in a climate of irrational exuberance, and many companies succumbed to the Winner's Curse. This volume takes a deep and nuanced view of the factors which lead to the Winner's Curse and offers suggestions for how to avoid it. We are convinced that if you are aware of this phenomenon and take the steps we have recommended, you can avoid becoming a victim of the Winner's Curse.

Where it all started

Economists who analyzed some of the Department of the Interior's early oil lease auctions in the Gulf of Mexico first coined the term *Winner's Curse*. When the U.S. Department of the Interior auctioned off-shore oil leases in the 1960s and 1970s, petroleum companies were confronted with the problem of deciding how much to bid for them. Each company had to estimate the reserves of oil in each lease site, and it is unlikely that they all had exactly the same seismic data or that they made the same estimates. So we ended up with Atlantic Richfield (ARCO) valuing a tract at a much different price than did Exxon. Clearly the company that won the bid was the most optimistic one. The problem was that the amount of oil underground was fixed, and its value did not depend on what was bid for it. (Economists call this the *common value* auction.) Given that the winning oil company had to have been the most optimistic, there was a good chance that it bid more (sometimes *much* more) than the lease was worth. In bidding for off-shore oil leases, a company that overvalues the oil or in the excitement of the auction bids higher than what it values the lease for, will experience the Winner's Curse.

ARCO's experience in 1967 in bidding for oil tracts initiated the study of the Winner's Curse by economists. Three ARCO engineers looked at the bidding process for several auctions and ran computer simulations of different strategies. Table 1-1 shows bids for a 1967 auction of leases off-shore from Louisiana and of leases in the Santa Barbara Channel in 1968.[1] The high bidder in Louisiana bid an amount that is almost ten times the lowest bid, while in Santa Barbara, the high bid is about seven times the low bid. The estimates of value for the tracts were not

---

1. E. Capen, R. Clapp, and W. Campbell, "Competitive Bidding in High-Risk Situations," *Journal of Petroleum Technology* 23 (June 1971): 641–653.

Table 1-1. Oil lease bids (in millions)

Louisiana (1967)	Santa Barbara (1968)
$32.5	$43.5
17.7	32.1
11.1	18.1
7.1	10.2
5.6	6.3
4.1	
3.3	

Source: E. Capen, R. Clapp, and W. Campbell, "Competetive Bidding in High-Risk Situations," *Journal of Petroleum Technology* 23 (June 1971): 641–653.

even close. Someone was being much too optimistic or much too cautious and risk-averse.

Next, the engineers looked at bids placed by ARCO and Humble Oil Company for Alaskan oil. The two companies were involved in a joint exploration agreement, and each company was thought to have about the same information on oil reserves for the 1969 Alaskan North Slope auctions. In the 55 tracts where the companies were bidding against each other, at one extreme Humble made bids that were 0.03% of Atlantic Richfield's bids, and at the other extreme, Humble bid about 17 times higher than ARCO for a different tract. How could these results happen? Humble and ARCO had to reach considerably different conclusions about the extent of the reserves in each tract and their value, even though the value would have been approximately the same no matter which company extracted the oil. Clearly, by being overly aggressive in order to beat ARCO, Humble was about to succumb to the Winner's Curse.

The value of a painting is personal and intangible, and deciding when to stop bidding is difficult. Overpaying for a painting, especially if one plans to keep it, may not matter that much. Overpaying for something like an oil lease, especially if one is talking about millions of dollars in 1967–1968 (table 1-1) or billions of dollars today, would have significant repercussions for a company and, in a number of cases, a country. The definition of the Winner's Curse in an auction is quite straightforward: the winner has placed too high a value on the asset being auctioned and will soon regret her actions.[2] In general, one runs the risk of encounter-

2. J. Kagel and D. Levin report this phenomenon in *Common Value Auctions and the Winner's Curse* (Princeton, N.J.: Princeton University Press, 2002), 107.

ing the Winner's Curse in any situation where you, and possibly others, are bidding for an asset whose value can only be *estimated* in advance, that is, you cannot be certain ahead of time about the value of the asset. In this book, we extend this definition to many different cases where companies have overestimated an asset, technology, business model, or even an individual in order to win a deal, only to find out that the long-term effects are quite detrimental.[3]

Winning one for the coach

Paying much more than a common value is certainly not limited to auctions; it can happen anyplace where there is uncertainty about value or future performance. Athletics offers a lot of opportunities for the Curse. When a coach or player has a great season, many teams will compete for his services. The team that wins is usually the one willing to offer the best contract. But we all know that past success is no guarantee of future performance. Unless one is willing to take the big risk of future performance into account before offering a lucrative contract or else include performance-based bonuses in the contract, the end result is likely to be the Winner's Curse.

The Curse seems to happen a lot to winners of the Heisman Trophy, the prize given annually to the best college football player. The trophy is said to bring fame and glory to the college as well as the player. When a student athlete is in the running to win the Heisman Trophy, his coaches generally design plays to improve his statistics. Very few Heisman winners do well in the professional ranks of the National Football League, however. Of the 67 Heisman winners through 2003, only 7 are in the Pro Football Hall of Fame. For every Heisman Trophy winner like Ricky Williams (Texas) and Charles Woodson (Michigan) who make it, there are many winning college football players who do not make it in the pros. The list of cursed winners includes Chris Weinke, Ron Dayne, Danny Wuerffel, Charlie Ward, Gino Torretta, and Rashan Salaam. Heisman Trophy winners tend to be offensive players, and professional defensive players target them mercilessly when they come into the NFL. It is said that Heisman Trophy winners get "special" treatment in the professional

---

3. A reviewer of this manuscript suggested that the Winner's Curse may also apply to reverse auctions. These auctions are generally business-to-business and are conducted on the Internet. It is likely that the firms bidding to sell a product to a company using the auction end up selling at too low a price to cover their costs.

field to counterbalance the preferential treatment they got in college. It is no wonder that few Heisman Trophy winners last long in the NFL. The biggest bust as a Heisman Trophy winner was probably Archie Griffin (Ohio State), who won it twice and did not make it in the pro ranks.

Another example is the deal simply referred to as "The Trade," which took place on October 12, 1989. Minnesota Vikings general manager Mike Lynn thought the team was only a big-time running back away from winning it all. He overpaid to acquire the famed Herschel Walker from the Dallas Cowboys for five Vikings roster players and six assorted draft picks. Trading away so many players decimated the Super Bowl–caliber Vikings squad. The Cowboys, perennial losers at the time, used the trade to build a two-time Super Bowl championship team. Herschel Walker was a great running back and led the National Football League in rushing in 1988. However, the Vikings paid too high a price to win him away from other teams, and they were cursed to not even make the playoffs for years after that. Walker never had a 1,000-yard season while with the Minnesota Vikings.

Football is not alone in encountering the Winner's Curse. In 1992 the Philadelphia Flyers and the New York Rangers entered a bidding war to acquire Eric Lindros, a talented center who had been drafted by the Quebec Nordiques. In the end, the Flyers won by handing over Peter Forsberg, Steve Duchesne, Kerry Huffman, Mike Ricci, Chris Simon, Jocelyn Thibault, and a pile of cash rumored to be in the neighborhood of $16 million to acquire Lindros. The following years saw the Flyers drop in the rankings to fifth and sixth positions in their National Hockey League division. They did manage to get to the Stanley Cup finals in 1997 while Lindros was with the team. He was eventually let go, and he signed with the New York Rangers. The Quebec Nordiques, however, really prospered. They moved to Colorado and were renamed the Avalanche. The Colorado Avalanche won the Stanley Cup in 1996 and 2001 with Forsberg and Chris Simon playing starring roles. As of 2003, Forsberg was widely considered to be one of the top five players in the National Hockey League.

Let's go buy something

American companies have a culture of growing at any cost. If you look at annual reports, the letters from chief executive officers (CEOs) focus on growth in sales, earnings, and profits. There are a variety of ways to grow; for example, a firm can expand the sale of existing products or introduce new products into the marketplace. Another way to grow, and to grow quickly, is to merge with or acquire another company. Mergers are popular with managers, and many mergers turn out to benefit shareholders. However, establishing the value for an acquisition is a difficult task, and it is easy to get into a situation where you pay far too much and later experience the Winner's Curse.

Merger seemed to be the theme of the late 1990s: almost $4 trillion of mergers took place from 1998 through 2000, more than in the preceding 30 years. In April 1998, Sandy Weill's Travelers Group announced a $70 billion merger with Citicorp. The next day, the insurance company Conseco announced it would buy mobile-home lender Green Tree Financial. The Monday after that, Bank One offered $28.8 billion for First Chicago, and NationsBank offered $59.3 billion for Bank America. A few weeks later, Daimler Benz picked up Chrysler for $38.6 billion.

Citigroup has been extremely successful, and its shareholders have done very well. On the other hand, Conseco's shares lost 47% of their value the year after it purchased Green Tree, and the company has been in financial distress ever since.[4] The Daimler-Chrysler merger has generally been acknowledged as a failure, with Chrysler experiencing heavy losses and Daimler finding the quality of the cars in its Mercedes group dropping.

There are a number of different kinds of mergers; some observers distinguish between mergers with a similar firm in the same kind of business and mergers with firms in a completely different market. A firm buys another in its line of business to get more market power, to acquire access to a new product line, or even to bring in new employees. Travelers' merger with Citibank provided a financial supermarket with products and services in insurance, banking, and brokerage. A manager might favor a merger with a different kind of company as a way to reduce risk. If the firms are in unrelated businesses, then a downturn in one sector of the economy will have less impact on the entire company. If a company builds itself through the purchase of unrelated businesses, it becomes a conglomerate like Textron many years ago and Tyco today.

How does a company approach merger or acquisition? There are many different stories about how firms have gotten together. Sometimes CEOs approach each other thinking that there might be a good fit between two companies, which is evidently what happened with Compaq and Hewlett

4. *Business Week*, October 14, 2002.

Packard. In most cases, a conglomerate has a staff whose sole function is identifying possible acquisitions. Large conglomerates such as General Electric and Tyco have been known to buy dozens of companies in a year. Some firms go to investment bankers to look for a company with which to merge or to sell their business to an acquirer.

How do these conglomerates put a price on a company? If they are buying a publicly traded company, the price is going to be related to the stock price, as they have to convince shareholders to sell. One possible measure of value is the market capitalization of a firm, which is the total value of all stock outstanding. There is also the book value of the firm, which is reflected in its accounting records, a value that is usually lower than its market value. There are many private companies for which there are no real market values. Investment bankers and others have procedures for estimating the value of a company, and there are many books and articles on the subject. The one thing that is clear is that a potential buyer has to estimate a value; there is no price tag here.

If you read about mergers, you have probably noticed that there is often bidding. Even in cases where only two firms are involved—the company interested in the acquisition and the target company—there could be many rounds of price negotiations. Most often the buying firm makes an offer, and the firm being acquired rejects it as too low. The two companies spar a bit in the press, and finally the buyer makes a "sweetened" offer, which the firm to be acquired accepts. Sometimes the action gets more interesting when a third company enters the bidding for the firm to be acquired, especially when the third company is a "white knight," rescuing the firm being acquired from an unwanted suitor.

There are a number of reasons for the valuation problem in mergers. There is the classic issue of trying to get sufficient information to perform due diligence in an acquisition. It is hard for the firms involved to learn about all aspects of each other's business. The competitive natures of managers and of businesses encourage the acquirer to continue after an acquisition target, even after the price has risen above what it planned to pay originally. Managerial optimism and hubris play parts as well; what manager does not want to be CEO of a larger company with more revenue? The manager's compensation may be based in part on growth in the stock price, which is what the CEO expects will happen after the merger. A manager with a string of successful acquisitions may also feel a sense of invulnerability; after all, the company has a long history of victories. Added to these forces that encourage the manager to acquire are market factors like the pressures from stock analysts and shareholders for growth. Investment bankers also encourage acquisitions because a significant part of their revenues comes from advising companies in merger negotiations.

It is little wonder that the acquisition process is biased to overvalue the target company. The acquiring company often wins its target, but at a price that it may soon regret.

The Winner's Curse defined

Figure 1-1 provides a succinct illustration of the Winner's Curse. The manager views the outcome of winning more positively than is likely to be the case. In the auction, the winner has overpaid for the value or utility of the good to him. In sports, star athletes are often paid much more than their eventual value to the team. In the case of the merger, the manager is overly optimistic about the value of the company or technology being acquired and also of the future of the merged companies. To realize full value, all aspects of the merger must go right, and this is rarely the

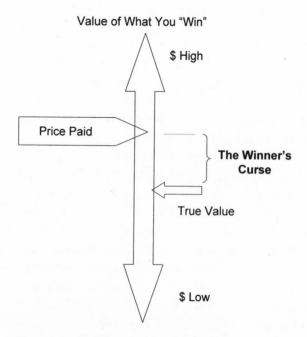

Figure 1-1. The Winner's Curse illustrated

outcome. The major point of this book is that we need to be aware of the Winner's Curse in many business decisions and find ways to avoid it.[5]

What forces promote the Curse?

Based on our research, we have tried to identify the most important forces that encourage business decision makers to overvalue a deal. These forces emerged from the examples contained in the rest of the book, and they fit into two major categories. The first of these we call *psychological and personal factors*, which are forces that come from within the individual or the nature of the organization. The second category of forces, *market factors*, is largely external to the decision maker. See table 1-2.

Psychological and personal factors

Many years ago, an antique car collector warned one of the authors to avoid buying a car at auction, saying, "You have this beautiful car sitting in front of you that you want to buy, and you go crazy with the excitement of bidding, forgetting what it's worth." There is a well-known tendency for people to get caught up in the excitement of an auction, finding it easier, as Mary Ashcroft did, to keep raising their bid rather than withdraw from the auction. We call this force *buying and bidding psychology*, and it is something that the auctioneer counts on to drive up prices.

"Winning isn't everything; it's the only thing," according to the great football coach Vince Lombardi. Western societies, especially the United States, are infused with competition and winning. All you have to do is look at the prominence of athletics in the United States and the revenues associated with sports at all levels to observe our competitive focus. The winners of the World Series or the Super Bowl are far more likely to receive an invitation to visit the White House than a prize-winning scientist and her laboratory team. The managerial focus on winning is responsible for a large number of instances of the Winner's Curse, especially in mergers and acquisitions.

There is a culture in different organizations; the feeling inside a high-tech firm is different from the feeling in a grocery chain. Regulated

---

5. We want to distinguish between the Winner's Curse, which results from mis-estimating the value of an asset, and a good decision that leads to a poor outcome in an uncertain world. The decision maker in the case of the Winner's Curse is led into a poor decision through a flawed process of assigning value to a desired asset.

Table 1-2. Factors that encourage the Winner's Curse

Psychological and Personal Factors
   Buying and bidding psychology
   Competition and winning
   Organizational culture
   Managerial optimism
   Hubris
   Compensation
   Invulnerability

Market Factors
   Pressures for growth
   Investment bankers
   Stock analysts
   Stock price
   Unrealistic business models

monopolies rely on rules and procedures, and employees value job security highly. A brokerage firm is different; the emphasis is on encouraging customers to buy and sell securities and to keep their assets with the firm. Some of the companies discussed later as "serial acquirers," firms that buy large numbers of other firms, exhibit an aggressive focus on growth. The culture of the organization can encourage managers to buy (win) a prize, increasing the size of the Winner's Curse.

A CEO once told one of the authors that "it is better to be a pessimist because you won't be disappointed so often." Most managers do not hold to this CEO's advice and are eternally optimistic. If it were not for optimism, would there be any innovation? It takes optimism to start a new company and to launch new products and services. However, managerial optimism can exacerbate the Winner's Curse when a manager is overly optimistic about the expected results of a purchase. Managers often overestimate the benefits that will come from a merger or acquisition, only realizing after consummating the deal that there are problems in realizing anticipated benefits.

The next factor in the psychology category is hubris, which is defined as exaggerated pride or self-confidence. Pride comes before a fall, and hubris is responsible for many a managerial misstep. The manager with too much self-confidence does not listen to others and is sure that her decision on value is the right one. Hubris encourages a manager to overpay for an acquisition and to persist in seeking an acquisition after it is clear to everyone else that it does not make sense to proceed.

What is the role of compensation in the Winner's Curse? The first way that compensation affects the Curse is by contributing to the manager's sense of confidence, power, and invulnerability. CEO salaries in the United States exploded in the 1990s, with senior managers making tens of millions of dollars annually in salary and bonuses, especially through stock options. The second impact of compensation is the incentive it provides for growth. Managers of large firms tend to make more money and the public views them as more important than the CEOs of small firms. Compensation encourages a manager to overpay for goods, services, and acquisitions in order to increase the size of the firm and justify a large salary package.

All of the forces that make senior managers feel powerful—compensation, perquisites, a string of victories, strong corporate growth, and the competitive spirit—can lead to feelings of invulnerability. When this happens, the manager is less likely to listen to disconfirming opinions or to pay attention to evidence that does not agree with her position. The manager who sees herself as invulnerable is likely to overvalue something that she wants to acquire, be it wireless spectrum, an oil lease, or another company.

Market factors

Market factors come from outside the company and can have a dramatic impact on how managers value goods, services, and acquisitions. Market forces certainly contributed to some of the embarrassing and disastrous CEO behavior that surfaced in 2002.

The first of these factors is pressure for companies to grow *quickly*. A significant part of CEO compensation in most companies is based on stocks and stock options. Wall Street rewards companies for rapid growth and punishes them for both slow growth and growth rates not matching expectations. Thus, CEOs have an incentive to grow companies quickly, either *organically* from trying to expand internal resources, or *externally* through acquisitions. Market-generated pressure for rapid growth encourages the CEO to overvalue target firms.

Investment bankers involved in mergers and acquisitions (M&A) also have market incentives to overvalue acquisitions. Investment bankers earn fees from underwriting stocks and from consulting in M&A activities. The investment banker is often retained to estimate the value of the acquisition as part of the due diligence process that an acquiring company must perform. By setting the value high, the investment banker helps to justify the high price that the acquiring company is paying. If it turns out later that the transaction led to the Winner's Curse, it is rare for the investment banker to be blamed; instead, the reasons given are usually problems related to integrating the new acquisition with the acquiring firm.

Stock analysts also contribute to companies' experiencing the Winner's Curse. Analysts have been known to write highly favorable reports on companies for reasons that are not entirely objective. Analysts are under pressure to produce overly optimistic reports in order to please the company's CEO so that the analysts' firms will receive the company's investment banking business. The incentive for analysts to drive initial public offerings to their own investment banks leads them to overvalue privately held technology firms and place a premium on them when they become acquisition targets. Such overoptimistic reports contribute to the Winner's Curse for the investor or buyer.

The dot-com era is littered with companies that had unrealistic business models. These firms were able to win investors and venture capitalists, who failed to determine if the underlying business model made any sense. It is clear in retrospect that the investors paid too much for their position in some of these companies, and they have experienced the Winner's Curse as a result.

How the forces apply

Table 1-3 presents the factors associated with the Curse arrayed against the examples described earlier in the chapter. The table suggests which forces were working in each instance. Not all forces apply in every situation; Mary Ashcroft and the football player are not as subject to external market forces as are oil companies and a conglomerate that acquires other firms. The acquiring firm in a merger will face all of the factors that can lead to the Winner's Curse, which may be why so many acquisitions seem to suffer from it.

It should be noted that recent trends encouraged by developing technologies like the Internet are likely to exacerbate the problems of the Winner's Curse. Firms have access to more global markets and suppliers, and information about potential acquisitions is readily available. Increasing globalization and outsourcing of key operations means that managers are faced with valuation decisions in many different countries.

Table 1-3. Reasons for overvaluing a deal

Force	Auction at Sotheby's	Auction for Oil Leases	Competition for Football Players	Business Acquisitions
Psychological and Personal Factors				
Buying and bidding psychology	X	X	X	X
Competition and winning	X	X	X	X
Organizational culture		X	X	X
Managerial optimism	X	X	X	X
Hubris	X	X		X
Compensation		X		X
Invulnerability		X	X	X
Market Factors				
Pressure for growth		X	X	X
Investment bankers		X		X
Stock analysts				X
Stock price				X
Unrealistic business models				X

The opportunities to encounter the Winner's Curse are expanding every day.

In addition to the first observations of the Winner's Curse in the off-shore oil lease auctions, there have been two books published, which treat the subject in different ways. Richard Thaler explores the Winner's Curse and other economic anomalies in a 1992 collection of academic articles.[6] His approach is grounded heavily in economics as well as individual psychology, which is responsible for some of the instances in which people do not behave as economic models predict. The book offers a good introduction to behavioral economics and to game theory. The other book, by Ferris and Pecherot Pettit, is a text on how to do valuations, especially for mergers and acquisitions.[7] It should be of interest to someone trying to value a company for any reason.

What's next

This chapter presented a series of examples to introduce the Winner's Curse and to describe the factors that encourage managers and others to

---

6. Richard Thaler, *The Winner's Curse: Paradoxes and Anomalies of Economic Life* (New York: Free Press, 1994).

7. K. Ferris and B. Pecherot Pettit, *Valuation: Avoiding the Winner's Curse* (Upper Saddle River, N.J.: Financial Times/Prentice Hall, 2002).

overvalue goods and services that do not have an obvious market price. The next chapter looks at the disastrous government auctions for wireless spectrum, auctions which we believe have contributed to the depression in the telecommunications industry. The global spectrum auctions are an example of the purest form of the Winner's Curse and provide a starting point for our investigation of other industries.

Part II of the book presents a number of examples of the Winner's Curse, and analyzes them using the factors in table 1-2. We begin with mergers and acquisitions, a field with great opportunity to encounter the Curse. Chapter 4 examines how the Winner's Curse extends beyond auctions to licensing fees for a cancer-fighting drug and lucrative contracts for a football coach. Chapter 5 looks at the optical networking industry, which experienced a frenzy of purchases as established telecommunications companies bought, and overpaid, for hundreds of start-ups. Chapter 6 reviews the failure of dot-coms through the lens of the Winner's Curse. Chapter 7 focuses on the securities industry. We examine how electronic brokerages attacked the established winners in the industry. Chapter 8 discusses the complacency of winning firms, in this case IBM and DEC. When new technologies threatened their markets, the CEOs of these firms suffered from their organizations' culture and hubris, among other problems, and did not respond fast enough.

The last section of the book is devoted to avoiding the Winner's Curse. Not every business deal results in the Curse, but the potential is present in enough cases that a wise decision maker keeps the possibility of the Curse in mind. In chapter 9 we discuss why winning is not everything and what conditions make us particularly susceptible to the Curse. In addition to the psychological and personal factors and market forces, our examples reveal additional factors that lead to the Curse. These include some personality traits of managers, particularly CEOs, aspects of decision-making psychology, and the interaction of market and financial incentives.

In chapter 10, we discuss approaches to avoiding the Winner's Curse and improving valuation decisions. To avoid the Curse, you need to curb the imperial CEO by creating a truly independent board that protects decision rights and enforces good governance practices. We offer a number of suggestions to reduce the hubris of the CEO and senior management; it is also important to look for a consensus on valuation decisions and to always seek a second opinion. The Securities and Exchange Commission (SEC) and others also need to find ways to reduce the conflict of interest that exists in the securities industry.

To improve valuation decisions, chapter 10 advocates adopting a systems approach to decision making, where a manager tries to identify cause-and-effect relationships. We also describe the use of scenarios to help understand the impact of making a purchase by looking at different possible outcomes. Finally, a company can employ an analysis approach called *game theory* to analyze decisions through the eyes of its competitors and to reassess its assumptions about decisions. You can use some or all of these suggestions to reduce the chances of encountering the Winner's Curse when making important decisions about the value of an asset where there is no agreed-upon price.

Our book presents a lot of evidence to convince you to beware of the Winner's Curse. It is easy to experience the Curse when bidding for a painting, a license, or another company. The Curse happens in a lot of places, ranging from Hollywood to the athletic field. The same factors that lead people to experience the Winner's Curse also contribute to a dangerous complacency in a firm at the top of its industry. There *are* ways to avoid the Winner's Curse: you can do a better job of determining the value of what you want to buy, and you can learn to walk away, to stop yourself from buying again.

2 • The spectrum auction fiasco

In 2000, the governments of several European countries auctioned licenses to telecommunications companies that planned to use the airwaves to provide third-generation wireless services. A new standard called UMTS (universal mobile telecommunications system) was expected to revolutionize wireless communications by using higher transmission rates, up to 200 times faster than the existing European GSM (Global System for Mobile Communications) standard. This new capacity would support an abundance of new services, including hotel and airline reservations; virtual banking; Internet access 24 hours a day, seven days a week; audio and video services on demand; and video conferencing on handheld wireless devices.

The first-generation mobile services, developed in the late 1980s, were built on wireless networks similar to the communications systems used by the military. The network was based on a system of communications towers, each of which handled callers from the area surrounding the tower. This area was divided into smaller parts called "cells," and thus the term *cell phone* came into being for this device, which was used to communicate without wires. In order to transmit the calls through the air, the telephone companies in the United States and other countries needed a license from the government, very much like FM radio stations need a license to broadcast entertainment through the airwaves. The governments in almost all countries charged for these licenses.

The second generation of wireless services, introduced in the mid-1990s, were true digital systems, communicating through a series of zeros and ones. The second generation provided voice services with some value-added services like voice mail, call waiting, call forwarding, directory services, and some text messaging. The third wireless generation (or 3G) was going to allow voice, data, and video services to be carried on a network.

In order to provide the state-of-the-art wireless third-generation networks, the telecom companies had to build and market new services, all of which would be costly. Because the new technology works at a much higher frequency than the European GSM standard, the physics of the system dictated that the range of each base station (that is, the towers with their antennas) would be much smaller than with GSM stations.

To make these third-generation networks operate seamlessly, a company would require 4–16 times as many base stations as current networks. Even though it was widely believed that the infrastructure to provide the new state-of-the-art services would be expensive, the UMTS license auctions generated an unsurpassed amount of revenue for governments.

The U.K. experience

The best example of the Winner's Curse occurred on April 27, 2000, in the government offices in central London where the U.K. government auctioned off five licenses for third-generation (commonly called 3G) wireless spectrum, originally attracting 13 bidders. In the largest auction in history, nine companies competed for 150 rounds and generated $35 billion in revenue for the British government. Four wireless incumbents—British Telecom, Vodafone, Orange, and One2One—each won a license, as did a new entrant, TIW. As Chris Anderson described it in a *Wired* magazine column in May 2002, "Bureaucrats fell over themselves with joy, economists toasted the success of auction theory, and British taxpayers celebrated the historic transfer of wealth to the public purse." Over the next year, a number of other European countries auctioned off UMTS licenses for 3G mobile wireless services, raising a whopping $100 billion for the exchequers of the respective governments.

In the U.K. auction, Vodafone's successful bid for one license was $9.5 billion, which translated to $160 per person. The other winners paid license fees that were roughly the same on a per person basis. The 1995 spectrum auction conducted by the U.S. Federal Communications Commission (FCC) netted $15.50 per person, less than one-tenth of the U.K. price. If this price is considered to be out of date after five years, consider the $8.3 billion bid by Nextel in early 2000 to buy the spectrum owned by the bankrupt Nextwave Communications, which translates to $80 per person, one-half of the U.K. number. Clearly, the U.K. spectrum auction led to a frenzy of overbidding, something that happened again in the auctions that Germany and the Netherlands conducted. The net result is that the European wireless industry is suffering, and some auction winners may go bankrupt. Further, the roll-out of 3G services has been extremely slow, mainly because the carriers cannot afford to build the new infrastructure.

The attraction of auctions

In the beginning, governments allocated wireless spectrum using an administrative process pejoratively called a "beauty contest." When the spectrum was up for grabs, the government asked all interested parties to send in a proposal that described their qualifications for developing wireless networks, how they intended to proceed with the license if they won it, how much they were willing to pay for the license, and other information that the particular government thought was relevant. After examining the proposals in minute detail and holding a hearing, the regulator awarded the spectrum to the most attractive proposal. In the beginning of the cable industry in the United States, regulators used the same procedure for providing community access television (CATV) franchises.

While the beauty contest ensured that those obtaining licenses had the wherewithal and the financial health to make the best use of them, the procedures in place to ensure that there was the widest possible participation and fairness were painfully slow. It took the FCC an average of two and a half years to award the initial 30 cellular licenses. In the CATV licensing procedures in most major metropolitan areas in the United States, it was apparent that those who received the allocations had the best political connections. Even in the cellular market, beauty contests lacked sufficient transparency so that losers further delayed the awards by filing lawsuits. Given these problems, and the urging of a number of regulatory economists, the FCC decided to first use lotteries and then moved on to auctions for the wireless spectrum.

Economists love auctions because they consider market-based approaches to be much better than administrative procedures for allocating licenses. They use three basic principles of resource allocation to justify auctions as a means for distributing wireless spectrum. The first principle is called *efficiency*, which means that a resource should be awarded to the one who values it most highly. Efficiency works well, provided that those who value the license the most are best able to use it. Social value is only enhanced if winners quickly move on to the business of building the network that can use the allocated spectrum and then offer wireless services to the population. The need to rapidly roll out telecommunications networks, whether wireless or wired, is essential for developing countries like India. The principle of efficiency does not always lead to the best outcome from the point of view of communications infrastructure development. Those who value the licenses the most might do so because of the opportunity gain of keeping others from getting them; that is, the value of building the network could be dwarfed by keeping the licenses for themselves.

Economists and governments also like auctions because, if they are designed correctly, the bidders truthfully reveal to the auctioneer what the resource is worth to them. Governments feel that by designing truth-revealing auctions they are able to get the maximum revenue for themselves.[1] Spectrum licenses are only given to those firms that participate in the process and reveal information about themselves and their bids. In the case of a beauty contest, after some preconditions are met to qualify for participation, the only thing revealed by the firms are their bids. Some auctions provide incentives for the firms to truthfully reveal the actual value of what they are willing to pay for the spectrum licenses, and some do not. For example, if the selection mechanism involves choosing the highest bidder among those that submit sealed bids and making them pay what they bid, one of two things might happen. Some firms respond in a risk-averse manner and low-ball their bids, and some get aggressive

---

1. There is a famous paper on auction theory by Roger Myerson, which shows that different types of auctions lead to the same expected revenue (that is, auction design is "revenue neutral"); see "Optimal Auction Design" in *Mathematics of Operations Research* (1981): 58–73.

and bid more than what they value the resource to be worth. In either case, the bids are not truthful.

How does one make people reveal the truth about what they are bidding? Let us try a simple experiment. Suppose you are competing with a number of others for an antique Grecian urn. You and your spouse have decided that it is worth $2,500 based on your expertise and budget. The auctioneer has set up a new rule: whoever bids the highest for the urn will get it, but *will have to only pay the second-highest price*. What would you bid? Suppose you decide to bid less than what you value the urn, say $2,000. Someone else could bid $2,250, less than what you could have bid, and get the urn. You would shake your head, because by bidding $2,500 truthfully, you could have beaten this person, and based on the rules of the game, you would actually have gotten the urn for the second-highest price of $2,250. Or, suppose you decide to be aggressive and bid more than your true value for the urn, say $3,000. Well, you could win the urn and pay less than $3,000 because of the second-price rule of the game. But if there were someone else who bid $2,750, you would end up paying more than the urn's true value to you. By truthfully bidding, you will lose the urn to the higher bidder, but you would not lose your money. The concept of this second-price auction was first proposed by Columbia economist William Vickrey in 1961, and he eventually won the Nobel Prize for this work. Spectrum allocation in the United States uses the principle of a second-price auction, and this mechanism is now being copied by most other countries as well.

An open-outcry auction like the ones used by Sotheby's and Christie's to sell precious art, satisfies the principle of second-price auctions and leads the participants to reveal the truth. In an art auction, no one reveals their true valuation, but they keep bidding until only one person remains. This person gets the prize at the price at which the next-to-the-last person drops out of the auction. This winning price is almost the same as the second price, that is, the price that the next-to-the-last person was willing to pay, plus an increment. Some spectrum auctions use a variation of the open-cry art auction called the *ascending price auction*, where the auctioneer "shouts" the bid increments and the bidders respond with their preferences electronically.

In practice, whether one is considering a Sotheby's art auction or an ascending-price spectrum auction, the participants could, and frequently do, get caught up in the passion of the moment and bid aggressively. Also, for the economic theory of truth revelation to work, one has to assume that the values that different bidders assign to the resource are independent of each other. In reality, most participants in spectrum auctions are not sure about the actual value and use the information revealed at the bidding stage to change and upgrade their estimate of what the spectrum is worth.

The final principle that makes auctions attractive to economists is that they are *transparent*, so that everyone knows what price is being bid at any particular time and, often, who is bidding. For the sake of transparency, it is important to know at the end of the process which firm bid what amount for the wireless spectrum licenses. The administrative beauty contests also revealed this information after the selection was made. However, auctions allow everyone to see how bid prices evolve, and this enables the participants to decide whether to continue bidding or to drop out of the race. This level of transparency also reduces waste by eliminating the overhead cost of tracking and processing numerous bid responses.

If the identities of the bidders were revealed at each stage, there is a strong possibility that new entrants might be scared off by aggressive established carriers because of the possibility of retaliation. Thus, complete transparency is a double-edged sword. In one set of auctions for personal communications systems (PCS) auctions, bidders were asked to use a ten-digit identity number, known only to the firms and the FCC, to hide their identities but at the same time ensure authenticity. However, some of the larger companies like Verizon (Bell Atlantic at that time) and AT&T used easily translatable identity codes to signal their interest in a particular set of licenses. After this debacle, the FCC now makes the bidders' identities quite opaque, thus safeguarding the smaller players and increasing competition.

In theory, auctions with the proper levels of regulation in place result in a high level of transparency. In practice, transparency also allows bidders to collude by signaling through their bids and establishing tacit agreements.[2] If such collusion happens, then the auctioneer, who in most cases in the telecommunications industry is the federal government, will receive lower revenues. Most governments have tried their best to put into place rules and regulations to increase competition and reduce collusive

---

    2. See P. Cramton, "Spectrum Auctions," in *Handbook of Telecommunications Economics*, ed. M. Cave, S. Majumdar, and I. Vogelsang (Amsterdam: Elsevier, 2001).

behavior in order to maximize the potential revenues from spectrum auctions.

Government avarice

The most important driving force that led to the Winner's Curse in the telecommunications sector was the avarice of governments throughout the world to increase their revenues by selling the airwaves. Economists are in agreement that auctions will raise much more revenue than either an administrative beauty contest or a lottery. At the urging of a number of prominent economists, the U.S. FCC was the first to use auctions to allocate wireless spectrum. In 1993, the U.S. government passed legislation giving the FCC the authority to auction wireless licenses. The first truly open spectrum auction was conducted in the Omni Shoreham Hotel in Washington, D.C., in July 1994 for licenses for paging services. John McMillan, an economist from Stanford, describes the process in exciting tones in his book *Reinventing the Bazaar*:

> After each round of bidding, the new bids were announced, to be greeted by some with cheers and by others with groans of disbelief. . . . as the bids rose tens of millions of dollars by the hour, the tension in the war room subsided somewhat, while in the ballroom it mounted. Wayne Perry of McCaw Cellular Communications said, "For once, the government is doing a great job dragging money out of people."[3]

The July 1994 auction went on for weeks and netted $617 million for the U.S. Treasury. The FCC and the U.S. government were so enthralled by the results that they continued auctioning spectrum for different uses, including digital wireless voice (PCS), wireless data, mobile fax, and so on, and raised a total of $42 billion by 2000.

This amount far exceeded the expectations of the U.S. government, which assumed, based on a study by the Office of Management and Budget, that the spectrum auctions would raise around $10 billion. Initially, the telecommunications industry was skeptical even about this number. In *Reinventing the Bazaar*, to show that the estimates of the stalwarts of the wireless industry were much lower than the $42 billion

3. John McMillan, *Reinventing the Bazaar: The Natural History of Markets* (New York: Norton, 2002).

eventually offered, McMillan quotes John Clendenin, chairperson of BellSouth, "There is no rational methodology on which the $10 billion was calculated," and Bert Roberts, chairperson of MCI, "The government is smoking something to think that they are going to get $10 billion for these licenses."[4] The question, of course, is: why did these companies end up spending much more than they thought the spectrum was worth? We will argue that the spectrum auction design and the act of participating in these auctions led to such extravagant behavior.

As further evidence of government avarice in the United States, consider the contrast between the wireless telecommunications industry and the television industry, which obtained the spectrum for high-definition broadcasting for a nominal amount, almost free. Allowing television to have access to the airwaves for a nominal fee is due to historical reasons; the industry lets the government take control over its networks in the case of emergencies or national security threats. After the financial success of the wireless spectrum auctions, the government is now eyeing the high-definition broadcast spectrum for enhancing the exchequer. The FCC has already studied the value of this spectrum and has concluded that it is worth around $70 billion. The government is looking for more ways to make money from public goods.

The success of the U.S. spectrum auctions did not go unnoticed by the governments of most countries around the world. While some countries, like France and Spain, continued to use beauty contests to allocate wireless spectrum, most other countries, including Mexico, Canada, Italy, Brazil, and the Netherlands, went the route of auctions. As we saw already, the British auctions netted the government more than $35 billion. The *Financial Times* called this process "the world's largest concerted transfer of money from the corporate sector to state coffers." Table 2-1 shows the results of some of these spectrum auctions, while table 2-2 shows their significance, including providing more than 4% of the government budgets in three European countries.

The German experience

The country that made the biggest splash in the 3G spectrum auction was Germany. While the U.K. Treasury earned €37.5 billion ($35.39 billion), the German finance minister received the record sum of €50.8 billion

---

4. McMillan, *Reinventing the Bazaar*, p. 84.

Table 2-1. Auctions for 3G spectrum in Europe, 2000

Country	Auction Date	# Bidders	# Licenses	Revenue Generated (€)	Revenue Generated ($)
U.K.	March–April 2000	13	5	37.5 billion	35.39 billion
Netherlands	July, 2000	6	5	2.7 billion	2.5 billion
Germany	July–August 2000	7	4–6	50.8 billion	45.85 billion
Italy	October 2000	6	5	12.2 billion	10.07 billion

($45.85 billion). The Germans chose a complex auction design: twelve blocks of spectrum were auctioned off, and the bidders could create licenses of either two or three blocks. So, for example, four firms could win large three-block licenses or six firms could win small two-block licenses. The licenses were sold using a complex scheme known as a *simultaneous ascending price auction*.

Unlike Britain, where there were 13 bidders initially, the German UMTS auction only attracted 7. However, since a license had to include at least two blocks, the auction could not end until at least one of the 7 bidders quit the auction. Early in the auction, one bidder (MobilCom) tried to make a smaller one (Debitel) quit by telling a newspaper that "should [Debitel] fail to secure a license [it could] become a 'virtual network operator' by using MobilCom's network while saving the cost of the license."[5] The government neither fined MobilCom nor did it exclude it from further participation because ejecting MobilCom could have ended the auction prematurely from Germany's perspective. As it turned out, no party quit the auction until after 126 rounds of bidding.

Table 2-2. Significance of spectrum auctions

Country	Spectrum Revenue ($)	$ as Percentage of GDP	$ as Percentage of Government Budget	$ Per Capita	$ Per Capita per License
Australia	352 million	0.08%	0.34%	18	?
Germany	45.85 billion	2.37%	4.43%	560	3,690
India	7 billion	0.61%	14.48%	7	?
Italy	10.07 billion	0.79%	2.01%	210	1,050
U.K.	35.39 billion	2.60%	6.93%	600	3,150

---

5. *Financial Times*, August 2, 2000.

Even then, the auction did not end because all players continued to demand large three-block licenses. One of the larger players, Mannesmann (Vodafone), tried to signal to the smaller players to reduce the size of their licenses or to quit. By round 147, the smaller players had reduced their demand to two-block licenses. However, the larger players decided to continue bidding to push the smaller players out. As the price kept going up, T-Mobile (Deutsche Telekom) panicked and stopped the bid increase just below the point where everyone thought that the smaller players would drop out. At round 155, the auction stopped with only six two-block licenses awarded, four acquired by incumbents and two by new entrants. The bidders paid a whopping $45.85 billion for the licenses.

Other countries

It was thought that blocks of spectrum were worth roughly the same amount per capita in different countries. As table 2-2 shows, the outcomes of the spectrum auctions in other countries clearly did not show this to be the case. Of course, smaller countries were said to be worth a little less because they did not give the network providers sufficient economies of scale. Also, countries centrally located in Europe were worth a little more because of the possibilities of expansion to neighboring countries and savings from sharing fixed costs.

Surprisingly, the auction held in the central European country of Switzerland at the end of 2000 was a complete flop because only four bidders showed up to bid for four licenses. The revenue generated was remarkably low in the Netherlands and Italy, both of which had the most profitable mobile phone markets in Europe.

By the end of 2000, the sentiment toward third-generation wireless had cooled somewhat, and many carriers were trying to provide some advanced data services using what is called 2.5G.[6] The major players had already incurred so much debt by winning in the earlier auctions that they were not inclined to participate in these "small" countries. Indeed by mid-2001, Belgium and Israel called off auctions due to marginal interest. Having been stung by the Winner's Curse in previous spectrum auctions,

---

6. The second-generation (2G) networks carried voice services using what was called "circuit switching" in which dedicated lines (and bandwidth) would be opened for each and every phone call. The 2.5G networks simply expanded the scope of the second-generation networks to also carry data traffic like e-mail and stock quotes.

many companies were disinclined to incur the overhead cost that was necessary to participate in future auctions.

Why was there a Winner's Curse in selected spectrum auctions?

Based on current law in most countries, if a company does not obtain spectrum, then it cannot provide wireless services.[7] There is a winner-take-all phenomenon here. The losing contestants are left with both the direct costs of competing in the spectrum auction, which consists of fees for legal, managerial, economic, and engineering consultants and the earnest or participation fee that most governments require, and the indirect cost of the missed opportunity for developing a leading-edge wireless service. Although many financial economists have discussed the issue of a sunk-cost fallacy, participants in telecom auctions want to recover these costs by winning.

Consider the entrapment game that was first described by Yale economist Martin Shubik; it provides some insights into why telecom companies bid so aggressively in spectrum auctions. An auctioneer announces to a group of people that he wants to auction off a $20 bill. The main twist in the *entrapment* auction is that once the bidding stops, the highest bidder will get the $20 bill, but both the highest and the second-highest bidders have to pay the auctioneer what they bid. In the context of telecom auctions, one can think of the highest bidder paying his bid, the second-highest bidder paying his opportunity cost, which is reflected in his bid, and both paying the bid-preparation costs.

Returning to the entrapment game, think about how such an auction would evolve in a competitive environment. Suppose at a particular stage of the auction, the highest bid is $10 and the second highest is $9. If the auction stops at this stage, the highest bidder will get the $20 bill for $10 and will make an instant profit of $10. The auctioneer will get money from both bidders for a total of $19, losing $1. Pity the second-place bidder, who will lose $9 because he participated in the auction. Continuing the scenario, if he just increased his bid by $1.50 to $10.50, he would win the $20 for a profit of $9.50, and the auctioneer would get $20.50 for a profit of 50 cents. The previous first-place bidder would lose $10, and thus, if the auction continued, would have the incentive to increase his bid to,

---

7. One could argue that the current technology allows a sharing of spectrum, but we shall not discuss this issue here.

say, $11. At this new point, the auctioneer nets $1.50, the difference between the total bids of $21.50 and the face value of the $20 bill. As one
can see, there is a significant cost of being the second-place bidder, and
this motivates the participants to avoid second place if at all possible.

In most classroom settings playing the entrapment game, students
escalate their bids even after they have paid more than $20 for the $20
bill. Psychologist Max Bazerman reports that he has earned more than
$17,000 auctioning $20 bills to MBA students at Northwestern University.[8] In the course of these simulations, no auction ended at less than
$39 in total bids, and one even fetched $407. All of this in an auction where
the actual value of the good is determined, that is, known for sure. A $20
bill is only worth $20. Just imagine a situation where the value of the good
being auctioned is not known for sure and where the opportunity cost of
not winning is high.

Many academic economists argue that the main reason for the
Winner's Curse in spectrum auctions was the design of the auction itself. The cynical among us would say that this argument is self-serving
as many of these individuals earn substantial consulting fees for designing auctions. There are two schools of thought on the design of spectrum
auctions. The first thinks that sealed-bid auctions, where the winning
bidder pays her bid, are best, and the second thinks that ascending auctions, where the bidders are allowed to revise their bids upward in every
round, are best. Theoretically, a multiple-round ascending price (English)
auction should end when the bidder with the second-highest valuation
for a spectrum license drops out. The one who has the highest value for
the license should win at a price which is a small increment above the
second-highest value. Many economists agree with the view that "there
is now substantial evidence that [the ascending price] auction design has
been successful."[9]

Most countries, like the United Kingdom, the Netherlands, and Italy,
have used a simple ascending auction, while other countries, like Germany and Austria, have used a more complex variable-price ascending
auction. We have already looked at the pros and cons of these design
mechanisms. The reality on the ground went beyond the academic theo-
ries of economists and the considerations of efficiency.

8. R. H. Frank and P. J. Cook, *The Winner Take All Society* (New York: Free Press, 1995), pp. 129–30.

9. Cramton, "Spectrum Auctions."

The problem with the ascending auction design from the perspective of the governments was that, after the significant level of bidder interest in the U.K. auction (13 bidders at the starting gate), new auctions did not attract many entrants. Part of the problem was the concern of the smaller players that the larger players, with deep pockets, would bid up the spectrum price significantly as in the U.K. and German cases. There was also skepticism over whether or not one could make money on 3G services. The valuations of telecom companies also fell dramatically between the British and the Swiss auctions; the Dow Jones European telecom stock price index fell by more than one-third, for example.

Given all of the problems, perceived or real, in the Swiss auction, the number of bidders fell from five to four for four licenses, thus reducing the chances for any real price-enhancement activity. In the Netherlands, six incumbent operators participated in the auction for five licenses. The Italian situation was much more dramatic. Six bidders paid the earnest money to participate in the auction of five licenses where the *reservation price*, the minimum the government would accept, was set at $1 billion. After just two days of bidding, one bidder, Blu in which British Telecom was the major partner, simply stopped just above the reservation price. The result was that the revenue generated for the Italian government was less than one-third that for the U.K. government (see tables 2-1 and 2-2).

Given the reluctance of the new entrants to join an auction where there were many rounds with ascending prices, Denmark decided to have a sealed-bid auction for spectrum allocation in September 2001. Given that, at the time, there was turmoil in the telecommunications market and a low expectation of the success of 3G services, the Danish government was happy that the licenses sold for an average of €95 per capita, a far cry from the €500 or so obtained by Britain and Germany, but double most expectations.

In any case, the primary motivating factor in the design of auctions has been the ability of governments to use them to generate significant amounts of revenue. For example, the Dutch government canceled its July 2000 bond issue in anticipation of receiving more than €600 per capita from its spectrum auction. It received, however, only €170. In order to use the auctions to enhance revenue, economists claim that the only "two issues that really matter [in auction design] are attracting entry and preventing collusion."[10] The more competitors, economists

10. P. Klemperer, "How (Not) to Run Auctions: The European 3G Telecom Auctions," *European Economic Review* (2002).

would say, the more efficiency, which is better for the government running the auction. Preventing collusion is also important in creating an efficient auction.

Much of the research on auction design has been based on trying to generate as much revenue for the government as possible. There is little interest in the consequences to the participants from bidding in the auctions. The issue of companies going bankrupt and causing significant problems for their employees and shareholders and, in the case of developing countries, slowing the growth of a vital infrastructure sector, is not perceived to be the concern of the auction designers.

Consequences of the Winner's Curse in spectrum auctions

How were all of these telecommunications companies able to bid such large amounts for the licenses to provide wireless services? Where did all the money come from? In the 1990s, commercial and investment banks were extremely bullish on the telecommunications industry. In the technology sector of this industry, all one needed to do was put together a credible management team and a reasonable business plan, and money would gush into companies like a Saudi Arabian oil well. Well-known banks like First Boston, Citicorp, and Deutsche Bank competed with each other to lend money to those bidding in spectrum auctions.

Almost all of the companies that won wireless spectrums have been burdened with significant amounts of debt. In a number of cases, the loans used to win spectrum auctions have led to the demise of the victorious companies. Table 2-3 highlights what happened to the 13 winners in the U.S. spectrum auctions between 1995 and 1997. Nine of the companies went bankrupt, lost their licenses because of their inability to pay the license fees, or else were acquired by other companies after having become insolvent.

In Europe, the situation was much worse. The telecom majors like British Telecom, France Telecom, and Deutsche Telekom have taken on significant amounts of debt because of the spectrum auctions and have jeopardized their futures. The net debt of British Telecom increased from around £9 billion at the end of 2000 to almost £28 billion in 2001. Deutsche Telekom saw its debt increase by 50% from €42 billion to €60 billion in the same period. France Telecom has seen its long-term debt increase steadily to some €14 billion at the end of 2001. Vodafone, which was rapidly becoming an important force in the European wireless mar-

Table 2-3. Status of PCS spectrum winners in the United States

Company	Spectrum Won (Amount Paid)	Status in December 2000
AT&T Wireless	Mar. 1995 ($1.684 billion) Jan. 1997 ($407 million)	Alive
AlTel Mobile	Jan. 1997 ($145 million)	Alive
NextWave Communications	May 1996 ($4.201 billion) July 1996 ($542 million)	Chapter 11 bankruptcy (June 1998)
Pacific Telesis Mobile	Mar. 1995 ($696 million)	Acquired by SBC Communications (1997)
PCS Primeco	Mar. 1995 ($1.107 billion)	Split up among Verizon, AT&T, and others (2000)
DCR PCS	May 1996 ($1.463 billion)	Chapter 11 bankruptcy (Mar. 1997)
GWI PCS	May 1996 ($1.06 billion)	Filed for bankruptcy (Jan. 1998)
BD-PCS	May 1996 ($874 million)	Missed downpayments; spectrum block re-auctioned
C.H.-PCS	July 1996 ($214 million)	Missed downpayments; spectrum block re-auctioned
OmniPoint	May 1996 ($509 million)	Merged with Voicestream (June 1999)
Magnacom Wireless	May 1996 ($109 million)	Chapter 11 bankruptcy (Oct. 1998)
SprintCom	Jan. 1997 ($544 million)	Alive
BellSouth Wireless	Jan. 1997 ($205 million)	Alive

ket, also increased its debt rapidly; at the end of 2001, its net debt was £6.7 billion on sales of £15 billion. This amount had grown to £12 billion by the end of 2002 on sales of £22.8 billion. The securities market reacted strongly to the weakening of the company's financials, and Vodafone's stock price dropped. Figures 2-1 and 2-2 show how the share markets have reacted to the winners of the spectrum auctions.[11]

Clearly, investors do not think much of the success of these companies in the spectrum auctions. If market valuation is the only issue, then the companies may not be that concerned. However, the steep reduction in share prices added to the high level of debt has drastically affected the ability of these companies to raise further capital to invest in the network itself. The auction winners are unable to buy equipment to expand the state-of-the-art wireless infrastructure necessary to provide 3G services.

11. In the graphs of stock prices in this chapter and the next, we compare a company's stock price with the S&P 500 composite market index to show the stock's change relative to the rest of the market. The S&P index is divided by 100 to better fit the scale of each graph. A comparison of the pattern of the stock price and the index shows that the stocks have fallen far more than the index.

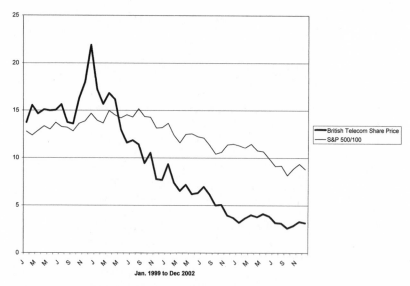

Figure 2-1. Stock prices of British Telecom

Telecommunications equipment manufacturers are suffering because of the sudden reduction in demand for their technology. Many of the vendors that had made massive investments in their production facilities to build third-generation wireless switches have been left in the lurch. Companies like Lucent, Ericsson, and Nokia have had to write off capital investments in their wireless divisions. Many of these companies had also designed 3G handsets, which have yet to appear in the marketplace. In fact, many of them have abandoned 3G altogether and have decided to focus on handsets with gimmicks like the ones used by NTT DoCoMo in Japan. This handset includes a camera to take and transmit still photographs, the ability to download tones and chimes, instant messaging, and so on.

The Winner's Curse has affected not only the companies involved, but also many of the countries that were eagerly awaiting state-of-the-art wireless services. Due to the burden of massive debt structures, many of the telecommunications companies that participated in the 3G auctions have tried to cut costs in order to boost income and enhance their ability to pay down their debt. The easiest way to cut costs is to reduce the labor force, and many of them have done so with a vengeance. British Telecom reduced its workforce by more than 10,000 people from 2000 to 2001, followed by another 5,000 from 2001 to 2002. All of the other major car-

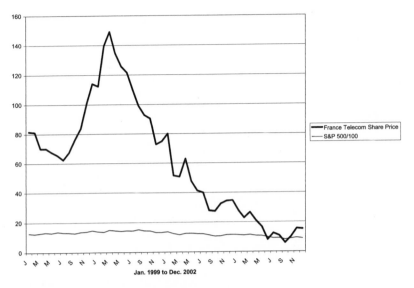

Figure 2-2. **Stock prices of France Telecom**

riers, including Deutsche Telekom and France Telecom, have cut their labor forces by 5–10%. The only exception to the rule is Vodafone. Although Vodafone also incurred significant amounts of debt due to its participation in the spectrum auctions, it is difficult to assess the debt's impact on the health of Vodafone's employment statistics. Due to the fact that it kept aggressively increasing company acquisitions in the telecom space, Vodafone actually doubled the number of its employees between 2000 and 2001; by 2002, it had close to 60,000 employees.

All in all, the exuberance of the telecommunications companies in aggressively purchasing wireless spectrum has had wide-reaching negative consequences for the companies, their shareholders, and individual countries. Many of the companies, especially in Europe, have yet to get out from under the massive debt burdens they incurred because of their license acquisition adventures. Shareholders of these companies have seen their investments erode significantly. Many of the shareholders of these previously staid companies were pension funds helping their clients save money for their retirements. The impact on these aging investors has been quite devastating. Employees of the wireless companies, who had looked forward to long careers, have been deeply disappointed. The large-scale layoffs also came at a time when the boom cycles of most economies had turned negative. Many feel that the telecom bust has been responsible for the economic downturn in the world. It is true that, like the automobile sector, infrastructure industries have a significant multiplier effect on the economy because of all the industries that supply them. One could argue that the Winner's Curse in the spectrum auctions has been partially responsible for the bear market of 2001 to 2003. The only happy participants in the spectrum auctions have been the different governments, especially the United States, the United Kingdom, and Germany. However, it may well be that the tax revenues these countries could have obtained from a healthy telecommunications market with widespread investment in third-generation telecommunications infrastructure and services would have surpassed the spectrum license revenues.

Factors leading to the Winner's Curse in spectrum auctions

The spectrum auctions are a pure example of the Winner's Curse. The companies involved were faced with an auction designed by experts to generate as much revenue as possible for governments. There was clearly a buying and bidding psychology in place; the telecom companies are highly competitive and focused on winning. There was no second place; if you failed to get a license, that meant a competitor owned that piece of spectrum and your chances of ever acquiring it were small.

Combined with the tense auction environment were market factors that pushed the telecom companies to bid more than the worth of the licenses. The auctions took place during a time of rapid growth in the telecom market and rapidly increasing stock prices. Investment bankers were happy to finance the bids, while stock analysts encouraged the companies to grow. Company officers kept increasing the bids during the auctions and failed to examine the business model that would result from winning. The telecom companies as a result had such high debts that they could not actually build the infrastructure to use the licenses.

What to do?

The spectrum auctions we have described are a classic case of the Winner's Curse: companies bid so much to win the rights to provide wireless services that they ended up hurting their own profitability. One of the authors has more than 15 years of experience studying the telecommunications industry. This industry, which was a pillar of stability for the first 90 years of the twentieth century, has gone through enormous ups and downs since the 1990s. The more recently developed wireless industry has also seen tremendous change over this period. Starting with analog telephony, wireless companies moved rapidly into digital voice and then data services in order to boost their revenues. At each stage, the governments of different countries seized on the ambitions of the telecom companies and set up auctions for the wireless spectrum needed to provide new services. Looking toward the future, the wireless companies need to take a systems approach when participating in spectrum auctions. Based on our knowledge of the industry, below is some advice that should help.

Be realistic about the wireless data market

Spectrum licenses do not provide revenue. They are simply a right-of-way *cost* that the companies have to pay before being able to provide wireless services, which generate revenue. Winning at all costs does not make any sense in spectrum auctions. The amount one spends on this right-of-way has to align with the amount of revenue one can generate after winning. The spectrum auctions that cost the telecom companies the most were for the 3G licenses, which companies thought they needed to provide complex data and video services. In order to avoid the Winner's Curse in spectrum auctions, one needs to be realistic about the size of the market for wireless data and video services.

The United States has probably the best landline connectivity in the world. Most businesses and many residences have computers and a connection to the Internet. There has been a fairly large annual, even monthly, increase in broadband (data and video) services over the wireline (fixed) networks. These services are much more sophisticated than any that a wireless carrier could provide; consumers can access a much larger variety and set of services and also have a better experience by being able to use large screens to interact with the services. Although wireless services have the advantage of mobility and the ability to access the Internet through handheld devices, these are seen by consumers to be niche applications. Thus wireless data services will likely play a secondary role to landline data services in the United States. Those bidding for spectrum licenses have to err on the side of caution when trying to estimate the size of the wireless data market.

Even internationally, one needs to be cautious about the size of the wireless data market. Although the penetration of cellular telephony in Europe and parts of Asia is much larger than in the United States, almost all of it is in voice services. Accessing data services using mobile wireless devices is not a good experience for most Europeans or Asians because of the simple fact that many Web sites are hosted in the United States; the latency (that is, download times) is simply too long. However, Europeans and especially Asians use wireless telephones for tasks like trading stock. Thus a limited set of data services is certainly of great interest internationally. The question then is: how big is this market given what one can realistically charge for these services? Again, "caution" should be the primary word.

Make your wish list into a market

In the mid-1990s, everyone in the wireless industry used the example of NTT DoCoMo, which seemed to have a lot of success in the Japanese market with its data services, including messaging, music clips, R-rated cartoons, and so on. DoCoMo also has a micropayment system in which consumers pay money for bandwidth used and time spent accessing the services. Based on DoCoMo's initial success, American companies hired consultants to help them brainstorm about different wireless data services they could provide to customers. The results of these exercises generated a number of possibilities, including location-based services, knowledge services, m-commerce (mobile commerce), telemetry, and so on, and estimates for the revenues that each of these applications would generate.

A wish list is not a market. For example, before location-based services can work, the wireless companies have to make sure that restaurants, movie theaters, and the like have installed technology to send wireless messages to customers who are in their vicinity. Further, there has to be a clear understanding as to who is paying and how service is measured. For example, who pays for the wireless technology installed at the cinema? If a customer buys a ticket after getting a wireless prompt, what commission does the wireless company receive? How does one know that a customer came to the movie because of the wireless prompt?

All of the potential data service revenue producers require additional investments of time and money to set up systems to make them work. This supply chain requires commitments from a number of content providers for there to be a financially successful application. In order to avoid the Winner's Curse of triumph in the spectrum auction, one needs to make sure that the wish list of potential services can be successfully marketed. Could the wireless companies have conducted some market research to evaluate the potential of new services? Their failure to test the market led to aggressive bidding for wireless spectrums.

Build it right and they will come

It was well known that data services could be built using the old spectrum. For example, NTT DoCoMo used a technology called iMode, which was a way to provide data services using a network built for voice services. Many of the data services provided by U.S. carriers in 2003, including imaging services like Sprint's PCS Vision, also use the wireless voice network. Data services that use voice networks are called 2.5G services.

Almost all of the wireless data services for which there are real markets can be provided by 2.5G technology. Building a 2.5G network is much less expensive than building a 3G network because one does not have to acquire 3G licenses. Build 2.5G networks, and customers will flock to them because they will have access to many data services without having to pay a lot for them. Thus if the main objective for the wireless carriers is finding new sources of revenue by providing data services, systems thinking would have enabled them to build the right network and avoid the 3G spectrum auctions altogether, or they might have been much less intent on winning these licenses at any cost.

Think locally, act globally

In 1984, a McKinsey report apparently dissuaded AT&T from getting into wireless communications because the consultants' projections showed that there would be no more than 1 million cellular users in the United States by 2000. This estimate was off by a hundredfold. At the end of 2002, there were about 1 billion wireless subscribers worldwide, many of whom were in Asia. China had close to 100 million subscribers but only a 10% penetration. In Latin America, the average wireless penetration was about 15%.

In addition to mobile wireless communications, many of these developing countries have embarked on a parallel path to provide telecommunications services using fixed wireless technology. In India, two of the largest companies, Reliance and Tata, have started building fixed wireless networks to provide limited mobile services. The International Finance Corporation, an arm of the World Bank, recently made a strategic decision to focus its investments in fixed wireless networks in Africa and Asia. Most U.S.-based wireless telecom carriers have experience with fixed wireless networks, and they should be able to generate revenue around the world using this technology as well.

In many countries, governments require spectrum licenses to provide fixed wireless services. If the local U.S.-based wireless companies want to boost revenues, they need to act globally to provide simple voice services to the rest of the world. In the global market for wireless licenses, their bidding behavior needs to be informed by their experience locally in spectrum auctions.

Know when to fold

Most important, in future spectrum auctions, companies should avoid the winning-at-all-costs syndrome. As we have discussed, there are many ways to make money in the wireless industry, and this variety should enable companies to exhibit more realistic bidding behavior in spectrum auctions. Losing some of the auctions may not be fatal because it is possible to provide good data services using the spectrum one already has. Knowing when to stop bidding is important in these auctions because winning simply gives one the right-of-way, and making a return on your investment involves more than just the acquisition of the license.

A bidder needs to set up a system of checks and balances so that it folds at the right time. For example, in the German 3G auction, there was enough information on the lack of demand for any of the larger companies to have ended the auction much earlier and saved everyone billions of dollars. In fact, Mannesmann and T-Mobile would have been better off had they done business in a secondary market after stopping bidding early in the government auction. If the team doing the bidding had people with different perspectives, the Winner's Curse in the spectrum auction could have been avoided. To paraphrase a Kenny Rogers song, "Know when to continue bidding, and know when to fold."

II ••• How Psychological and Market Factors Promote the Winner's Curse

3 • Hubris and the urge to merge and acquire

Mention mergers and acquisitions, and the typical CEO's eyes light up with the possibilities. A merger increases the size of the firm and makes the CEO's position more important. CEOs of big firms generally have larger salaries and bonuses than the CEOs of smaller firms. Unfortunately, the record when one combines the operations of two firms is mixed at best. Some mergers have been successful while others have turned into disasters. We believe that many mergers and acquisitions have failed because they experienced the Winner's Curse. Senior management officials in the acquiring company paid too much for the merger and were far too optimistic about their company's ability to successfully combine two firms and obtain the benefits promised to their shareholders.

This application of the Winner's Curse begins a series of extensions we will make throughout the rest of the book. Like an auction, some mergers involve bidding, especially when two firms compete for the same acquisition target. The majority of acquisitions do not resemble a competitive auction; the acquirer is bidding against itself, trying to find a price that is acceptable to the board of the firm it wants to acquire. However, the end result is similar to the result of an auction where the firm pays too much. Eventually, the public realizes that the acquiring company placed too high a value on the target, and the price of the acquiring company's shares drops. In other cases, the target generates large losses and leads to a substantial write-off for the merged firms. In these instances, the actual amount of the Winner's Curse, the overpayment, can be estimated by combining the amounts of these two kinds of losses.

Managers like to buy other companies to expand the sales of their firm and often to diversify into other product lines. Pharmaceuticals firms buy rivals to become larger and to obtain drugs that the target firm has developed. Banks buy other banks to expand their customer base and their geographical reach. Some managers have a vision that involves acquiring a large group of related companies to create a dominant firm. Sandy Weill, CEO of Citigroup, has assembled a variety of companies, including retail, commercial, and investment banking, brokerage services, finance companies, and others to create a huge financial services business.

One of the major challenges in acquiring another company is figuring out the value of the target and deciding how much to offer for it. The risk of overpaying is substantial. In this chapter, we analyze specific mergers and acquisitions that illustrate the Winner's Curse and discuss managerial and financial research that looks at patterns across multiple M&As. Managers need to be aware of the Winner's Curse and ways to avoid encountering it when considering a merger or acquisition.

The serial acquirers

A group of firms in the 1990s became known as *serial acquirers* in their efforts to become growth companies and impress their investors and the stock market.[1] These companies, like Tyco, WorldCom, Vivendi Universal, and AT&T, bought tens, scores, and even hundreds of other companies. The champion in the contest to acquire companies in 2001 was General Electric, which spent $18 billion on takeovers; in the 1990s the company completed 534 deals. Another acquisition-oriented company is AT&T, which purchased a large collection of cable companies for more than $90 billion in the 1990s. Vivendi spent $100 billion in the media business during this time. Cisco Systems is one of the leading acquirers in the technology sector, having made more than 70 acquisitions in the 1990s. It seems that no sector is immune; the financial services industry

1. *Wall Street Journal*, August 6, 2002.

is represented by Bank One and by First Union Corporation, which has bought more than 90 banks since the early 1990s.

What motivated these serial acquirers? Why did they adopt this strategy? The emphasis was on growth; their senior managers felt that growth was the best approach to increasing the stock market valuation of their companies. As growth led to increases in stock prices, managers had to convince analysts that their stock price was justified. Much managerial compensation is based on stock price and stock options, so the CEOs of these companies benefited directly as the companies grew. As managers purchased more and more companies, they reinforced the feeling of being winners in their industries. We believe that winning in these companies led to excessive hubris on the part of management as well as feelings of invulnerability.

The rise and fall of Tyco

Tyco built itself into a conglomerate with four major business groups. Its chairperson, Dennis Kozlowski, said that Tyco would become the next General Electric. In the three years prior to 2002, Tyco acquired 700 companies at prices ranging from several hundred thousand dollars to $9.5 billion.[2] This frantic pace made Tyco one of the fastest growing stocks on Wall Street, some 20% a year. This growth occurred in spite of a collection of businesses that were rather dull, including adult diapers, clothes hangers, and water hoses. See table 3-1 for a list of some of these acquisitions.

A review of some of Tyco's recent annual reports documents the company's obsession with growth:

We grew diluted earnings per share 29 percent in fiscal 2001. (CEO letter, Tyco 2001 Annual Report)

Tyco's internal revenue growth in fiscal 2000 was 14 percent, a remarkable feat for a company of our size. Put another way, our business units delivered $3.7 *billion* in incremental sales last year alone—not counting acquisitions. That is what I call a growth company. For the seventh consecutive year, we increased revenues and earnings substantially. (CEO letter, Tyco 2000 Annual Report)

2. *Wall Street Journal*, August 6, 2002.

Table 3-1. Selected Tyco acquisitions. From Tyco annual reports. Investment figures in bottom row are approximate and include all acquisitions during the year. Acquisitions are listed in the calendar year rather than fiscal year.

July 1996 to Aug. 1997	1998	1999	2000	2001
ADT	US Surgical	AMP	Thomas & Belts	CIT Group
Carlisle Plastics	Sherwood	Raychem	General Surgical Innovations	Mallinckrodt
Rochester Group	Confab	Temasa	Critchley Group	CIGI
AT&T Submarine Systems	Holmes Protection	Graphic Controls	GSI	Interdyne
Electrostar	Wells Fargo Alarm	Sunbelt Plastics	AFC Cable	Lucent Technologies Power Systems Group
Arbo Medical	CIPE	Balts		Simplex Time Recording
INBRAND	Crosby Valve	Alarmguard		Scott Technologies
Sempell Valve	Bayard	Glynwood Metal Processing		Cambridge Protection Electronic Security Business
Henry Pratt	Rust Engineering	Central Sprinkler		
James Jones	Sigma Circuits	Siemens Electromechanical Components		
Edward Barber		Entergy Security		
Keystone International		Pragetizer		
American Tube & Pipe				
T. J. Cope				
$10 billion	$4.2 billion	$6.9 billion	$5.16 billion	$19.5 billion

We have grown our earnings at a 35% compounded rate for the past five years. . . . For the sixth consecutive year, we increased revenues and earnings substantially. (CEO letter, Tyco 1999 Annual Report)

Our over 100 acquisitions during the past six years have been very successful . . . and there are many more great companies that would fit snugly with businesses we already own. We plan to increase shareholder value by continuing to make smart, disciplined acquisitions and integrating them while simultaneously maintaining our strong organic growth. (Tyco 1998 Annual Report)

How did Tyco generate growth? As one example, it acquired ADT, the burglar alarm company, in 1997. One kind of ADT dealer is a small company that sells alarms and monthly monitoring contracts. The alarms connect to ADT centers via phone lines. ADT pays the dealers a one-time fee of about $1,000 for the monitoring contracts and makes its money from monthly monitoring fees of about $30 a customer. ADT was founded in 1874 and has more than 7 million customers worldwide. Prior to its outside dealer program, ADT sold most of its systems itself to businesses and affluent home owners, generally via telemarketing. Tyco rapidly expanded ADT's outside dealer program and began to pressure local managers to increase sales in poor neighborhoods. Tyco encouraged local dealers to use high-pressure, door-to-door sales tactics. One local manager complained that all Tyco wanted was numbers; it didn't care if customers dropped the accounts later. Many of these poor credit customers did stop paying, and Tyco is now under investigation for the way it accounted for these canceled accounts.[3] In January 2003, Tyco fired the chief financial officer of its fire and security division, and in March 2003, it fired the division president.[4]

One might ask how does a company evaluate and conduct due diligence on a large number of acquisitions? Reportedly, Tyco had a substantial group of acquisition experts, who specialized in finding, valuing, acquiring, and then integrating new companies into the conglomerate. In addition to purchasing companies, there are notes in the annual reports which indicate that some subsidiaries were sold. However, overall, table 3-1 and the annual reports show a frantic level of acquisitions activity. Given the

3. *Wall Street Journal*, November 15, 2002.
4. *Wall Street Journal*, March 13, 2003.

difficulty of valuing companies, it appears that Tyco ran a considerable risk of overpaying for some of its acquisitions.

When a company like Tyco acquires a firm, it frequently pays for the acquisition with cash and with company stock. Some or all of the cash is likely to be borrowed, leading to a high debt load for the acquirer. A serial acquirer is under great pressure to keep its stock price high in order to facilitate further acquisitions. As a result, the quest for growth generates more pressures for future growth and acquisitions. If, at some point in time, the investing public loses faith in a serial acquirer, then its stock price drops, which makes it hard to acquire additional firms. If this happens, a company like Tyco is in deep trouble because it is unable to continue its acquisitions strategy to grow revenues, while at the same time it is likely to be faced with a high level of debt from previous acquisitions.

In 2002, investors lost confidence in Tyco and its chairperson, Dennis Kozlowski, and Tyco's stock price dropped 60% in three months, erasing $86 billion of market value. The stock plummeted from above $62 a share in January 2001 to $16.05 in June 2002. The stock price's decline, coupled with a huge debt load, created major problems for Tyco (see figure 3-1).[5] The CEO announced a plan to sell Tyco's newly acquired CIT Financial and to break the company into five smaller firms based on its existing business groups. Shareholders objected, and Kozlowski dropped the plan. Shortly thereafter, New York state prosecutors indicted Kozlowski, first for sales tax evasion and then for evidence tampering related to his purchases of artwork. Subsequent investigations have resulted in charges that Kozlowski "looted" the company, spending large amounts of company funds for personal expenses. His trial ended with a hung jury and a mistrial. Prosecutors plan to hold a second trial.

What does Tyco illustrate about the Winner's Curse? First, the market believes that Tyco as a whole was overvalued. Much of Tyco's value came from the hundreds of acquisitions it made from 1997 through 2001. It seems safe to infer, given Tyco's dramatic loss of value in the stock market, that it overvalued some of its acquisitions. Given the extremely large number of acquisitions, there must have been a feeling that the company

5. One might argue that Tyco was a victim of a general stock market decline. However, Tyco's stock suffered more than the S&P 500, as investors became concerned about its accounting and business model. Regardless of changes in the market or investor perceptions, management should be considering risk when it formulates strategy, and the risk of a market decline is real. Did Tyco ever consider how its business model would perform if its stock dropped in value for any reason?

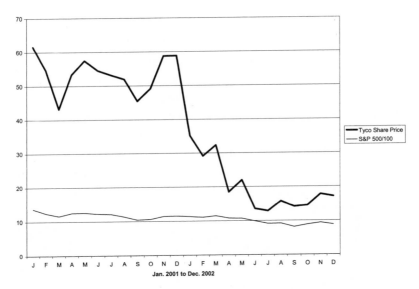

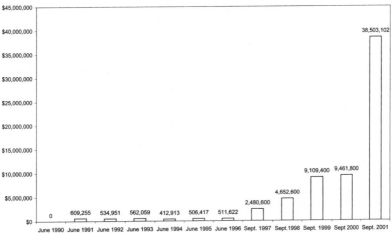

Figure 3-1. Tyco share prices (top) and the S&P 500/100 and Tyco long-term debt (in thousands) (bottom)

was "on a roll." Since Kozlowski took over Tyco in 1992, its revenue had grown twelvefold.[6] Certainly the acquirers within Tyco were focused on winning the companies they sought. There is also ample evidence of pressure for growth, fueled by stock analysts and investment bankers.

Was Tyco's business model unrealistic? At the strategic level, with its primary focus on acquisitions, it would appear that the model is

6. *Wall Street Journal*, June 4, 2002.

unsustainable, particularly in a stock market that is not experiencing continuing growth. There is much debate about whether the conglomerate model is viable and whether it represents the best interests of shareholders. Financial experts suggest that management should not purchase unrelated firms for the purpose of diversification; instead, the investor should diversify by purchasing stocks in different kinds of companies.

Dennis Kozlowski was one of the most highly paid executives in the world. In the three fiscal years up to 2002, Tyco paid Kozlowski about $97 million in cash, restricted stock, and other compensation. He also made another $240 million through stock options.[7] Kozlowski's annual letters to shareholders exude unbounded optimism. Whether ultimately convicted or not, Kozlowski's behavior demonstrates considerable hubris and a sense of invulnerability.

Edward Breen, the new chairperson at Tyco, must now try to deal with $27 billion in debt piled up during its acquisitions spree. First to go was CIT Financial, acquired in 2001 for $9.5 billion. In the summer of 2002, Tyco made an initial public offering of CIT, which underwriters priced at $23 a share, below the $25–29 a share they had originally indicated. The total value of the offering was $4.6 billion, and Tyco took a $2.4 billion charge to write down the value of the unit.[8] It would appear that Tyco overvalued CIT when it purchased the firm and now can assign a dollar value to its Winner's Curse overpayment of $4.9 billion (the difference between the $9.5 billion the company paid and the $4.6 billion sale price).

The trials of WorldCom

WorldCom also fits the profile of a serial acquirer, having undertaken more than 70 acquisitions since it was founded. Unfortunately, the company is most noted for an accounting scandal, which surfaced in the summer of 2002. An internal auditor at WorldCom found that network expenses had been sprinkled across various capital accounts, thereby allowing the firm to report higher earnings. The chief financial officer (CFO) had charged the costs of renting lines from other networks as capital, rather than as an operating expense. Capitalizing an expense postpones its impact on earnings until the capital investment is depre-

---

7. *Wall Street Journal*, June 4, 2002.
8. *Wall Street Journal*, July 2, 2002.

ciated in future years. The auditor contacted the board of directors, which brought in a public auditing firm to determine the extent of the problem. The current estimate is that WorldCom hid expenses and therefore inflated its cash flow by $9 billion; when corrected, it was enough to wipe out its reported profits for a number of years. The board immediately fired the vice president of finance and the financial controller. Table 3-2 presents the historical highlights of WorldCom's rise and fall.

WorldCom reached its peak value of more than $115 billion in June 1999 with a share price of $62. The company in 2002 was worth less than a billion dollars, and its stock was down more than 94% from 2001.[9] Shares dropped low enough that WorldCom was at risk of being delisted by NASDAQ (see figure 3-2). In July 2002, WorldCom filed for bankruptcy.

The architect of WorldCom, Bernard J. Ebbers, resigned abruptly in April 2002, owing more than $366 million for loans and loan guarantees to the company. WorldCom made these loans to Ebbers as its stock price dropped so that he would not have to sell his shares on the open market. Currently there are charges that Ebbers used company loans for far more than covering his stock investments, and the scandal is not over yet. Today, Worldcom is in the process of emerging from bankruptcy with a new name, MCI.

Table 3-2. A short history of WorldCom

Date	Event
September 1983	Ebbers and colleagues launch Long Distance Discount Service; they change its name to WorldCom in 1995.
August 26, 1996	WorldCom announces $12 billion merger with MFS Communications, an operator of business networks.
November 10, 1997	WorldCom merges with MCI for $42 billion after beating out British Telecom.
October 5, 1999	WorldCom and Sprint announce $129 billion merger.
July 13, 2000	Sprint merger dropped due to opposition from government regulators on antitrust grounds.
April 30, 2002	Ebbers resigns as CEO due to SEC inquiry of company's accounting practices and personal loans to Ebbers.
June 25, 2002	WorldCom announces $3.8 billion accounting error and fires its CFO.
July 21, 2002	WorldCom files for bankruptcy.

Source: *Business Week*, July 8, 2002.

9. *New York Times*, June 26, 2002.

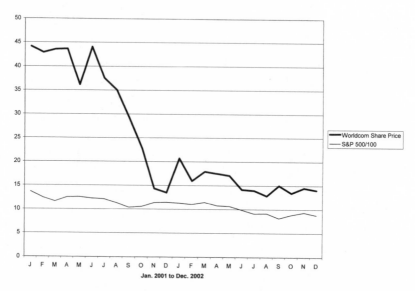

Figure 3-2. WorldCom share prices and the S&P 500/100

In 1998, WorldCom had purchased MCI, the long-distance carrier, for about $42 billion. Now WorldCom is faced with $30 billion of debt, $6 billion of which belongs to MCI. Analysts once believed that WorldCom was preparing to sell MCI, whose revenues fell 15% in 2000 and could drop even further in the future.[10] WorldCom was unlikely to receive anywhere near the price it paid for MCI in 1998.

Prior to the MCI purchase, WorldCom had been buying small telephone companies that did not attract much notice. In the same pattern seen with Tyco, investors bid up the price of WorldCom's stock, giving it the currency to go after MCI and other large acquisitions. In 1999, WorldCom attempted to purchase Sprint Corporation for $129 billion, but the deal fell through when the government opposed it on antitrust grounds. This means that one year later, WorldCom was valuing Sprint at more than three times what it had paid for MCI. The MCI purchase is another illustration of overpayment; imagine the subsequent blow to WorldCom if it had succeeded in buying Sprint and its value dropped the same percentage as MCI's.

WorldCom illustrates a number of the factors contributing to the Winner's Curse of overvaluing a purchase. Because of its accounting

10. *Business Week*, June 24, 2002.

scandals, these lessons will probably be lost as the focus now is on bankruptcy as creditors seek to salvage as much as they can. WorldCom was under pressure to grow and increase its stock price so the company could continue to add businesses, which in turn increased its annual revenues. There is evidence that stock analysts and investment bankers were happy to participate in this effort. Salomon Brothers underwrote WorldCom's bond offerings and advised the firm on billions of dollars of mergers and acquisitions. Salomon's top telecommunications analyst, Jack Grubman, advised the company and only changed his rating of WorldCom stock to "underperforming" after the announcement of the accounting misstatements.[11] Ebbers's compensation and the huge loans the company made to him are certainly signs of managerial optimism, hubris, and a sense of invulnerability.

The mother of mergers

During the height of the Internet boom, on January 10, 2000, America OnLine, led by Steven Case, bid $166 billion in an all-stock offer for Time-Warner. At the time of the merger, AOL was a delivery company with little content, while Time-Warner was a content company without a strong online presence. The expected results were those famous "synergies" that justify so many mergers. The two companies were complementary, and together they would be more than the sum of their individual parts. Company executives promised a 30% increase in operating profit the first year, adding $1 billion to what the two companies would have earned without a merger.[12] AOL issued new stock and took on more debt for the purchase.

AOL had another significant reason for wanting to merge: the Time-Warner cable properties. AOL is primarily a dial-up service; a small minority of its subscribers use broadband. Yet to distribute content that includes a lot of graphics like photographs, music, and movies, subscribers need broadband. Data compression helps, but it is not enough to enable a viewer to download a movie at the speed of a modem connection.

The timing of the merger turned out to be bad for the shareholders of both companies; AOL was paying for 55% of Time-Warner with inflated stock. When the Internet bubble broke a few months later, the benefits of the deal for shareholders became less obvious. Gerald Levin,

---

11. *Wall Street Journal*, June 27, 2002.
12. *New York Times*, October 14, 2002.

Time-Warner's CEO, had participated in other mergers, most of which turned out reasonably well, including the 1995 $7.5 billion merger with Turner Broadcasting and acquisitions in the cable television business. Neither he nor Case anticipated what was coming in the next two years, including a 60% decline in the value of AOL Time-Warner stock.

AOL has not been able to make a dramatic improvement in Time-Warner's business. It has been hurt by the end of the dot-com boom; advertising revenues have fallen; and Microsoft Network (MSN) is turning out to be a formidable competitor. One analyst thinks that AOL would be better as a division of Time-Warner than as a merger partner.

The two CEOs were overly optimistic about merging the companies. They promised a lot more than they, or possibly anyone, could deliver. The new company was supposed to induce 35 million AOL subscribers to purchase more Time-Warner movies, magazines, and music while subscribing to Time-Warner cable broadband Internet services. Resistance from existing business units meant that many of the promised synergies did not happen. One example of how poorly the integration of the two companies progressed was a mandate that all employees switch to AOL e-mail. Time-Warner employees rebelled; they complained that AOL's mail system could not handle large digital images and occasionally lost messages. Executives rescinded the e-mail mandate, now a symbol of the overoptimism about synergies that helped motivate the merger.[13]

It is easy to understand the difficulty in cross-selling, but it is much more difficult to grasp why AOL did not make a major push to sign up broadband customers. It only has 5% of the high-speed Internet services market compared to 37% of the dial-up market.[14] Did the company delay because cable customers are about half as profitable as dial-up subscribers?

Finally, in late 2002, AOL announced a new strategy to encourage broadband as well as to improve customer satisfaction. It began marketing a $14.95 per month service to customers who have broadband access from other companies. Someone with a cable modem from Comcast or a DSL line from a communications carrier can have access to all of the features that AOL offers. The question is whether people will be willing to pay this much given the nature of the services, though AOL says it will be improving content greatly. A comparable deal from MSN is only $9.95, and it remains to be seen how this new strategy will work. Much of the

13. *New York Times*, July 21, 2002.
14. *New York Times*, July 21, 2002.

outcome depends on whether Time-Warner management will make its content available on AOL. Time-Warner has not been particularly cooperative to date.

Further benefits of the merger were to come from centralizing advertising sales and developing packages that would include most Time-Warner units. "Time-Warner would entice advertisers with the promise of space in Time magazines, air time on Turner cable networks, spots on AOL, and licensing opportunities with Warner Brothers film studio."[15] Some Time-Warner executives did not think their ads would be more valuable if combined with online ads on AOL. There are stories of bitter infighting at the company and reports that powerful Time-Warner division heads felt they could do better by selling their own ads, which finally doomed the effort. Another potential synergy went unrealized.

In the first quarter of 2002, AOL Time-Warner took a $54 billion write-down for its decline in value since the merger. By this time, the company's stock had dropped more than 60%. AOL Time-Warner reported a net loss for the year 2002 of $98.7 billion after taking a fourth-quarter charge of $45.5 billion, mostly as a write-down of the value of America OnLine. When Robert Pittman (AOL) and Richard Parsons (Time-Warner) co-chief operating officers, visited company locations, they found employees and shareholders almost in open revolt against senior management, especially Pittman.[16] Most of these executives watched helplessly as their savings in company stock disappeared.

There are a number of reports of tremendous discord among executives of the merged companies. The first managerial casualty of the merger was Gerald Levin, who stepped down in December 2001. In July 2002, the company announced a major change in management during which Robert Pittman left, and former Time-Warner executives took over all of the key positions in the company. The top three managers after Steve Case were Richard Parsons (chief executive), Don Logan (chairperson of media and communications), and Jeff Bewkes (chairperson of entertainment and networks); all three are from Time-Warner. With Pittman's departure, the board of directors was now evenly split between AOL and Time-Warner representatives.

It is reported that at high-level strategy meetings in May 2002, the company moved away from a focus on synergies between the Internet

15. *Wall Street Journal*, July 18, 2002.
16. *New York Times*, July 7, 2002.

and content businesses and toward stressing divisional autonomy.[17] Parsons supposedly decided to let operating divisions operate in their own best interests, as they did at Time-Warner before the merger with AOL.[18] In less than two years, the company had given up on the original premise of the merger.

In January 2003, Steve Case announced that he would step down as chairperson of AOL Time-Warner after the May board meeting, though he would retain his seat on the board. The reason for his resignation was shareholder anger over the disappointing results of the AOL and Time-Warner merger. AOL, which was flying high at the merger, has been dragging down the stock of the combined companies. Many of the firms that advertised on AOL went out of business, and others cut back on online advertising. Revenues plummeted, and the stock price went with them. Case has floated the idea of spinning off AOL, which would undo the merger after a tremendous loss in value for shareholders.

What went wrong with the AOL and Time-Warner merger? Figure 3-3 shows the stock price of the company versus the Standard and Poor's (S&P) 500 following the merger announcement in January 2000. AOL

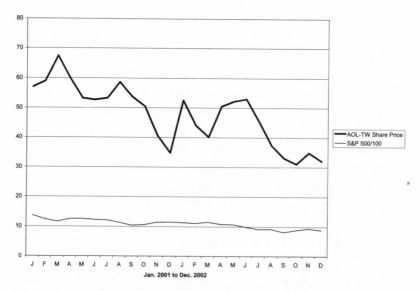

Figure 3-3. AOL Time-Warner share prices and the S&P 500/100

17. *New York Times*, July 27, 2002.
18. *Wall Street Journal*, July 18, 2002.

made its offer for Time-Warner when its stock was near its highest point, and Time-Warner accepted. Was the offer too low or too high? Holders of Time-Warner stock may argue that Levin sold out for too little, while AOL stockholders complain that AOL took on too much in trying to merge with a company like Time-Warner.

Whoever is right, it is clear that, so far, the shareholders of both companies are worse off than before the merger. The S&P 500 is down about 30% since the merger while AOL Time-Warner shares are off about 75%. Measured from the last trading day before the merger plans were announced, January 7, 2000, as of January 2003, AOL stock is down 80% while Time-Warner shareholders have seen 65% of the value they had in the company disappear.[19] This gigantic merger is another telling example of the Winner's Curse; AOL Time-Warner has already taken a $54 billion write-down, which is a strong sign that the two companies greatly overvalued their combination. The company has dropped "AOL" from its name. The two men behind the merger suffered further from the Curse as both ended up losing their jobs.

What factors from our model of the Winner's Curse affected this largest merger of all time? Certainly there was a sense of competition and winning. AOL had fought skeptics all of its life, and over 15 years Steve Case had demonstrated that they were wrong. He built AOL into the largest online service provider. Case and Levin thought there would be synergies with AOL providing the delivery mechanism for Time-Warner's content; both exhibited excessive managerial optimism, hubris, and feelings of invulnerability. Excessive managerial optimism contributed to the belief that the two chairpersons could successfully merge the strategies and operations of an Internet company like AOL with Time-Warner, a company with autonomous divisions and powerful executives. The two chairpersons, in their optimism and enthusiasm, did not adequately consider the organizational challenges of achieving the synergies predicted for the merged company. Levin felt that digital communications offered more opportunities for growth than "old economy" businesses like publishing and movies, and the pressures for growth fueled another merger. Other growth pressures include the need for America OnLine to provide high-speed cable access and to grow its subscriber base. AOL's inflated Internet stock price made the purchase possible, helped by stock analysts and investment bankers.

19. *New York Times*, January 14, 2003.

The story is that Case and Levin worked out the merger in a short time period with little input from other managers in either company. One Time-Warner top manager reported that the deal was announced on a Monday morning, and he had found out about it only the previous Sunday night.[20] His question was: how could the chairperson sell 55% of the company without consulting with top managers? When managers rush a deal, they do not have time to conduct a careful analysis, and they invite the Winner's Curse. The results in the AOL Time-Warner merger have been a huge write-off and a great deal of suffering for the shareholders and employees of the two companies.

Tales of two banks

Bank One corporation

In the late 1980s and early 1990s, Bank One of Columbus, Ohio, made more than 100 acquisitions. In 1996, its chairperson, John B. McCoy, announcing a rest period, said, "We're not going to overpay, and we're not going to do dumb deals."[21] In January 1997, Bank One ended its slowdown in acquisitions and bought First USA for $7 billion. The price was 20 times estimated earnings, while Bank One's stock was priced at about 14 times earnings. McCoy defended the purchase and said "you're going to pay more" for a target likely to grow swiftly.

Shortly thereafter, Bank One bought First Commerce Corporation for $2.97 billion, some 24 times annual earnings. Less than a year later, Bank One merged with First Chicago, paying with $21 billion in stock. McCoy promised to produce more than $930 million of savings from the merger and to find more than $270 million in new revenue—a total of $1.2 billion in synergies over three years.[22]

First USA is a large credit card issuer, and Bank One soon encountered problems as it pushed the unit for an even greater contribution to its profits. (First USA in a good year generated one-third of the total corporation's profits.) Under pressure, First USA mistreated cardholders by increasing interest rates to 19.9% if they paid one day late on two occasions. The competition for credit card accounts is fierce, and customers simply abandoned First USA.

20. *New York Times*, May 17, 2002.
21. *Wall Street Journal*, June 6, 2002.
22. *Barrons*, March 15, 1999.

John McCoy was forced out as chairperson shortly after the First Chicago merger. A Bank One spokesperson said, "We did a poor job of integrating them effectively." As for overpaying, "It is so hard to know whether the prices were right."[23] The poor performance of Bank One is shown by its stock price in comparison to the S&P 500 in figure 3-4.

Jamie Dimon became the CEO of Bank One after a falling out with Sandy Weill at Citigroup. Dimon has worked hard to turn the bank around, but he faces a number of problems from all of the bank's past acquisitions. The bank still has not linked together all of the computer systems from its acquisitions; for example, there are seven deposit systems. And, of course, Dimon has made acquisitions of his own; most notably, he paid $8 billion for Wachovia's credit card operation, making Bank One number two in the credit card business after Citigroup.

After years as an acquirer, Bank One found itself on the other side of a deal; in January 2004, J. P. Morgan announced a takeover of Bank One in a $58 billion merger. William Harrison, CEO of J. P. Morgan Chase, had been under pressure to find a successor; one was not obvious from within the bank. As a part of the deal, Harrison is CEO and Dimon is chief operating officer (COO) of the merged banks. Dimon is scheduled

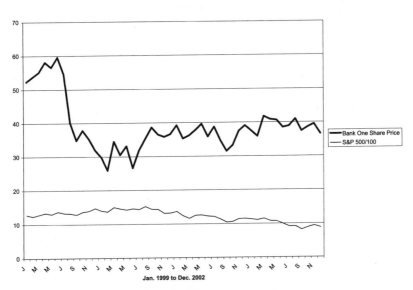

Figure 3-4. Bank One share prices and the S&P 500/100

23. *Wall Street Journal*, June 6, 2002.

to inherit Harrison's title in 2006.[24] It will be interesting to see if this final Bank One merger experiences the Winner's Curse.

It would seem to us that the prices for its purchases were not reasonable and that Bank One is another serial acquirer that overpaid for its acquisitions. What is interesting about Bank One and the other examples in this chapter is that they are not only serial acquirers, they are serial victims of overpayment. The pressures for overvaluation seem to have become more intense over time, as these companies grew through acquisition and needed to constantly increase their stock prices to pay for further acquisitions that would feed earnings and growth. We see a vicious cycle in which overly optimistic valuations led the acquirers to win the companies they purchased. When the stock market dropped in 2001 and 2002, could it be that investors caught on to the overpayment before management did? The firms' drops in market value illustrate the cruel results of paying too much when investors realize that a company has overvalued its purchases.

First Union and two troublesome acquisitions

First Union is a bank that acquired other banks and financial services companies to fuel its growth. Its chairperson for 27 years, Edward Crutchfield, made 90 acquisitions as First Union became the sixth largest bank in the United States. As a part of the shopping spree, First Union purchased CoreStates Financial and the Money Store (a consumer finance company), both in 1998, and the Wachovia Corporation in 2001. First Union adopted its latest purchase's name and is now Wachovia.

First Union paid $19.8 billion for CoreStates and then had a great deal of trouble integrating it with other operations. Management decided to free banking staff from mundane processing tasks in order to sell more products. To accomplish this time savings, they directed clients who needed help to computerized call systems rather than branch employees. About 20% of CoreStates' 2 million customers left the bank, forcing it to lay off 5,800 workers to cut costs. These layoffs and cost cutting led the bank to replace more tellers, further angering customers.[25] First Union management was overly optimistic about its ability to integrate CoreStates into its operations, and both employees and customers paid the price.

24. *New York Times*, January 15, 2004; *Business Week*, January 26, 2004.
25. *Wall Street Journal*, June 27, 2000.

The Money Store purchase led to even greater problems, though the purchase cost was only $2.1 billion. The Money Store is a subprime lender, a company that lends to customers with poor credit histories. Its advertisements appeared regularly on late night television with noted athletes as spokespeople. Crutchfield felt that the Money Store would give the bank experience in lending at high interest rates to borrowers who were not good credit risks. In addition, First Union's investment banking arm could earn fees by securitizing Money Store loans and selling them to investors.

First Union's due diligence study of the Money Store before its acquisition missed some important signals. The Money Store followed the normal practice of subprime lenders, which is called *gain-on-sale accounting*. The company booked earnings from loans as soon as they were made, rather than after they were paid off. A bank like First Union would book earnings after the loan was paid off. The Money Store's approach works fine as long as the loans perform as expected. However, if there are an unusually large number of defaults, already booked earnings disappear.

Interest rates fell in 1998, and Money Store borrowers paid off their loans early, reducing profit margins. The Money Store then cut its own rates and loaned money to customers with even worse credit histories. At the same time, the market for mortgage-backed securities diminished, so the lender had to absorb the risk of these loans itself.

Diagnosed with cancer, Crutchfield stepped down as COO, but remained chairperson. Ken Thompson became the chief executive, and he soon sent a team to the Money Store to find all of its loans that were sure to default. The results were pretty discouraging: the Money Store was capable of "sucking the life" out of First Union. The investigators found that credit controls did not exist or were ineffective, and accounting was lax. Loans originated in 2000 would be $3 billion instead of an expected $5 billion. Thompson tried to find a customer for the Money Store, but there were too many other subprime assets for sale at the same time.[26]

In June 2000, First Union announced that it was closing the Money Store, selling two other units, closing 80 branches, and taking a $2.9 billion charge. The bank laid off more than 2,300 employees at the Money Store. (Remember that the bank had bought the Money Store only two years earlier for $2.1 billion.)

26. *Wall Street Journal*, July 25, 2000.

The CoreStates and Money Store acquisitions are two more examples of the Winner's Curse. In the case of CoreStates, the bank was overly optimistic about its ability to integrate the acquisition into First Union's operations. The strategy behind the Money Store purchase was questionable as the business model for a combined full-service bank and subprime lender is not well defined, and the due diligence before the purchase was flawed. Was this hubris and invulnerability on Crutchfield's part after 90 acquisitions? Were there pressures for growth from analysts and investment bankers? First Union is another serial acquirer that eventually paid too much and suffered the consequences.

Mergers, movies, booze, and three billion lost dollars

Vivendi started out as Compagnie Generale des Eaux, loosely translated as the General Water Company in France. Jean-Marie Messier joined Vivendi in 1994 and decided that this old-line utility should become a large conglomerate and that it would become best known as a media company. *Business Week Online* described Messier and Vivendi on June 11, 2001:

> Not since Napoleon has France produced an empire-builder as ambitious as Jean-Marie Messier. In five years of voracious deal making, the 44-year-old dynamo has transformed a financially ailing French utility into Vivendi Universal, the world's No. 2 media company behind AOL Time Warner. Last year, Messier acquired Seagram Co., adding Universal Studios and Universal Music Group to his portfolio.
>
> Since then he has scooped up a bevy of online music and game businesses. And on June 1 he sealed a $1.7 billion acquisition of U.S. education publisher Houghton Mifflin. "Worldwide, we want to be in the top three of any content business we are in," Messier says. "If we aren't in the top three, we won't stay."

Added to this list in 2001 were the cable TV holdings of Barry Diller's USA Networks, which Vivendi acquired for $11 billion.

Messier's mad acquisition spree produced a company that pipes water in Paris and hauls garbage in Bogota. Vivendi Environment does all of these things as a separately listed company, but it is 63% owned by Vivendi Universal, which rolls Vivendi Environment's financials into its own. Vivendi's utility business produces close to $25 billion in revenue. Did the utility mask weaknesses in other Vivendi units? It is hard to tell as the analysts and investors criticize the company for its convoluted and murky accounting. As another example, one of Vivendi's fastest growing units is Cegetel, a French phone company. It is only 44% owned by Vivendi, however, Vivendi books 100% of Cegetel's operating earnings when computing its EBITDA (earnings before interest, taxes, debt, and amortization).[27]

One of Vivendi's largest and most famous purchases was Seagram's in June 2000. Edgar Bronfman, a member of the storied Bronfman family of Canada, controlled Seagram Company, a liquor and entertainment powerhouse that owned Universal Studios in Hollywood as well as Universal Music, the largest music company in the world. The price tag: $34 billion. The deal combined Seagram's film and music business with Vivendi's European cable TV, satellite, and Internet service providers to create Vivendi Universal. Vivendi also owns Canal Plus, a pay-television company.

Messier's motivation was to create scale and to continue to expand Vivendi, which was now second only to AOL Time-Warner in size. He would gain a foothold in Hollywood and add music to his media empire. The claim was that Vivendi Universal would have $55 billion in revenue and no debt. This outcome was possible because the deal was an all-stock transaction valued at $77.35 per Seagram's share. To help pay for the deal, Vivendi planned to sell $7–8 billion of Seagram's drinks business and to float 30% of Vivendi Environment's stock.[28]

In total, Vivendi spent more than $50 billion in less than three years on acquisitions. Soon Vivendi's stock began to plummet (see figure 3-5). By 2003, Vivendi's market capitalization had dropped more than $70 billion compared to the summer of 2002. No one noticed this decline more than Edgar Bronfman. He had bought 80% of MCA Corporation, the owner of Universal Studios, in 1995. Bronfman hired a former talent agent, Ron Meyer, to run the studio. Meyer lured the best talent to the studio and began turning out hit movies like *The Mummy, Meet the Parents*, and *The Fast and the Furious*. By the time Bronfman sold Seagram's to Vivendi, Universal had doubled the size of its music operation and had returned its movie studio to prominence.[29] By the end of Messier's tenure at Vivendi, the Bronfman family stake had dropped in value from $6.5 billion to $3 billion on paper.[30]

27. *Business Week Online*, March 4, 2002; *www.businessweek.com*
28. Associated Press, June 20, 2000.
29. *Business Week Online*, December 27, 2001.
30. *Business Week Online*, January 13, 2003.

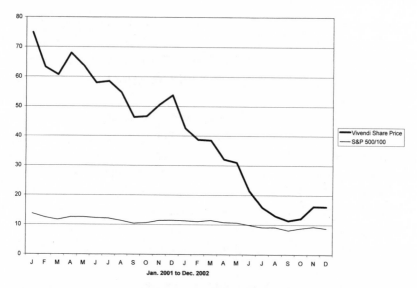

Figure 3-5. Vivendi share prices and the S&P 500/100

By mid-2002, it was time for Messier to exit Vivendi. He tried to present a survival plan to the board to cut Vivendi's €17 billion ($15.6 billion) debt and halt the slide in the company's stock, which lost 45 percent of its value in 2003 alone. The company also posted a €13.6 billion net loss in 2001.

His plan is likely to include the partial sale of Vivendi Environment, France's biggest water and sewage company, along with other assets. Environment, which has seen its share price fall by one-third in the past 12 months—has been a source of cash to help pay down the group's debt and fund acquisitions. . . .

After winning much praise as a deal maker—chalking up a string of acquisitions, including Canada's Seagram and French pay-TV and film company Canal Plus—Messier has come under growing criticism for not delivering a clear picture of his plans for the expanded company.

Most recently, he came under fire for his sudden dismissal of Canal Plus boss Pierre Lescure. Canal Plus is responsible for producing the majority of French films, and his handling of the matter prompted concerns over the unit's editorial independence as well as Messier's commitment to French culture.[31]

31. *www.CNN.com.europe*, May 29, 2002.

On July 2, 2002, news sources reported that Messier had resigned from Vivendi, supposedly with assurances that a French person would be its new head. Messier left a company that at one point was worth $100 billion, but was valued at less than 20% of that amount on his departure.[32] Jean-Rene Fourtou, Messier's successor as head of Vivendi, found that the company would run out of money within several days of his assuming the position because banks did not want to lend to Vivendi if Messier was still in charge, and the financial picture of the firm remained so unclear. Fourtou successfully sold bonds to provide cash to tide the company over while he worked on plans to sell off pieces of Vivendi, unwinding many of the mergers and acquisitions that Messier undertook during his reign.

Vivendi, its shareholders, and Edgar Bronfman suffered from the Winner's Curse during the company's acquisitions spree. Messier was obsessed with buying and winning other companies; he wanted Vivendi to become the biggest media conglomerate in the world. Messier continually exuded managerial optimism up until he was forced out by the board of directors. His hubris shows in Messier's observation that his ouster was a blow to French capitalism. As Vivendi grew, the market pressured it for further growth. Investment bankers and stock analysts questioned the financial information the company provided, but they also seemed happy to do business with it. Looking at Vivendi and AOL Time-Warner, we would say that the Winner's Curse has not been kind to large media companies.

The overall merger picture

We mostly concentrated above on the so-called serial acquirers, companies that have undertaken numerous takeovers of other firms. The analysis suggests that many of these acquirers experienced the Winner's Curse repeatedly. But for those companies that merge infrequently, are the results any different?

Business Week on October 14, 2002, published the results of research conducted on mergers that was designed by the head of Boston Consulting Group's mergers and acquisitions practice. The staff examined 1,000 deals worth at least $500 million announced between July 1, 1995, and August 31, 2001. The M&A activity during this period was five times larger

32. BBC News, July 2, 2002.

than any previous boom; from 1998 to 2000, deals totaled nearly $4 trillion, more than the preceding 30 years combined. To be part of the study, the merger had to include at least one U.S. company, and the study excluded mergers with private sellers or where the buyer paid less than 15% of its own market cap or made another major acquisition within a year. These requirements reduced the sample to 301 deals. To evaluate the outcome of a merger, the researchers determined the returns to the shareholders of both acquiring and acquired firms in two periods: one week before the deal was announced to one week after, and one week before to one year after. The final number was the difference in percentage points between the companies' returns and their peers' in the S&P 500 stock index.

   Business Week's major conclusion was that "most big deals don't pay off." Some examples:

   Travelers Group and Citicorp in a $70 billion merger.
   Insurer Conseco with a $7.1 billion bid (an 86% premium) to buy
      mobile-home lender Green Tree Financial. (Conseco has since
      filed for bankruptcy.)
   Bank One Corporation and its $28.8 billion offer for First Chicago
      NBD Corporation.
   NationsBank's bid $59.3 billion for BankAmerica.
   The merger of Daimler Benz and Chrysler Corporation for $38.6
      billion.

Using the methodology described above, the analysis showed that 17 out of the 21 mergers in the spring of 1998 did not pay off for investors. In the year after the Green Tree bid, Conseco shares lost 47% of their value, and its relative performance lagged behind its peers by 55%. Its stock dropped to 10 cents in a subsequent restructuring. Looking at the numbers, 61% of buyers destroyed their own shareholders' wealth; a year after the deals, the losers' average return was 25 percentage points below peers in the industry.

   What do the researchers think went wrong? First, the expansion of the stock market inflated stock prices, providing cheap currency for acquisitions. (Interestingly, the performance of mergers that involved cash was better than for those employing stock only.) Basically, *Business Week* contended that the bidders paid too much, which sounds a lot like the Winner's Curse. The CEOs offered an average premium above the target's market price of 36%. The *Business Week* analysis showed that sellers collected over 19% extra returns on their stock value compared to peers in their industry. The other factors from our model also applied: "Executives were brimming with confidence and rich stocks." It also appears that CEOs were overly optimistic about the synergies that would result from a merger, and they discounted the difficulties of integrating two companies.

There have been a number of academic studies of mergers and acquisitions. The studies take quite different perspectives; they come from faculty in organization and management departments and from finance. The finance literature has a number of studies of mergers, most often examining the stock prices of the acquiring and the target firms around the time of the announcement of the deal. In general, the results show that the stock price of the acquiring firm drops, while the price of the target firm's stock goes up, though the results are not as strong as the *Business Week* study shows. Investors are expressing their pessimism about the potential of the merger by selling the acquiring company's stock. Other investors feel that the price offered for the target will increase, so they purchase its stock in advance of the merger.

Many of the finance studies look just at the time around the announcement of a merger or takeover and ignore the longer term. Agrawal and Jaffe reviewed 22 studies of long-term stock returns following acquisitions and concluded that long-run performance is negative following mergers. However, long-run performance is neutral or positive following tender offers.[33]

Hubris defined and measured

We have suggested that hubris on the part of managers contributes to overpaying for an acquisition.[34] Two Columbia University professors, Matthew Hayward and Donald Hambrick, set out to define and measure managerial hubris and see how it affected the prices paid for merger targets.[35] These two researchers argue that takeovers primarily reflect deci-

33. A. Agrawal and J. Jaffe, "The Post-Merger Performance Puzzle," in *Advances in Mergers and Acquisitions*, ed. C. Cooper and A. Gregory, vol. 1 (Amsterdam: Elsevier Science, 2000), 7–41.

34. J. Kagel and D. Levin discuss hubris in *Common Value Auctions and the Winner's Curse* (Princeton, N.J.: Princeton University Press, 2002), 107.

35. M. Hayward and D. Hambrick, "Explaining the Premium Paid for Large Acquisitions: Evidence of CEO Hubris," *Administrative Science Quarterly* 42, no. 1 (1997): 103–127.

sions on the part of the acquiring firm's managers, and the key decision maker is the CEO. The dictionary definition of *hubris* is "exaggerated pride or self-confidence, often resulting in retribution." The term comes from Greek mythology, where hubris was considered man's cardinal sin. Those who were excessively confident, presumptuous, overly ambitious, and lacking in humility were struck down by the gods. (One might see signs of Greek mythological retribution in the fates of some CEOs at places like Enron, WorldCom, Tyco, and Vivendi.)

How does hubris apply to a merger? Extremely confident managers are overly optimistic about their abilities to extract the benefits anticipated from a merger, and they consequently pay too large a premium for the target company. These researchers identified a number of sources of managerial hubris, including:

1. recent organizational success (think of the serial acquirers),
2. media attention for the CEO,
3. exaggerated sense of self-importance, and
4. weak boards that defer to the CEO.

These two faculty members conducted a study in which they measured hubris and looked at the composition of company boards, company performance, and takeover premiums that companies paid for acquisitions in 106 transactions between 1989 and 1992. The transactions had to involve prices of more than $100 million since these acquisitions were major and would involve the CEO. The degree of managerial hubris was associated with the size of the takeover premium. The results on average were losses in shareholder wealth for the acquiring firm, and the greater the CEO hubris and acquisition premium, the greater the shareholder losses.

Conclusions

It is important to stress that not all mergers have failed. Our point is that any merger or acquisition is subject to the Winner's Curse, but not all M&As experience it. One economist has argued that mergers in general are prone to the Curse;[36] unlike a lot of economic activities that include the decisions of many buyers and sellers, takeovers reflect individual decisions. These decisions are usually made by CEOs.

36. Richard Roll, "The Hubris Hypothesis of Corporate Takeovers," *Journal of Business* 59, no. 2, pt. 1 (April 1986): 197–216.

One can look at a potential acquisition as an auction in which the first bid is the market price of the target company. If you believe in the efficient markets hypothesis, then this market price is the real value of the firm, but no one ever buys a firm without offering a premium to induce shareholders to sell. The acquiring firm, then, is subject to the Winner's Curse similar to the winner of an art auction at Christie's. Managerial hubris leads the CEO and the acquiring firm to generally overpay for the target.

To illustrate the Winner's Curse, this chapter has presented evidence of mergers that did not work out as planned. The objective is to warn those involved in merger activities to be careful. There are a number of things that have to go right for a merger to succeed; experiencing the Winner's Curse will certainly make a positive outcome more difficult.

Managers in M&A situations should be wary of getting into a bidding psychology that drives the price of an acquisition far above its subsequent value. Do not be caught up in winning a contest for another firm. Managers need to temper their optimism about the synergies of a merger, how easy it will be to meld the cultures of two organizations, and the cost savings that will result. Excessive hubris and feelings of invulnerability are a good way to get into trouble in a merger. CEOs like Kozlowski, Levin, and Case illustrate these traits.

Managers also need to be wary of the market; investment bankers profit handsomely from representing either side in a merger. We have seen inflated stock prices encouraging firms to become serial acquirers. Since the serial acquirer has to estimate the value of a lot of companies, statistically some of its estimates are going to be too high and it will overpay. Finally, unrealistic business models contribute to overpaying; the digital convergence business model of AOL Time-Warner proved to be impossible to realize given the nature of the two organizations, the state of the technology, and their customers.

What to do?

Beyond being wary of the problems in mergers illustrated by the Winner's Curse, what else can management do to increase the probability of a successful acquisition? We have talked to managers and experts in the field and examined reports on a large number of mergers and acquisitions. Given the evidence on merger failures, it is clear that there is no formula that will guarantee success. Here is what some experts and practitioners have found helpful:

Examine your own experience with mergers and acquisitions

Successful companies take a good hard look at their own experiences with past M&A activities. As first coined in *Alice in Wonderland,* this "through the looking glass darkly" strategy goes a long way toward ensuring that senior management does not get carried away in an M&A frenzy. It is imperative to perform a postmortem analysis one, two, and five years after every victory in the acquisition battle. A CEO should also see that the staff gathers postdeal intelligence on competitors' experiences after M&A victories. The acquisitions team and the board should use this information to examine which acquisitions worked and which failed. Why did some of these mergers succeed and others become a disaster? What can be learned?

Based on this analysis, the company can decide when to go for the M&A victory, when not to, and how to make a merger work. A firm that analyzes the reasons for its successes and failures can use that knowledge to judge a new acquisition and to plan for postmerger integration of the two firms. The more similar that past mergers are to the current target, the more valid the transfer of knowledge from the past.

Do not get carried away by your suitor

The folklore in the investment banking community is that when deals come their way, the first and most important thing the bankers look at is the management team. After that, they examine the "space" in which the company operates, what unique product or service it offers, and whether or not it can be profitable within a specific period of time. In the case of M&As, the management team plays a paramount role. An acquisition or merger is triggered by a CEO calling another about a potential partnership. A management team that has been successful in the past is always a good draw, and if the CEO has a good track record, for whatever reason, then the chances of pulling off a successful marriage are higher.

It is important, however, not to get carried away by the "beauty" of your suitor. There is no substitute for doing due diligence, no matter how attractive the management team might be. The track records of the lead executive and management team have to be examined carefully. At the end of the day, the merger has to make sense from the point of view of long-term profitability. It is important to ask the following questions about M&A suitors:

Is the positive "buzz" associated with the suitor justified by past performance?

Is the management team successful in engineering mergers only to fail to keep the newly acquired business going?

Have they been successful in actually building profitable companies?

Does the team work to make the postmerger company succeed, or do they leave at the first possible opportunity to cash in on financial rewards from the merger?

Analyze the operations of the postmerger company before the merger

Managers too often focus on the deal and forget about the complexity of a corporate marriage. In many respects, the deal is the easy part; the success of the merger depends on management's ability to integrate merged or acquired firms. Even before the deal is made or the potential acquisition is initiated, it is important to perform an operations analysis of the postmerger company. In most cases, this involves taking a good look at the operating principles and style of the acquisition target. In some cases, in order to get a good grip on future operations, one might develop different operating scenarios for the postmerger company. Even better would be to set up an effective operating structure before the merger is finally inked.

As an example, consider the merger of Burroughs and Sperry to create Unisys. Burroughs manufactured large mainframe computers, and Sperry made minicomputers and computer-control equipment. The merger's aim was to create a computer giant with the ability to provide products for every segment of the computer industry at that time. These synergies notwithstanding, each company had a distinct style of operations. Burroughs had a few very large orders every year and worked to keep these customers happy. Sperry recruited new customers heavily and was in the business of marketing and selling equipment all the time. Had senior management done an operations analysis of the future Unisys, it would have been obvious that the merger would create a heterogeneous company with many different cultures and operations and that different organizational structures would be needed to successfully manage this diverse company. Instead, after the merger, management tried to create a homogeneous style too quickly, and this approach proved to be disastrous. Common marketing, operating, and incentive systems created a lot of stress for those who came from Burroughs and from Sperry. There was infighting among executives and managers about what needed to be done, who was responsible for what, and who contributed what to the company. It took Unisys more than ten years to get on track.

Conversely, Cisco has been a master in acquiring and integrating companies. Even before a deal is finished, Cisco sends an executive team to examine postmerger operational issues. In some cases, the company being acquired fits in well with the culture and operations of Cisco. In these cases, during postmerger the new company is completely folded into Cisco's organizational structure. Where the assessment is that post-merger operations will work, Cisco leaves the day-to-day operations management intact. In other instances, the potential acquisition target operates in a different mode and perhaps in a different geographic region. If the executive team decides that postmerger operations are going to be difficult to manage, Cisco is likely to decide that winning is not everything and will walk away from the acquisition. In both cases, the focus is on ensuring that the company being acquired adapts to Cisco's information and operating systems before the execution date of the deal.

Shearson Lehman Brothers at one point in its history frequently acquired other brokerage firms. Most brokerage firms operated pretty much the same way, and thus it was not that difficult to integrate the operations of the acquired firm. To make the transition smoother, Shearson Lehman Brothers decided to create "the play book," a detailed set of manuals for how to convert the systems at the acquired brokerage to its own systems. A broker at the acquired firm could go home on Friday and come back Monday to a new owner and continue working as if nothing had happened.

The compatibility and integration of information technology (IT) in companies that are merging are too often forgotten. Today, with the technology pervasive and key to the operations of most organizations, it is important for management to have IT experts assess the compatibility and the ease of integrating the technology of the two firms involved.

Make sure that your employees count

Desh Deshpande, the CEO of Sycamore Networks, was asked by a Wharton MBA class in 2000 to explain why his small company was valued more highly than Cisco. His explanation was telling; he said that the value of his company "walks away every night." He hopes that they (meaning, the employees) walk back in. Managers may experience euphoria if they win a merger or an acquisition, but they need to make sure that the employees in the new firm count. M&As are synonymous with layoffs, yet in most mergers, especially in the high-tech industries, skilled employees are a key resource for the new firm. If the merger results in a demoralized workforce and an outmigration of the most valuable employees, then no matter how good the prospects of synergy or how streamlined an operations structure, the potential of the merger is unlikely to be realized.

It makes sense to plan ahead for any restructuring and, if there are to be layoffs, to announce one round as soon as the merger is complete. Most important, the CEO should also announce that it is the final round of layoffs. This strategy will ensure that the employees who remain behind know that they are part of the M&A victory, rather than a future casualty. At this time, management should also announce changes in organization structure and reporting responsibilities to remove as much uncertainty for employees as possible.

In addition to removing uncertainty, it is also important to provide incentives for the employees to really make the merger a success. In many cases, and the high-tech boom of the 1990s is a prime example, managers of the target firm come into the acquiring firm with lucrative financial packages, including stock options. This windfall can cause morale problems within the organization. It was an open secret that highly respected Lucent employees were unhappy after every new acquisition because the management team of an upstart company, probably with an average age in the mid-30s, made millions from the acquisition. Many highly qualified Lucent employees, making far less, left the company. You do not want to lose key people from your own firm because employees are unhappy about the amount of money spent on the acquisition or on the employees of the acquired firm. Making sure that all employees count will go a long way toward seeing that a victory in an M&A battle is not short-lived.

Don't forget about your competitors

By winning an M&A contest, it may seem that you have given competitors a "black eye." It is unlikely they will take the loss lying down. Recently, PeopleSoft announced plans to acquire J. D. Edwards, a vendor of supply-chain software, to strengthen itself against Oracle. Shortly after the announcement, Oracle offered to buy PeopleSoft for $7.5 billion. While a competitor may not react that drastically, it is important to keep in mind that competitors are unlikely to maintain the status quo given your M&A activities. In chapter 10, we discuss game theory as a way to anticipate moves by competitors.

Keep your focus on revenue growth

The stated motivation for many mergers is cost reduction and synergies. For example, HP and Compaq dramatically pared their combined list of products to reduce duplication and laid off a large number of employees. To the outside world, it looks like the merger is about eliminating duplication of positions and products. As we have mentioned before, at the end of the day, the merger has to make sense from the point of view of long-term profitability. While cost reduction does help, it is vital to not forget about revenue. You do not want to become so fixated on costs that you forget that the combined business has to have a way to generate money.

In fact, how one needs to pursue cost-cutting measures is usually different from how one enhances revenue. From the employee perspective, cost cutting is usually demoralizing, while revenue generation is energizing. A cost-cutting regime (including layoffs) that continues day to day will make employees wonder what or who is next. This approach could well make the best and brightest leave the company to work for competitors that lost out on the M&A sweepstakes, but have a more conducive work environment. We have already addressed the issue of keeping up employee morale. A revenue-generating regime will provide employees with goals to meet and paths to follow, and it will also give them a sense of having a stake in the company's success.

In addition to the effect on employees, keeping a focus on revenue growth will help the company take a more dynamic view of the future. It will bring out the creativity of the management team in product and service innovation. It is easy for chief executives to claim revenue and market share growth by simply engineering a merger or acquisition. If this is a sufficient yardstick to the board, then the energies of the executives will be on winning the M&A game. Changing the benchmark to the revenue growth of the *postmerger* company will shift the focus to making the merger a success.

The evidence is pretty overwhelming: a large number of mergers and acquisitions fail, and they do so for a variety of reasons. Carefully consider the recommendations in this chapter and look closely at the suggestions in chapter 10 before making an offer to buy another company. You will be glad you did.

4 • The Curse can appear anywhere

We have discussed examples of the Winner's Curse in places like the auction for wireless communications spectrum and mergers and acquisitions. These kinds of decisions are for a lot of money and affect everyone in the organizations involved. But the Curse goes beyond auctions and businesses; it has the potential to pop up in a variety of contexts, from licensing a product to the hiring of your favorite team's next coach. In this chapter, we depart further from the economist's strict definition of the Winner's Curse in an auction setting. We are expanding our view of the Curse to situations where an individual or organization overvalues a purchase, pays too much for it, and suffers the consequences. The organization has won what it wanted, but it has experienced the Curse in doing so.

Bristol-Meyers Squibb, Erbitux, and Martha Stewart

Pharmaceuticals companies have a straightforward business model. They invent, buy, or license high-priced prescription drugs that have patent protection and market them anyplace someone will pay for them. At the end of the patent period, generic drug manufacturers quickly enter the market, and the profits on the drug in question drop dramatically. The keys to success in the industry, then, are drug development, obtaining regulatory approval, and marketing.

Bristol-Meyers Squibb (BMS) had a drought of discoveries from its own laboratories; it had not had a blockbuster of its own for more than a decade prior to 2000. Its highly successful cancer drug, Taxol, was about to come off patent. BMS needed a cancer-fighting drug to generate sales and to maintain its reputation for anticancer drugs. A company named ImClone looked like it might have the answer in its drug Erbitux. But BMS encountered the Winner's Curse when it agreed to pay a high price to ImClone to share the rights to Erbitux prior to its approval by the U.S. Food and Drug Administration. When this approval did not materialize in the expected time frame, shares of BMS fell dramatically as the market reflected its overpayment and its failure to assign a reasonable value to Erbitux when negotiating with ImClone.

Dr. John Mendelsohn and his colleagues at the University of California, San Diego, created Erbitux in the 1980s. The research team's approach was based on the discovery that many types of cancer cells need certain proteins to multiply. The proteins attach to receptors on the surface of the cell to promote tumor growth. They fit into receptors like a key in a lock, and they send signals that tell the cells to grow. The San Diego researchers genetically engineered a version of the proteins that fit the receptors but that would not send the signals to grow.[1] Erbitux is one of a group of drugs called *epidermal growth factor receptor blockers,* which are aimed at the biochemical switches that signal normal cells to become malignant.

Dr. Samuel Waksal learned of this research in the early 1990s, and his company, ImClone, acquired the license for the drug by 1993. ImClone reportedly invested $200 million in developing Erbitux, but the company has never had a profit. Mendelsohn is president of M. D. Anderson Cancer Center in Houston, and he became a board member of ImClone. The company began clinical trials of Erbitux, and in June 2001 it reported a 22.5% response from severely ill colon cancer patients. At this point, the company started filing what is known as a *rolling application* for approval with the FDA. In this procedure, the pharmaceuticals company sends in portions of the application as they are completed, rather than sending all documents at once. During the approval process, the drug company and

---

1. *Wall Street Journal,* February 7, 2002.

the FDA are in frequent communication, discussing the design of trials and the results.

In September 2001, Peter Dolan, CEO of Bristol-Meyers Squibb, negotiated a deal with ImClone for a share of Erbitux. At that time, analysts estimated that Erbitux would have sales of $500 million to $1 billion a year upon approval. Under the terms of the agreement, facilitated by investment bankers from Lehman Brothers and Morgan Stanley, Bristol-Myers would acquire a 19.9% stake in ImClone for $70 a share or about $1 billion. This price represented a 40% premium over the current price of ImClone shares. Bristol-Meyers also agreed to pay ImClone $200 million on executing the agreement and another $800 million as Erbitux reached milestones on the way to the market. At the time, all parties expected FDA approval of Erbitux by the spring of 2002.[2]

On December 15, 2001, the FDA extended its 45-day deadline for a decision, and on December 28 it rejected the Erbitux application (for reasons elucidated below). At this point, the Winner's Curse hit Bristol-Meyers Squibb with a vengeance. Its due diligence in spending $2 billion on a drug was called into question, and this embarrassment was compounded by charges of insider trading on the part of Sam Waksal, his family, a well-known stock broker at Merrill Lynch, Peter Bacanovic, and Martha Stewart of Martha Stewart Living Omnimedia fame.

First, what happened in the insider trading scandal? In the month before the FDA's action, directors and officers at ImClone sold more than $70 million in stock.[3] It appears that Sam Waksal had early warning of the FDA rejection and realized that when the news became public, the value of ImClone's stock would drop dramatically. He notified family members to sell their stock, and he also tried to sell. His brokers would not accept the order since they knew he was an insider. Martha Stewart and Waksal had a phone conversation one evening, and the next day she sold shares in ImClone. Stewart has denied that Waksal gave her a tip to sell, but she has been indicted and convicted for being untruthful about the sale of stock (obstruction of justice), giving new meaning to the term "designer drugs." Waksal reached a plea bargain and is serving time in prison in return for prosecutors not indicting family members who sold stock. In addition to insider trading accusations, stockholders have filed suits alleging securities fraud.

---

2. *Wall Street Journal*, February 7, 2002.
3. *Washington Post*, October 20, 2002.

What happened to the drug? It appears that ImClone's trial had a number of flaws, and some observers contend that BMS should have been aware of problems as it monitored the trial. ImClone ran the trial without a control group of patients receiving a placebo or nothing at all. ImClone's argument was that it selected patients who had failed to respond to the chemotherapy drug generally used for colon cancer. The FDA and ImClone had agreed that the trial had to meet a number of criteria: (1) patients had to have tumors that had grown larger despite taking irinotecan (a chemotherapy drug used for colon cancer); (2) at least 15% of the patients had to respond to a combined treatment of irinotecan and Erbitux; (3) the tumor size reduction had to be at least 15%; and (4) there had to be statistical validity in the findings. The data ImClone submitted claimed that tumors of 23% of the patients in the trial shrank by more than 50% using a combination of Erbitux and chemotherapy.

Part of the problem with the FDA rejection was that ImClone had failed to document that patients had not just responded to chemotherapy with irinotecan; without this evidence it was not safe to conclude that Erbitux was effective.[4] The FDA wanted ImClone to separate out the effects of each medication; it needed to know how much Erbitux had contributed to the trial's positive results. In defense of the trial, ImClone believed that Erbitux and irinotecan should be given together; their combination was more effective than either alone.

The FDA's position is understandable; it wanted to know if all of the benefits came from irinotecan when the two drugs were used together. The FDA rejection letter said there was evidence that some of the patients should not have been in the trial and that ImClone failed to provide needed X-ray images on patient tumors. The study was relatively small, and ImClone tried to show the drug was effective by finding a positive response in 27 of 120 patients in the trial. In 15 of these 27 cases, the two reviewers, who evaluated the effects of the drugs, perceived discrepancies.[5]

Doctors who have participated in trials or have been able to administer the drug under the "compassionate use" category for unapproved drugs are enthusiastic about it. The consensus in the medical field seems to be that Erbitux has great potential and that it is important to provide evidence to obtain approval. The FDA said that it would not demand a new trial, but would look at additional data and at a trial that the German

4. *Wall Street Journal*, February 7, 2002.
5. *Wall Street Journal*, February 11, 2002.

drug manufacturer Merck KGAA (which is unrelated to the U.S. Merck) was running, which was more traditional than the ImClone U.S. trial. Merck is studying Erbitux in combination with chemotherapy in 96 patients with head and neck cancer; these patients have not responded to standard treatments. Merck reports that the preliminary results look encouraging. The company is also testing Erbitux for colorectal cancer in a 225-patient study.[6]

On the business side of Erbitux, Dolan of BMS made a series of demands of ImClone to revise its agreement based on the FDA's initial rejection of the drug. Even if ultimately approved, sales of the drug would be delayed, giving an advantage to AstraZeneca's competing cancer drug, Iressa, which is also under FDA review.[7] Dolan's demands included the removal of Sam Waksal and his brother (the chairperson) from management, the release of BMS from $800 million in future payments, an increase in BMS's share to 39% of Erbitux sales, and control over the FDA trials for BMS. ImClone's board rejected these demands outright.

After negotiations, Bristol-Meyers Squibb and ImClone came up with revised terms to their original agreement, reducing the BMS payments by $100 million. Instead of paying $300 million on FDA acceptance of the Erbitux application, BMS has increased its upfront investment by paying $140 million in March 2002, and it will pay an additional $60 million in a year. Bristol-Meyers Squibb will also be able to stagger the $500 million it was to pay ImClone upon FDA approval of the drug. ImClone's share of the revenue from Erbitux sales is now capped at 39%. Most important, BMS's senior vice president of medical and external affairs, an ImClone board member, will head the team seeking FDA approval for Erbitux.

In early 2002, Bristol-Meyers Squibb wrote off $735 million of its $1.2 billion investment in ImClone and said that it may write off more in the future. One year and a quarter after signing an agreement with ImClone, BMS had written off more than 60% of what it paid for Erbitux. It certainly looks like Bristol-Meyers Squibb has experienced the Winner's Curse. The conditions were ripe for such an outcome: BMS was under great pressure to come up with new products to make up for expected declines in the sales of existing products and to fuel growth. Lehman Brothers and Morgan Stanley were only too happy to help BMS and ImClone reach a $2 billion

---

6. *Wall Street Journal*, February 13, 2002.
7. *Chemical Market Reporter*, January 7, 2002.

agreement. The company did conduct due diligence, but the rigor of that effort is questionable. BMS must surely have reviewed ImClone's plans for the Erbitux trial as that was key in getting FDA approval to market the drug. A medical newsletter obtained a copy of ImClone's original plan for testing Erbitux and asked three oncology researchers to evaluate it. Their response was that the trial was poorly designed and looked incapable of demonstrating that Erbitux was effective.[8]

Bristol-Meyers Squibb had no way of predicting the behavior of Waksal and other ImClone employees, relatives, and friends when the FDA did not accept the Erbitux application. The scandal that resulted helped to drive down the share price of ImClone, and it is difficult to separate its effect from investors' disappointment over the FDA action. Some of the Bristol-Meyers Squibb write-down is due to factors that it could not anticipate. However, even without the scandal, the poorly designed and executed trial and the FDA decision are events that could have been predicted if BMS had done a more careful evaluation of ImClone and Erbitux. One report characterized the test as "unusual" because there was only one clinical trial and characterized the study design as "risky."[9] Why didn't anyone at Bristol-Meyers Squibb look at the proposed study and reach the same conclusion? A $2 billion deal deserves a fair amount of due diligence.

In May 2002, ImClone, after discussion with the FDA, decided to initiate a new U.S. trial of Erbitux for treating colorectal cancer. The new trial would have sufficient patient numbers to provide compelling statistical evidence and would include at least two experimental groups. One group would be treated with Erbitux plus irinotecan and one with Erbitux alone. It is expected that the new trials will extend product launch into late 2004 or early 2005 instead of the original 2003 date.[10] Dolan's and BMS's rush to acquire rights to Erbitux included inadequate due diligence. This failure has been costly in terms of money and reputation in the short run, though in the longer term Erbitux may turn out to be successful. The more immediate benefits that Dolan promised with BMS's $2 billion investment in Erbitux, however, have not been realized.

Clearly BMS has experienced the Winner's Curse and has been forced to take a large write-off. With Waksal in jail and new management, at least one analyst is very positive about ImClone's future. In early 2004, the FDA

8. *Barrons*, February 25, 2002.
9. *Pharmaceutical Executive*, March 2002.
10. *Chemical Market Reporter*, May 27, 2002.

finally gave approval for Erbitux to be marketed, which will make ImClone a strong buyout target.[11] We have to wonder if the next company that looks at ImClone will experience the Winner's Curse, or whether Bristol-Meyers Squibb will bid for the company in an attempt to recover some of what it has had to write off from its first deal with ImClone.

The Winner's Curse goes to Hollywood

Hollywood presents abundant opportunities for the Winner's Curse; there is a collection of artists and business managers competing for talent surrounded by huge sums of money. In making a decision to "green light" a proposed movie, studios have to estimate two things. First, how much will the movie cost to make, and second, what are the likely proceeds from theaters in the United States and abroad and from video sales and rentals?

The Curse sinks a studio

Michael Cimino is a film director who scored a huge success with the Oscar-winning movie *The Deer Hunter*, which was released in 1978. The movie has been described as gorgeous, though controversial. Today, it is thought of as a masterpiece and probably the best movie on the Vietnam War. Having an Oscar does wonders for one's bargaining power in Hollywood. Cimino convinced United Artists to back a film called *Heaven's Gate* in 1978. The original budget was around $10 million, a large sum for a movie in the late 1970s.

Stars, including Mary Pickford, Douglas Fairbanks, and Charlie Chaplin, founded United Artists (UA) in 1919; their objective was to have a studio where there would be artistic freedom that was not influenced by financial constraints. In 1978, Transamerica bought United Artists, and the owners since 1951, Arthur Krim and Robert Benjamin, soon left to start Orion Pictures. So Transamerica had to find new managers and replace the knowledge and experience of Krim and Benjamin. It also wanted to prove that it could attract major talent. Michael Cimino seemed to be the answer, so Transamerica gave him a $10 million budget to make the movie.[12]

The film was originally going to be called *The Johnson County War*, and the script was described as a "mishmash" of classic western themes.

---

11. *Business Week Online*, January 21, 2004.
12. *Wall Street Journal*, July 12, 1985.

The basic story line involved a massacre of immigrant farmers by cattle-men in Wyoming in 1970. It was unlikely from the start that $10 million could support the movie. United Artists did not assess the risks of the movie adequately, and it banked too much on Cimino's ability to dupli-cate his first big success, *The Deer Hunter*.[13]

"In the first six days of shooting on 'Heaven's Gate,' Michael Cimino had fallen five days behind. . . . He had shot almost 60,000 feet of film and had approximately a minute and a half of usable material, which had cost roughly $90,000 to expose," according to a book by Steven Bach, the UA production chief at the time.[14] The movie came in at 5 hours and 10 minutes in its first viewing. A few months later, Cimino man-aged to reduce the film to 3 hours and 39 minutes, but by this time the budget had ballooned to $35 million, an unheard-of amount at that time for a movie.

This huge overpayment might have worked out all right had the movie performed as one would expect from an Oscar-winning director, but "'Heaven's Gate' was derided so violently by critics after its first show that distributors withdrew it immediately for radical alterations."[15] Critic Vincent Canby wrote that the "movie was something quite rare in movies these days, an unqualified disaster." The distribution chief of United Artists said, "It's as if somebody called every household in the country and said, 'There will be a curse on your family if you see this picture.'"[16] Steven Bach, the UA production chief, was fired.

Not only did the picture fail, but it took United Artists down with it. Transamerica Corporation shuttered the studio and took a $44 million write-off. Cimino wandered in the wilderness for five years before he was able to make another movie, *Year of the Dragon*, which was reviewed more favorably. Managers at UA had decided to fund *Heaven's Gate* based on Cimino's Oscar for *The Deer Hunter*. After all, he was a big winner. Trans-america, the management at United Artists, the actors, and UA's employ-ees all experienced the Winner's Curse, and they suffered terribly as a result.

13. *Variety*, April 30, 2001.
14. *Final Cut*, rev. ed. (New York: Morrow, 1999).
15. *Wall Street Journal*, August 30, 1985.
16. *Variety*, April 30, 2001.

Trouble in the Magic Kingdom

"Mouse House Loses Big Cheese"[17] was the headline in *Variety* when Michael Ovitz stepped down as president of the Walt Disney Company, a little more than a year after assuming the position. Ovitz, who started in the mailroom at the William Morris Agency, had become one of the most powerful men in Hollywood. He eventually cofounded Creative Artists, another talent agency in Hollywood, in 1975. During his career, Ovitz represented stars such as Tom Cruise, Dustin Hoffman, Kevin Costner, Michael Douglas, Sylvester Stallone, and Barbra Streisand. He counted prominent directors like Steven Spielberg, Barry Levinson, and Sydney Pollack as his clients. Ovitz also was an advisor for entertainment industry deals, including Sony's purchase of Columbia Pictures in 1989 and Credit-Lyonnais' rescue of MGM in 1993.[18] Everyone raved about Ovitz's ability to have a human touch when dealing with difficult people. "He is a winner with his stars" was a common theme.

In 1995, his friend of 25 years, Michael Eisner, the CEO of Disney, lured Ovitz away from his agency to become president of Disney. In addition to assisting the CEO to make strategic decisions about which films to produce and which properties to pursue, the main job of the president was to ensure that all of the producers, directors, and actors worked together to make successful films. Who could be better at a job like this than a proven winner with people? Ovitz gave up a lucrative job at Creative Artists in exchange for a five-year contract at Disney. This contract provided Ovitz with a $1 million annual salary, options to purchase 5 million shares of Disney stock (with 1 million shares vesting each year from 1998 to 2002), and a discretionary bonus of up to $7.5 million per year.[19]

Eisner had recently lost two managers who reported to him. Frank Wells, a well-regarded president, died in a vacation accident in 1994. Eisner underwent open heart surgery in 1994, but had trouble sharing power with a likely replacement for Wells, Jeffrey Katzenberg. Because he was not moving into the president's position, Katzenberg quit Disney and formed DreamWorks with Steven Spielberg and David Geffen. In 1995, Disney

---

17. *Variety*, December 13, 1996.
18. *http://www.museum.tv/archives/etv/O/htmlO/ovitzmichael/ovitzmichael.htm*.
19. Stephen Radin, "Court Refuses to Overrule Disney's Severance Package," *Directorship*, December 1998.

completed a $19 billion acquisition of Capital Cities/ABC, and Eisner was faced with new responsibilities and no second in command.

Enter Ovitz. Ovitz had been a powerful agent, and he was used to demonstrating that power dealing with studios as the agent for his sought-after clients. Is this the kind of background needed to run a company with more than $18 billion in revenue a year, and to run it as the second in command? From the outset, it seems that Eisner had his doubts.

Both of the principals, despite their long friendship, misread the other's intentions. Ovitz thought that Eisner believed he needed help and was ready to delegate some power to a second in command. Eisner thought that Ovitz could make a successful transition to a large corporation like Disney. But Ovitz pursued individual projects with seemingly no concern about their impact on the company as a whole. Eisner, on the other hand, looked over Ovitz's shoulder and second-guessed Ovitz's decisions. For example, Ovitz wanted to buy a record company, but that idea received a veto from above. And it is likely that neither man understood the fierce autonomy of Disney's four principal division managers.[20] It appears in retrospect that both Michaels were wrong. Rather than using his winning skills in dealing with people, Ovitz ended up in clashes with the division heads.

Ovitz worked on Disney's planned expansion in China and then undid his efforts with the green light he gave to the movie *Kundun* about the Dalai Lama and his struggle against China when it annexed Tibet. MCA and Universal passed, but Ovitz picked it up with Martin Scorsese as director. Beijing hinted that if Disney went ahead and made the movie, it would have problems with a planned theme park near Shanghai.[21]

Steve Bollenbach, the chief financial officer at Disney, said that he offered to meet with Ovitz and talk to him about how the company actually worked, but Ovitz did not come to the meetings. Other senior executives evidently told Eisner that if Ovitz stayed, they would not; he was considered impossible to work with. Bollenbach eventually quit and became CEO of Hilton Hotels, saying that he left because of Ovitz. Eisner reportedly complained that instead of helping to relieve him of operating responsibilities, Ovitz became a source of added stress. Ovitz also created unrest among other executives at the firm. Eisner finally admitted that hiring Ovitz had been "a mistake."[22]

20. *Variety*, December 13, 1996.
21. *World Tibet Network News*, December 13, 1996.
22. E-online, November 19, 2002.

On December 12, 1996, Ovitz left Disney "by mutual consent" and caused an even greater ruckus than when he was an employee. What caught everyone's attention was the size of Ovitz's severance package. The original five-year employment agreement provided that if Disney terminated Ovitz's employment lacking a good cause, or if Ovitz resigned with Disney's approval, called a *nonfault termination*, 3 million of his shares would vest immediately. He also was to receive a $10 million lump-sum payment, the present value of all remaining salary through September 30, 2000, plus $7.5 million multiplied by the years remaining in the agreement (the maximum bonus he would have earned had he stayed).[23] Ovitz negotiated an agreement with the board that his resignation was a nonfault termination and that he was eligible to receive the full severance package. There were a number of estimates of the total value of this package, all depending on the value of the stock options. These estimates ranged from $70 million to more than $140 million—not bad for 16 months of work.

Did the Walt Disney Company and Michael Eisner experience the Winner's Curse? Clearly, Ovitz's winning ways when he represented Hollywood megastars did not carry over to dealing with the executives at Disney. The size of the contract and the generous severance terms suggest to us that Disney overpaid considerably for the short tenure of Michael Ovitz as president. We are not alone. The Supreme Court of Delaware in one ruling on a suit brought by shareholders to stop the severance agreement from being implemented noted that the "casual, if not sloppy and perfunctory" process of Disney's board in approving the compensation package and agreeing to the nonfault termination were "hardly paradigms of good corporate governance practices." The size of the payout "pushes the envelope of judicial respect for the business judgment of directors in making compensation decisions."[24]

Hollywood will persevere

Heaven's Gate and Michael Ovitz's brief role starring as president of Disney are great examples of the Winner's Curse, and Hollywood seems

---

23. Radin, "Court Refuses to Overrule Disney's Severance Package."
24. "Del. Sup. Ct. Grants Disney Shareholders Leave to Replead Complaint to Challenge Application of Business Judgement Rule Deference to Ovitz' Compensation Package," *FindLaw*, March 2000.

primed for many more performances. Some enduring actors who command large salaries have never won an Academy Award, and there are Oscar winners who never seem to achieve anything close to that level of success again. Yet an Oscar or a single hit movie makes an actor or producer a winner, and the next deal their agent negotiates will be huge. The studios, producers, and directors exhibit incredible optimism and hubris in creating these packages. There are also incredible pressures from the investment community as the studio's performance is reflected in its stock price or the stock price of the company that owns it.

Play ball!

Sports provide abundant opportunities for the Winner's Curse to plague teams and their fans. University-level and professional sports teams are under great pressure to produce winning teams. While the faculty would like to see donors support a college because of its academics, the fact is that athletic success produces far more donations than academic success. For the professional team, winning is about attracting fans and the revenue they generate in ticket and concession sales.

The Winner's Curse seems endemic in sports. In the National Basketball Association draft of 2001, many teams jostled to get the number one pick because a high school phenomenon named Kwame Brown was going to be available. The Washington Wizards were lucky enough to get the pick and did not hesitate to use it on Brown, signing him to a three-year, $12 million contract. The 6'11" power forward, who averaged more than 20 points a game in high school and led his team to championships, simply flamed out. During 2002 and 2003, he averaged a little more than 6 points and fewer than 5 rebounds a game. Another example is Vin Baker, who was the eighth pick in the 1993 draft and was a star with Milwaukee and Seattle. The Boston Celtics aggressively sought him out and gave away three starters (Kenny Anderson, Vitaly Potapenko, and Joseph Forte) to get him. For a number of years, Vin Baker turned out to be a bust.

Baseball has its fill of examples of the Winner's Curse, especially pitchers who fail to win games. Steve Avery was considered an excellent pitcher who went 18–8 in 1991 for the Atlanta Braves in his second year in the majors. He repeated this performance in 1993 and took the Braves into the National League playoffs. Although he lost both games he started to the Philadelphia Phillies, he was given a lucrative multiyear contract, first by the Braves and then by the Boston Red Sox. Over the next six years, Avery only had one winning season (10–7 in 1998). Rick Ankiel was the St. Louis pitcher whose pain all of America felt during the 2000 National League championship. The college star and sophomore phenomenon, who had gone 11–7 in the regular season, could not get a pitch over the plate. The hubris and stubbornness of the Cardinals' manager, Tony LaRussa, who "[knew] a winner when he [saw] one," ensured that Ankiel embarrassed himself, and the team lost the series to the Mets.

Orlando Hernandez, a Cuban phenomenon, was so dominant in 1999 that people started to call him "El Duke." He went 17–9 and powered the Yankees to a World Series title. After signing a lucrative contract in the off-season, El Duke never was able to reproduce this performance. He went 12–13 the next season and then kept getting onto and off of the disabled list. Eventually, the Yankees traded him to the Cleveland Indians, which traded him to the Montreal Expos, which signed him to a $4 million contract. He went back onto the disabled list right away. With this experience behind them, the Yankees were so sure of their ability to pick winners that they competed with many teams to sign another Cuban winner, Jose Contreras, to an $8 million-a-year deal. Although Contreras was expected to perform from his arrival, he started really badly with a 1–1 record and an earned run average of 8.74; he had to be sent to the minor leagues.

There are also many stories of coaches with successful records being lured away by other teams, usually with huge salaries, only to fail in their new settings. Clearly, it is never easy to correctly predict the future performance of an athlete. As athletes age, their skills do deteriorate. In professional sports, where everyone performs at an extreme level of intensity, the chances of getting injured are high. Also, with the exception of baseball, an athlete's success depends on how the rest of the team is performing. Many people would argue that Terry Bradshaw had very good statistics with the Pittsburgh Steelers because of the wide receivers Lynn Swan and John Stallworth. Despite the superior statistics of Wilt Chamberlain, most sportswriters consider Bill Russell of the Boston Celtics to be the best center to ever play the game because he made his teammates better; the Celtics won 12 championships in a row.

The main problem is not that the athletes do not perform to expectations; it is that owners, in their excitement to get star players, never seem to take into consideration the risks involved. When the stakes are high and the pressure to succeed is great, teams try to win potential "saviors" at any cost.

A case in point is the debacle of 2001 at the Washington Redskins professional football team. Daniel Snyder owns the Redskins; he grew up as an avid fan in the greater Washington, D.C., area. Snyder dropped out of the University of Maryland to start a business that published a magazine for college students. He was adept at getting well-known investors like Mort Zuckerman, publisher of U.S. *News and World Report*, to finance this venture, but it bombed. Then Zuckerman helped Snyder launch Snyder Communications, which started life as a marketer of baby products in doctors' offices and moved on to bigger and better things. Soon, Snyder Communications had become the king of direct marketing, and the company grew to more than $2 billion in revenue by 1999. By the age of 34, Dan Snyder was said to be worth more than $500 million. Toward the end of 1999, a group of investors headed by Snyder bought the Redskins for an unprecedented $800 million and took over for the 2000 season.

Getting so rich so quickly tends to make people feel invulnerable and impatient. The Washington Redskins had won their division in 1999 and had gone two rounds in the playoffs. Snyder decided to "juice up" the team and went after aging stars like Dion Sanders and talented but troublesome players like quarterback Jeff George, in spite of the concerns of the coach, Norv Turner. The team chemistry suffered, and the Redskins sputtered through the season. Even before the 2000 season ended, with the playoffs in sight and with a 7–6 record, Snyder fired Turner. The team proceeded to lose two of the next three games and missed the playoffs. During the season, one sports commentator, long-term former coach of the Kansas City Chiefs Marty Schottenheimer, had said that he would never coach for a "meddlesome" owner like Dan Snyder. This turned out to be a challenge for Snyder, who proceeded to make the deal to get Schottenheimer as the coach for the 2001 Redskins. In order to make him eat his words, Snyder contracted to pay Schottenheimer $10 million for four years, making him one of the highest paid coaches in the National Football League. The new coach lasted, however, just one year.

Dan Snyder had long coveted Steve Spurrier, the coach of the University of Florida football team, the Gators. Spurrier had a reputation as a cocky, brash college coach who was supposed to have the Midas touch. He seemed to care neither about his own players nor about the opposing teams in his quest to score points. In a number of games, even in situations when Florida was up by a massive score with just minutes until the end of the game, Spurrier had the reputation of going for one last touchdown when most coaches would simply run the clock out. Whenever a quarterback made a mistake and did not run a play Spurrier called, he yanked the offending QB and substituted the back-up quarterback. The conventional wisdom was that Spurrier did not believe in one quarterback for his team, only in his system. Certainly, Spurrier had the reputation for being aggressive and even macho in the college arena. From the moment Spurrier announced that he was resigning from college football to try the professional ranks, Schottenheimer's number was up. It did not help matters that the Redskins went 8–8, the same record as in 2000. Given that Schottenheimer had three more years on his contract, Snyder had to restructure it to force him out. Then Snyder went after Spurrier.

Spurrier had an enviable history in the college ranks: in 12 seasons, he had a 122–27 record with 7 Southeastern Conference championships, 6 bowl wins, and 1 national title (1996) with Heisman Trophy winner Danny Wuerffel. Spurrier himself was the Heisman Trophy winner from Florida in 1966, but he had mixed experience as a quarterback for the San Francisco 49ers (1967–1975) and the Tampa Bay Buccaneers (1976). He then started his college coaching career, first with Duke (1987–1990) and then with Florida. Spurrier's Florida team was full of fireworks, averaging more than 35 points a game along with 310 yards passing. However, he had no experience coaching in the NFL.

Despite the fact that past successes cannot easily be reproduced in the future, that Spurrier had no experience in the NFL, and that college coaches had seldom found success coaching in the NFL (Miami coach Jimmy Johnson being the exception with the Dallas Cowboys), Dan Snyder aggressively went after Spurrier. At the start, Spurrier made clear his intentions to live and coach in warmer climates, and he interviewed with the Carolina Panthers and the Jacksonville Jaguars. Snyder did not want to lose his prize and immediately offered Spurrier $25 million for a five-year contract, an unheard-of sum in the NFL for anyone. The $5 million annual salary was almost 50 percent higher than the next highest paid coach. Spurrier just could not say no, and it was a big win for Snyder.

The Washington Redskins and its large loyal fan base proceeded to suffer the Winner's Curse for the next two years. Spurrier thought that his college playbook would easily work in the professional game, and he chose to bring his former Florida quarterbacks to the Redskins despite the fact that they had been relegated to second and third strings on their current teams. Spurrier was sure that he would soon be showing the world how a football offense is really run, and Snyder backed him fully. They were sadly mistaken. The defense on their opponents' teams soon figured out the "fun-and-gun" offense and had plays to prevent it. Spurrier was too egotistical to try anything different; the team went 7–9 during the first year, 2002. To make matters worse, and against all advice to the contrary, the Redskins let their star running back, Stephen Davis, leave and proceeded to sign "faster" backs with the potential ability to catch footballs from the back field. The team did even worse in 2003 and ended 5–11, losing 11 of their last 13 games.

Even with more than $15 million remaining on his contract, Steve Spurrier resigned from the Redskins to escape the continual vilification from the media, the fans, and even many of the professional football minds who commented on his decisions from television-broadcasting booths. Dan Snyder, the extremely successful businessman who accumulated hundreds of millions before he was 35, let hubris get in the way of good decision making and thought that spending lots of money could buy a championship. Unfortunately, during the past four years of his ownership, a once-proud sports franchise with three Super Bowl championships has reached depths that it had not experienced in a long time.

It can happen to anyone

The stories in this book include a lot of companies and well-known people because they generate newspaper and magazine articles that illustrate the Winner's Curse. But the Curse can strike anyone, anywhere, though it may be little noted by the rest of the world. Most of the authors' personal experience is in academia, and even we have seen the Curse manifest itself in various ways.

The most famous of universities, whether Harvard or Stanford in the United States, or Cambridge or Oxford in the United Kingdom, have multiple missions. The public would generally say the mission of the university is to educate, but a research university also has the mission to create new knowledge. It expects faculty members to be successful in research and hopes that they will bring the results of this research into the classroom. Much of the fame of the best universities is due to professors who are research "stars," whom the students seek in the classrooms because of the halo effect of publicity. Who would not want to be taught by a Nobel Prize–winning physicist, a Pulitzer Prize–winning English professor, or a business professor who has a bestselling book?

Most good universities seek academic stars and are willing to pay a lot to move them from their current institutions. This phenomenon was examined in 1981 by Sherwin Rosen, a University of Chicago economist, in a famous paper entitled "The Economics of Superstars."[25] In his article, Rosen discussed how talent and the scale of the market affect the amount of money those considered stars are able to make. For example, someone like opera singer Luciano Pavarotti might be just a little bit better than another talented tenor, but because Pavarotti's audience is so large, just that little difference means that he will be able to sell many more CDs and receive income many times that of his nearest competitor. Many universities have tried to build their academic reputations by purchasing so-called stars. For example, Duke University built itself one of the premier English departments by paying unprecedented sums of money to star professors from places like Yale, Princeton, and the University of Pennsylvania in the hot field of deconstructionism.

The only problem is that in academia, where professors have lifetime employment, it is easy for these stars to either misbehave or simply to reduce their productivity because they have arrived. Having been anointed as stars, many of these academics make demands on the institutions and their colleagues, demoralizing everyone, making their hires more expensive than the universities had originally thought. Some of the stars had name recognition for past achievements and had really slowed down even before trading places. Universities generally get star-struck and hope that their great catch will be a catalyst for attracting productive, younger colleagues and alumni funding.

Thus, many universities have experienced the Winner's Curse by going after those who have had a good reputation and using large salaries as the lure. In many cases, getting the prize turns out to be a Pyrrhic victory. Indeed, at Duke, after years of turmoil, many of those deconstructionist English professors left the institution for different pastures.

You will find examples all around. The potential results of the Curse suggest being very careful in seeking victory.

---

25. Sherwin Rosen, "The Economics of Superstars," *American Economic Review* 71, no. 5 (1981): 845–858.

Conclusions

Licensing a new product, making a movie, winning a teaching award, hiring a company president, or hiring a pro football coach are all subject to the Winner's Curse. It can literally happen to anybody faced with uncertainty when making a decision that requires them to invest money or time now in anticipation of future performance. Often, all we have for judging the future is a person or company's past history, and in these examples, that history was misleading, or decision makers relied on it too heavily. Is it excessive optimism to believe that an untested drug will be a blockbuster? Is the studio that believes a director who won an Oscar will produce another hit film being too optimistic? The same question can be asked of the management of a football team about a successful coach. Isn't the coach's past success heavily influenced by circumstances beyond his control, like the quality of the players he inherited? The message in this chapter is twofold: first, the Winner's Curse can strike almost anyone; and second, beware of extrapolating past performance too far as history may not repeat itself just when you are counting on it to do so.

What to do?

There are some important lessons from the examples in this chapter, and they suggest some steps to take in comparable situations.

The past may not predict the future

One clear lesson is that past performance is no guarantee of future performance. The movie director who did well on one movie may produce a bomb the next time around. The bestselling author does not necessarily write a bestseller for her second novel. Drug companies come up with a blockbuster, followed by years of mediocre products that do not make it to market or that fail to generate huge sales.

What's your causal model?

Did a player lead a team to victory, or was it a group effort? What were the reasons for a person's or a company's past success? Can you figure out what caused a hit book or movie? Why was Michael Ovitz a great success as a talent agent and a failure as president of Disney? Was it just a conflict with Michael Eisner, or is there more to it? What is responsible for success in an agency? What leads to success in a large studio? Are the same factors necessarily responsible? Think about cause-and-effect relationships before buying into a deal.

Watch out for successes that are contingent
on something else happening

Not knowing if it was going to receive FDA approval of an experimental drug was a big risk for Bristol-Meyers Squibb; Erbitux had to have approval before it could be sold in the United States. It looks like management did not factor in that the drug might not be approved, or that its approval might be delayed, in figuring out what to invest in ImClone. What roles do the teammates of a Heisman Trophy winner play in his success? Is his success contingent on their performance, or does it come solely from his own efforts and talents?

Protect yourself with contracts that involve pay for performance

A few smart team managers have crafted contracts that pay only if a player meets certain performance goals. They offer a large salary, but the player only receives it each year when he plays up to the specifications in the contract. Could Bristol-Meyers Squibb have protected itself with a contract that specified one level of investment in ImClone until FDA approval of Erbitux and another level after approval?

The key concept to remember here is that history may not repeat itself and that you want to protect your investment in case it does not. You will have to be creative in figuring out how to do so, but you will not be sorry that you made the deal more complicated.

5 • The mad scramble to acquire optical technology

During the heady 1990s, those in the telecommunications industry thought that the sky was the limit. The Internet was going to transform businesses and become the new medium for leisure and entertainment. Forecasts were that residences and businesses would demand high-speed broadband services to download Web pages and entertainment from the Internet. Until the mid-1980s, almost all networks only carried voice traffic: people used the telecommunications networks to talk to each other. Beginning in the late 1980s, individuals started sending messages and files to each other through the network. By 1993, business was using the Internet widely, leading to an explosion in data traffic that bypassed voice traffic by 1998.

Incumbent long-distance companies like AT&T and MCI (later acquired by WorldCom) and regional Bell operating companies (RBOCs) like Verizon, SBC Communications, and BellSouth started to upgrade their networks to accommodate the burgeoning demand for telecommunications services. In response to the need for fast, cost-effective communications equipment, many companies started working on the next generation of optical technology. From the late 1980s, the core and backbone of telecommunications networks the world over were built using fiber optics instead of copper cables. Indeed, in most countries, the long-haul network currently is made up of *only* fiber-optic cabling. Fiber optics employs lasers to send signals by light; fiber cables are faster than copper and have a much greater capacity to carry information.

Telecommunications companies, which own the "last mile" of the network that reaches the actual premises of residences and businesses, were much slower to embrace fiber optics. There were a number of reasons for this. First, the amount of communications traffic sent between a cluster of homes and offices and the first switching station, often called a *central office* or a *local exchange*, is not that great, thus obviating the need for large-capacity (that is, large bandwidth) fiber optics. Second, there were millions of these last-mile, or *local loop*, connections, and it would be expensive to refurbish them with fiber. In the United States, monopoly carriers controlled many local exchanges; they had little or no incentive to rapidly improve the technology in the local access networks. Even in the 1990s, when applications using the telecommunications network, especially e-mail and the Internet, were expanding rapidly, the incumbent local exchange carriers were not sure how to extract payments and enhance their revenues to pay for the investment in fiber in the local loop.

The long-haul telecommunications carriers were not that reluctant. Carriers invested heavily in fiber optics networks. Even as recently as 2001, telecom companies extended their networks by 93 million miles of fiber optic cables, a 210% increase over 1999. In 2000, worldwide vendors sold optical transport equipment of $32 billion in terrestrial cables (a 31% increase over 1999). Ironically, in 2001, the global terrestrial optics market declined to $28.2 billion. Thus, the seeming paradox was that while there was an increase in fiber buildout, the revenue for vendors was on the decrease.

The main reason was that significant innovations entered the fiber optics market, making it easier to build networks and extend fiber at a much lower cost. Innovations in fiber optics occurred in all segments of the value chain: the lasers that generated the light signals, the amplifiers and regenerators that enhanced the signals periodically, the switches that moved billions of signals from place to place, and the components that went into all of these systems. The technology game plan was to increase the amount of information carried by the fiber optic network and to move it around the communications network at low cost.

There are basically two ways of increasing information flow. One is to increase the amount of bits and bytes that a laser can produce at any point in time. For this, one needs to build better and better lasers. The second is to increase the amount of bits and bytes carried by each strand of fiber. For this, one needs to be able to combine the signals from different lasers together in a single strand of fiber optic cable. The technology for the latter is called dense wave division multiplexing (DWDM), and the trick is to be able to combine as many different colors of light as possible, each color carrying the signal from one source to one destination. The potential innovations in DWDM technology excited engineers and investors alike.

In order to reduce the cost of carrying the signals, one needs to have only a few light amplifiers and regenerators in the network. Prior to 1993, the industry used electronic regenerators every 40–80 kilometers to amplify the light traversing the network at the cost of about $40,000 per channel. The emergence of a new technology called EDFA (erbium-doped fiber amplifier) allowed the companies to amplify up to 100 channels for the same cost. Thus, an 80-channel system would cost $3.2 million using electronic regenerators but only $40,000 using EDFA, a savings of millions in the whole network. The entire industry saw such deep cost savings due to innovations in optics.

Thus, in the long-haul network, innovations in fiber optics really transformed the dynamics of an industry that had been stable for almost a century. The telecommunications industry, like many infrastructure industries, was subject to economies of scale and economies of scope, which proved to be formidable barriers to entry. Once an incumbent had many customers, economies of scale and scope ensured that the per-customer cost would be low. Advances in fiber optic technology helped aggressive new firms to enter the long-haul telecommunications industry with impunity. Innovations occurred in both cabling and switching technology, which allowed a significantly larger amount of traffic to be carried in these networks. This increase in capacity, in turn, significantly reduced the average cost of bandwidth. New firms building their networks with the latest in fiber technology had a cost structure that compared favorably with the incumbents' low cost created by economies of scale and scope. In fact, the newer the fiber optic technology, the lower was the per-bandwidth cost, and this allowed a number of new companies to enter the long-haul communications sector.

Thus, in the 1990s, companies such as Qwest, Level-3, and Global Crossing crashed the exclusive party of AT&T, MCI, and Sprint. The new companies had to obtain the right-of-way to build their networks, and they were off to the races with the latest and best in optical fiber technology. Each company used different mechanisms to obtain the right-of-way; Level-3 used the agreements that its main investor and one-time parent, Kiewitt, had in the construction industry, and Qwest signed up with railroads that crisscrossed the United States. These firms also carved out different business strategies for their presence in the telecommunications industry. Then the new entrants went shopping for state-of-the-art optics.

Venture capitalists (VCs) backed any optics start-up with a seemingly good idea and a management team that had some experience in the telecommunications industry. Companies with plans for producing new optics technology sprouted in many places, predominantly in the San Francisco Bay area, around Route 128 in Boston, and in greater Washington, D.C. In the mid-1990s, the joke in industries competing for funding was that they should use the word *optics* in the names of their companies or their technology in order to have an easier time with the venture capitalists. It was not unusual for VCs to think in terms of turning over companies at 100 times their initial investment within three years of funding them. Large vendors were also in the hunt for new and exciting optical technologies and tried to leapfrog into leadership roles in the optics space by acquiring start-ups with revolutionary potential. This chapter is about the sad story of optical technology and describes the folly of Lucent, Nortel, and Cisco in the drive to acquire this technology.

Lucent's lunacy

Lucent Technologies was formed in late 1995 when AT&T split into three publicly traded companies "to serve the increasingly divergent business needs of its customers." In the beginning, Lucent did really well. During 1996–1998, share prices increased fivefold, and revenues jumped threefold. The primary reason for this success was that the Internet, a *data* network, ironically, increased demand for its traditional 5ESS switches, which were used to power *voice* networks. When someone uses the telephone for a voice call, typically the conversation lasts about 5 minutes. When someone connects with the Internet, the data call lasts about 30 minutes on average. Until the late 1990s, most people connected to the Internet using modems and local telephone lines. Thus, there was an enhanced demand for voice switches to manage this large volume of persistent traffic. Being the global leader in voice communications equipment, Lucent cleaned up in this business environment. Thus, within three years of its divestiture from AT&T, Lucent seemed perched at the top of an exciting telecommunications equipment market.

Based on this financial success, Lucent went shopping. During 1996–2001, the company completed 38 acquisitions totaling more than $46 billion. In the beginning, Lucent wanted to enter the data networking market and sought out companies that produced routers and other data switches. Lucent paid $24 billion in 1999 for Ascend Communications, which was its biggest acquisition and which helped position Lucent as the leading data networking equipment supplier to service providers. Given the tremendous expansion of the Internet, it made a lot of sense for Lucent to go shopping for data networking companies.

The acquisition of Ascend provided Lucent with a plethora of technologies that could be marketed to the different segments of a data network.[1] However, what was lacking was a large router (called a *core router*) that could move Internet traffic at the core of the network where the quantity of communications traffic was the largest. In data networking technology, Lucent's primary competition, Cisco, had yet to supply core routers to the market and was in catch-up mode. The only company that the venture capital community thought had a product was Juniper Networks. On the morning of Juniper's planned initial public offering (IPO), June 25, 1999, and a day after the completion of the Ascend acquisition, Lucent announced its intention to acquire Nexabit Networks, a privately owned start-up that developed high-end switching/routing equipment. On July 19, 1999, the acquisition was completed with the offering of 14 million shares of Lucent common stock, valued at $900 million. This was the largest acquisition in history for a "prerevenue" company because the acquisition occurred before Nexabit had sold any of its routers.

How did Lucent decide what to pay for Nexabit Networks? At the time, Cisco was trading at 22 times its revenue. Based on cursory analysis, Lucent was convinced that Nexabit could ship $40 million worth of "boxes" in 2000, and this multiplied by 22 gave $880 million, which was rounded up to $900 million. Although a number of analysts were skeptical about the deal, Lucent was certain that this merger would provide it

---

1. This equipment ranged from modems to frame relays to ATM (asynchronous transfer mode) switches.

with a leading product for ultra high-speed core information processing (IP) networks, which could connect directly into the physical fabric of backbone optical networks.

It took only a year for Lucent to realize that it had experienced a classic Winner's Curse. It may have won Nexabit, but the company had overestimated the value of this acquisition in the hurry to fill a gap in its communications technology. Lucent also seemed to have had too much faith in what the Nexabit team had revealed about potential orders and how close the company was to delivering products. After the acquisition, Lucent had a tough time fitting Nexabit's IP solutions into its product line as originally planned. The management team at Nexabit could not see eye to eye with the senior managers at Lucent. To exacerbate these problems, by December 2000, one year after Lucent's Nexabit acquisition, the entire management team at Nexabit decamped to form another telecommunications equipment company. In March 2002, Lucent announced a new switching unit to further enhance the technologies obtained from Nexabit Networks. Yet less than eight months later, citing unexpected cutbacks in network equipment spending by big telephone and Internet companies, Lucent canceled the product. The winners of the Nexabit acquisition were the senior management and staff of Nexabit Networks. The losers, as would be the trend in many of Lucent's optical acquisitions, were the Lucent shareholders.

Between Bell Labs and its own development teams, Lucent had more than 2,000 patents in optical technology alone. Lucent had market leadership in what is called the OC-48 market where the bits and bytes of communications traffic would move at 2.5 giga (billion) bits per second. By the end of 1998, Lucent found itself losing market share in the optical networking space. A small start-up company called Ciena stole a march on Lucent in DWDM equipment. As we explained earlier, DWDM technology allows the telecom system designer to combine optical signals from many different sources into one fiber optic strand. By late 1998, Ciena had a number of major customers, including Sprint and MCI. Then Nortel made a technological leap into the 10 giga (billion) bits per second (OC-192) technology and started getting business from Lucent's own customers.

At the time, Lucent had the largest share (34% or approximately $1.3 billion) of the fast-growing global sales of optical equipment, but it was worried. Although its foray into the technology acquisition strategy in data networking was mixed at best, Lucent decided to aggressively play catch-up in the optics equipment market. In fact, Lucent decided to pursue optics in every segment of the communications market and to provide customers with a portfolio of technologies with which to build or expand their networks. Lucent New Ventures, a venture enterprise that was formed from within the company, provided the leadership for technology acquisitions.

One area where Lucent faced severe competition was in optical equipment for the local loop of the telecommunications network. Lucent had been the major supplier in equipment called add-drop multiplexers (ADM), which allowed different optical rings to connect to each other and decide how to switch traffic. A new company called Cerent, which was later acquired by Cisco, took the traditional ADM boxes, added functionality, and cut the cost by a factor of three. This new access switch provided efficient data transport and guaranteed quick response times for both voice and video traffic simultaneously. The switch allowed telecommunications carriers to deliver cheap fiber connections to customers over the local loop. Many telecom companies, both incumbent local exchange carriers like Verizon and new entrants like XO Communications, showed a lot of interest in this technology because of its low cost, flexibility, small size, and full compliance with the way in which the switches in central offices should be configured.

In order to compete in this business segment, Lucent New Ventures invested money in 1999 in a company called Ignitus, which it folded into its Optical Network Group in March 2000. In June 2000, in a surprising move to both Lucent customers and Ignitus, Lucent Technologies purchased Chromatis Networks for $4.5 billion. Chromatis was developing a product similar to Ignitus's, and it was widely believed that the architecture of the switches was identical. Soon after this, the Ignitus team was folded into Chromatis, and the Ignitus switch was eliminated from Lucent's portfolio of products. It was not surprising to anyone that much of the Ignitus senior management left Lucent for other ventures, licking their lips over the amount of money they had made from their brief romance with Lucent.

The worst part of it for Lucent shareholders was that the Chromatis product did not live up to the expectations of Lucent's strategic planning team. Although its U.S. headquarters was in Herndon, Virginia, Chromatis was an Israeli company based in Petah Tikvah, cofounded by Rafi Gidron and Orny Petruschka, and funded by Jerusalem Venture Partners (JVP). The eye-popping $4.5 billion that Lucent paid for Chromatis would yield for JVP's 15% holding a return of $675 million—over 100 times the $6.2 million that JVP invested in Chromatis for one of its funds in 1998, and 200 times the $3.2 million investment made in 1999. Each founder received Lucent shares worth more than $700 million, with another couple of hundred million going to other staff members. The amount Lucent paid for Chromatis was actually less than the $6.5 billion spent a year earlier by Cisco on Cerent, also an optics company, that had allegedly an inferior networking product.

Lucent was excited about Chromatis's flagship product, called the metropolis system, which the company claimed was the first in the industry to integrate packet, voice, and video services together on metropolitan (that is, citywide) networks and to combine this traffic with a wave division multiplexing (WDM) system. Chromatis also sold Lucent on a concept called selective wave division multiplexing (SWDM), which Chromatis claimed was revolutionary because it allowed network providers to deploy only the optical wavelengths that they needed, where and when they needed them, thereby realizing huge savings in start-up costs. Lucent, in its press release announcing the acquisition, quoted its CEO, Richard McGinn, as saying, "With Chromatis, Lucent is one step closer to bringing the speed and power of fiber optics all the way to a customer's desktop."

However, in August 2001, 15 months after its acquisition, Lucent closed Chromatis and dismissed all 150 employees. Lucent's stock had fallen 86% from $60 in May 2000, when it purchased Chromatis, to a little under $8 by August 2001. In pure valuation terms, then, Chromatis was now worth only $590 million. At the end of 2000, Lucent had reversed its acquisition trend and started spinning off companies to recoup much-needed liquidity. It first sold its enterprise networking group in September 2000 and successfully spun it off as Avaya. Lucent then created Agere Systems from its microelectronics division and completed an initial public offering for it in April 2001. However, none of these divestitures seemed to pacify Wall Street. In July 2001, Lucent announced the dismissal of 17,000 employees worldwide and its intention to shut down several production lines that did not yield revenue. Clearly, Chromatis fell into the latter category.

There are differing opinions on what went wrong. Some critics argue that the Chromatis product simply did not work. Some Lucent insiders state that despite claims of superior technology, the Chromatis team failed to deliver the product on time and within budget. Others claim that the Chromatis failure was symptomatic of Lucent's inability to manage, integrate, and commercialize promising new technologies. These critics also argue that there was a pattern at Lucent of suffocating promising new technologies, including those from other companies like Ignitus, Nexabit, and Ascend, under a complex and bureaucratic operating structure.

It appears that Lucent's acquisition strategy was driven by an intense focus on growth and on meeting Wall Street expectations and a critical need to signal that it was staying on the cutting edge of new telecommunications technology. Advances in optics were hot in the mid-1990s, and Lucent was under pressure to stay ahead of companies like Nortel, Alcatel, and Cisco in this arena. Two fundamental weaknesses obviously existed—inadequate due diligence and the inability to properly integrate and commercialize new technologies. Of course, a Wall Street insider told one of the authors that "Lucent was simply a poor acquirer of companies."

What is clear is that in its acquisition of optical and even IP technology, Lucent succumbed to the Winner's Curse. It paid far too much for technology that was a long way from commercialization just to ensure that it beat potential rivals by either acquiring the same firm or getting into a particular technology space before it. There was considerable hubris associated with this winning and overoptimism about the potential of integrating the new technologies into Lucent's portfolio of products. In the Chromatis disaster, Lucent initially wrote off a loss of $500 million prior to the shutdown. In the fourth quarter of 2001, the company announced plans to record an overall $7–9 billion charge for closed business units. This amount approximated $6 billion in lost shareholder value less any recoverable tangible assets.

Nortel's nightmare

Until the mid-1980s, Nortel was a "sleeper" in the telecommunications equipment market. Although it was a leader in digital circuit switches, few people outside the industry had heard of it. After AT&T's divestiture in 1984, Nortel (which was called Northern Telecom at the time) became the primary equipment provider for Bell Canada. The rules of the divestiture also mandated that the RBOCs (regional Bell operating companies) would buy 40% of their voice-switching equipment from Nortel. Thus, although it did not supply technology to the long-haul carriers like AT&T and MCI, Nortel had a little more than 40% of the stable central-office equipment market. In the 1990s, Nortel became aggressive and entered new business areas: wireless networks, wire line networks, enterprise networks, and optical networks. Its adventure into the optics market gave it the most prominence.

In 1995, Nortel found that Lucent had a stranglehold on telecommunications carriers in the long-haul segment of the network. Lucent had helped build these networks using an optical technology called OC-48, which operates at 2.5 gigabits per second. Nortel was the first-to-market in the newer generation OC-192 (10 Gbps) technology, but found no takers. So, Nortel pioneered what is called *vendor financing* in the telecommunications infrastructure market. Nortel wrote contracts with Qwest and MCI-WorldCom saying that it would finance and build customer networks using OC-192 and that the carriers only had to pay OC-48 costs until the traffic in the networks exceeded OC-48 rates. Many carriers, which were already seeing eroding revenue streams, found this proposition quite attractive and moved away from Lucent to a long-term relationship with Nortel. Having stolen optics from Lucent, Nortel embarked on a path of building an all-optical network. Of course as events would eventually show, vendor financing would turn out to be a Pyrrhic victory for Nortel.

Nortel considered first-to-market and hence the speed of technology development to be essential. In the race to be the leader of the optical industry, rather than relying on inhouse development, Nortel embarked on a strategy of acquiring needed technologies, integrating newly acquired employees quickly, and gobbling up market share. Table 5-1 provides a list of Nortel's prominent acquisitions of optical technology companies. In the case of the large acquisitions, in. terms of valuation, Nortel suffered the Winner's Curse pretty much like Lucent, although perhaps not as spectacularly.

One of the first major companies that Nortel acquired was Qtera Corporation, which was a privately held company in the business of produc-

Table 5-1. Nortel's optical company acquisitions

Date	Company Name	Amount
Dec. 15, 1998	Cambrian Systems	$300 million
Jan. 28, 2000	Qtera	$3.25 billion
Feb. 13, 2000	JDS Uniphase Zurich	$3 billion
May 23, 2000	Photonic Technologies	$35.5 million
June 2, 2000	Xros	$3.25 billion
June 23, 2000	CoreTek	$1.43 billion

ing ultra long-reach optical networking systems. The promise of the technology was to enable optical signals to be sent as far as 4,000 kilometers or 2,500 miles without the need for opto-electrical regeneration, delivering advantages in cost and reliability to long-range networks. Qtera's solutions could operate at 10 Gbps, the line rate used by leading-edge high-performance Internet backbone networks.

Nortel paid $3.25 billion in Nortel common shares to acquire Qtera. When the acquisition agreement was announced on December 15, 1999, Qtera had been in business for little more than a year and did not have a completed product. After the acquisition, Nortel made an effort to integrate Qtera's innovations into Nortel's product line but failed completely. Qtera's technology turned out to have many technical problems, which led Nortel to write down a large portion of its goodwill obtained from the acquisition. Wall Street industry analysts argued that Qtera was one of Nortel's biggest disappointments. By June 2001, it was clear that the acquisition had failed to meet specific business performance objectives that would have result in increased shareholder value.

The dream of developing an all-optical switch propelled Nortel in June 2000 to acquire Xros (founded in Sunnyvale, California, in 1996) for $3.25 billion in Nortel common shares on a fully diluted basis. The technology that was being developed at Xros would allow data to be switched through optical networks by reflecting light with tiny, movable mirrors. Nortel also thought that buying Xros was a good move because the technology allowed it to have a product on the market at the same time Lucent was expected to start selling its own all-optical network product. At the time of the Xros acquisition, Nortel was criticized for paying such a large amount for a start-up with no substantial revenues. The deal for Xros, which had all of 90 employees, set a new premium on talent in a notoriously deep-pocketed industry: $36 million per worker.

Problems started right away. At the time of the acquisition, Xros was not close to having completed any prototype switches, and its first systems were not scheduled for field trials until later in 2000. Nortel considered combining Xros's switching technology with its existing optical products and the long-haul technology acquired from Qtera to help carriers build all-optical networks. But in the following years, it was discovered that Xros's technology had some severe drawbacks; it was based on a type of component that was not popular any more because it was too complex to integrate into existing networks. Further, Nortel realized that Xros's technology would be difficult to manufacture at a reasonable cost.

Thus, Nortel postponed the release of a large-scale switch for optical networks based on Xros's technology. This acquisition marked another failed attempt by Nortel to pioneer in the optics market by acquiring companies with cutting-edge technologies.

During this technology acquisition spree, also in June 2000, Nortel acquired CoreTek, a leader and pioneer in the use of a new type of laser and MEMS (micro-electromechanical systems) technology for optical networking. This acquisition cost Nortel $1.43 billion, much less than the Qtera and Xros acquisitions. To justify the acquisition, Nortel stated that CoreTek's solutions would complement Nortel's products, as CoreTek's components were designed to operate in 10 Gbps systems, the speed that Nortel had already set as the standard for optical Internet communications.

CoreTek's products use tiny, movable mirrors to alter the wavelength of light emitted by semiconductor lasers and other optical components. CoreTek developed these laser-transmitting devices, which can be tuned to any of 60–80 different channels, so that a single device can be used to replace dozens of different devices in the optical switches made by Nortel, Lucent Technologies, Sycamore Networks, and other companies. This innovation dramatically improved the speed, performance, quality, and economics of the optical Internet, as tunable laser technology has had a big impact on the cost and complexity of manufacturing the switches.

Initially, Nortel used some CoreTek lasers in its own products and sold some to other equipment makers, but with the softening of the telecom market, carriers delayed upgrading their networks and buying new equipment. Unable to sell its product, Nortel decided to shut down CoreTek's optical components business and lay off the company's 160 workers in early September 2002. Nortel thought that CoreTek's technology was way ahead of market demand.

The most egregious acquisition of Nortel's was not in optical technology; it was in data networking. In the late 1990s, a number of companies started to work on a new technology called *content switching*. When different types of content (data, video, voice-over IP) enter a Web environment, it is important to be able to decide which servers service the traffic and which part of the network is used to deliver the traffic. Content switches can make decisions on how individual Web pages and images are served from a company's site. By balancing the load among the different resources, one can improve the performance of the content services. In 1997, a company called Bay Networks moved aggressively into building content switches.

Given the explosion of Internet and broadband traffic, many companies, including Cisco and Lucent, were interested in getting into this marketplace. In June 2000, in addition to going on an acquisition spree for optical technology, Nortel also bought Alteon WebSystems, a content switching company, for a whopping $7.8 billion. At the time, Alteon was a public company with revenues of around $400 million, so the price-earnings ratio of 20 did not compute. The expectation was that revenue would grow to more than $4 billion by 2004, but this just did not happen. Although Nortel was selling Alteon switches even in 2003, the market for content switches was just not there. The price paid for the acquisition was so out of proportion with reality that a telecom insider told one of the authors, "Alteon was the camel that broke Nortel's back."

In early 2001, market research figures indicated that Nortel had won the optics race. RHK industry analysts and the Dell'Oro Group ranked Nortel number one in the optical market for the year 2000. According to Dell'Oro's investigation, Nortel grabbed 71.1% of the metro DWDM market as well as a market-leading 44.6% share in the long-haul business. Among telecom equipment suppliers, Nortel was particularly aggressive in broadening its product portfolio and getting into new markets as quickly as possible. Nortel thought that having the first-mover advantage was essential in the dynamic, competitive telecom equipment market and that all of its acquisitions made strategic sense. All in all, Nortel had bought 18 companies since 1998, with a combined worth of more than $43 billion (not including X-CEL Communications, the price of which was not disclosed). Among the 18 deals, the 6 acquisitions of optical companies reached a combined $11.7 billion. Even more stunning is that Nortel bought several unknown start-ups that had little—or, in some cases, no—revenues.

After proclaiming in early 1999 that it would double its optical networking production capacity, Nortel announced in late 1999 that it would triple it. The stock price of Nortel soared from a low of $13 in January 1999 to $86 in mid-July 2000. At that time, Wall Street analysts forecasted an estimated 80% growth rate in Nortel's optical revenue in 2000, compared with about 40% for its closest competitor. In the year 2000, many Wall Street analysts also believed that Nortel looked like a good bet to go higher as it frantically expanded its optical systems and components manufacturing. Unfortunately for Nortel, the years following its acquisition binge were filled with more strife than success. In 2001, Nortel announced that the company would have a $19.2 billion second-quarter loss.

Some $12.4 billion of the loss came from the write-offs of goodwill associated with its purchases of Alteon, Xros, and Qtera in 1999 and 2000. This news sent Nortel's stock to a low of $8.75 on the New York Stock Exchange.

What went wrong when Nortel's acquisition strategies were once viewed as ambitious and reasonable? In hindsight, it's easy to blame the industry slowdown across the board. Telecom carriers had overbuilt, and excess capacity allowed them to defer spending on building out and upgrading their networks. In the late 1990s, especially 1999 and 2000, the telecom boom seemed to be a sure thing: "if they had brought on enough customers, they would have eventually become profitable."[2] The boom contributed to the severity of Nortel's Winner's Curse, but it is clear that the company badly overvalued its acquisitions regardless of industry trends.

Cisco's challenge

Cisco is an admired leader in Silicon Valley and Wall Street; its business is data networking. Cisco had built itself by pursuing an aggressive acquisition strategy. By the early 1990s, it was the largest player in routers with more than a 70% share in many enterprise data services markets. Even so, compared with the likes of Lucent and Nortel, which had long histories in the traditional voice-switching market, Cisco was a small supplier to the telecom services provider market. One of its most successful acquisitions was Stratacom, which allowed it to supply service providers with a technology called *frame relay*. In late 1998, the demand for optical equipment soared, and Cisco turned its attention to this market. Cisco was considered by many business scholars to be the paragon of virtue when it came to acquisitions. Before buying a company, it supposedly did due diligence well to ensure that the newly acquired company could be integrated into the mainstream of Cisco's product lines, culture, management, and customer service practices. However, in the mad scramble to get optical technology, Cisco seemed to have left its principles behind.

In March 2000, Mike Volpi, the head of business development at Cisco, proclaimed that in optical networking, the spoils would go to the most

---

2. K. Cheng and J. Ikram, "Nortel Acquisition Analysis," BMCT 798X Report, University of Maryland, December 2002.

nimble. He stated that Cisco's acquisition strategy had shifted in view of quickly moving markets to one of acting once it identified a suitable acquisition and using its $500 billion market cap as a currency to enter new markets. Implied in his comments was Cisco's growing indifference to the price tag of acquisitions, so long as the acquisitions were sizable and allowed Cisco to enter a new market rapidly (see table 5-2).

One of the first companies that Cisco acquired in the optics industry was Cerent.[3] Cerent was supplying technology for the access networks and had many of the CLECs (competitive local exchange carriers) as its customers. The company's first product was shipped in October 1998 and enabled network service providers to manage the flow of data from customers to the optical network core while lowering costs and increasing efficiencies. This product allowed customers to increase the amount of data in their networks by 400–500% while simultaneously cutting costs. Right around this time, Cisco made a strategic investment in Cerent of $13 million for a 9% stake.

Cisco, at the time, did not have any optical products in its portfolio and did not sell in the transport market at all. Although Cisco saw the widespread acceptance of the product, it did not develop any real feel for the product's potential. In March 1999, Cisco made its first offer to acquire

Table 5-2. Some of Cisco's optical acquisitions

Company	Price	Status	Analysis
Cerent	$6.9 billion	Alive and well	Although Cerent has generated $1 billion in estimated sales for Cisco, nearly two decades will be needed at current revenue run-rate to recoup the cost.
Pirelli Optical Systems	$2.2 billion	Alive but struggling	A disappointing attempt to bolster Cisco's long-haul optical networking strategy, but the technology is too far behind that of rivals.
Monterey Networks	$500 million	Written off in April 2001	This promising optical start-up never produced a viable product, and Cisco cut its losses.

3. This information is mostly based on a case study published by Stanford University's Graduate School of Business, "Cerent Corporation," April 2000.

the company for $300 million, which the CEO, Carl Russo, and the board rejected outright. At the time, the market was near its peak, and optical transport solutions companies like Carrier Access, with similar revenues to Cerent, had valuations of $1.5 billion. By June 1999, 30 companies had their networks running on the Cerent system. Several optical networking equipment companies also went public, including Juniper Networks, Copper Mountain Networks, Extreme Networks, and Redback Networks.

The recent emergence of optical networking companies had changed Cisco's perception of the market, and at the same time, Cerent had established an effective sales channel into the transport market. Further, the economics of the optical networking market seemed incredibly compelling at the time. Eventually, Cisco made a $6.9 billion offer for Cerent, and the board of the company accepted. Russo became the head of optical networking products at Cisco. The acquisition of Cerent was done over a period of time during which Cisco used its initial investment to learn about the optical business and the company. It is widely accepted that Cisco's acquisition of Cerent was a success in the long run.

Conversely, Cisco's acquisitions of Monterey Networks and, Pirelli Optical Systems were flawed and subject to the Winner's Curse.[4] In 1999, Cisco wanted to move aggressively into the optical transport market and tried to acquire an established vendor of DWDM equipment. It also threatened to go to a competitor if its overtures were turned down. Having been spurned by the competition, Cisco ended up buying Pirelli partly to follow through with its threat.

Founded in 1995, Pirelli was a leading developer of optical technology, with 1999 sales of $225 million, 700 employees, and operations in France, Germany, Italy, and the United States. The company was the first to ship open standards-based 10-Gbps optical transport systems and boasted customers such as France Telecom, Deutsche Telekom, Brazil Telecom, and Global Crossing. The hope was that this acquisition would allow Cisco to market a broader array of solutions to large national carriers, particularly the ability to extend the capacity of their fiber-optic networks, adding line capacity as needed. In December 1999, Cisco made an offer of $2.2 billion for the business in a stock deal. During December 1999, rival Nortel made an offer for start-up Qtera, which made simi-

---

4. Information based on articles in C-Net News (http://news.com.com) and Lightreading (www.lightreading.com), December 1999.

lar equipment, for $3.25 billion. Thus, the price Cisco paid did not seem out of line.

This victory, however, turned out to be ephemeral. Pirelli's optical technology was much further behind that of the leading companies, Ciena, Lucent, and Nortel. Cisco has yet to develop any significant market share in any of the product lines that the Pirelli acquisition promised.

One of the most egregious acquisitions Cisco made was not in optics technology; it was in data communications technology where Cisco should have had the best knowledge in the industry. In May 2000, Cisco acquired ArrowPoint Communications, which made content switches that were designed to manage Web content and traffic. When ArrowPoint was a privately held company, Nortel had tried to buy it for around $2 billion, but failed because the founders would not accept the price. Cisco could have bought the company then, but waited too long. ArrowPoint went public in March 2000 at the height of the stock market boom. After its initial offering of $34 per share, Wall Street frenzy over technology stocks resulted in the company closing its first day of trading up 250% to almost $120 per share. When Cisco acquired the company, its market capitalization was around $5 billion, and Cisco paid $5.7 billion for it, almost double what it could have paid before the initial public offering.

In the quarter before the Cisco purchase, ArrowPoint had a loss of around $5 million. However, some analysts projected that revenues would grow to about $60 million by year's end. This level of sales never materialized. In fact, the content switching market failed to take off. Cisco's acquisition of ArrowPoint has had the same fate as Nortel's acquisition of Alteon: a big bust.

Conclusions

The change in the climate for investors in optical technology can be summarized by two statements: "You're in optics? Let me get my checkbook" (c. January 1998), which changed to "You're in optics? You must be an idiot or from another planet" (c. December 2002). While everyone was excited by the potential for innovations in optics technology and many different companies sprouted like mushrooms in the 1990s, investors were poisoned by the reality that the devil was in network implementation.

Propelled by the stock market, analysts, and investment bankers, many of the major equipment manufacturers in telecommunications like Lucent, Nortel, and Cisco went on shopping expeditions to acquire optical technology as quickly as possible. In the excitement that clouded everyone's judgment, companies paid enormous sums of money to purchase start-ups with unproven technology and incomplete products. A buying and bidding psychology developed which produced a logic that you had to buy a new technology or risk being left behind. And you had better buy a company now, whatever the price, so that a competitor does not acquire it first. The focus was on winning and beating competitors. Managerial optimism and hubris helped fuel the mad race for acquisitions. One gets the impression that the entire optical industry felt invulnerable as it raced ahead, acquiring companies and overbuilding capacity. All of these factors combined to create extreme pressures for growth.

This money transfer gave a signal to many budding entrepreneurs that being in opticals was the surefire way to become rich very quickly. Many engineers, especially in Silicon Valley, left their companies to flock to start-ups developing optical technology. A number of these people were quite risk-averse to begin with, but the signals they were getting in the marketplace completely obscured the real risks of being in optical start-ups. The investment community, especially investment bankers who had been in the business of building companies, got into the game of flipping them. Even blue-blood venture capitalists started investing in small optical companies with the sole purpose of hyping them for sale to the major vendors. As we have seen, established firms like Lucent, Nortel, and Cisco bought and sold the wrong companies for huge sums of money, resulting in devastating losses all around.

The financial implications of this Winner's Curse meant that the new employees of the large companies, who had come with the acquired start-ups, were getting paid much more than the employees who had been there for a long time. This inequity led to a huge loss of morale and an intense struggle for control of the acquired technology. It was no wonder that, in many cases, the parent company had to abandon the integration of the new product line into its business. Also, optical systems are inherently skilled-labor intensive, and the notion that one could simply implement an innovation in a manufacturing facility as fast as one could negotiate a merger was wishful thinking. Excitement about new technology in a seemingly fast-growing segment of the economy won the day, and in the process companies lost all sight of the effort that would be needed to make the technology work. The Winner's Curse was alive and well in the optical technology market of the late twentieth and early twenty-first centuries.

What to do?

The telecommunications industry in the 1990s was awash in great excitement and optimism. The Internet captured the imagination of everyone. Governments in many countries, especially the United States, deregulated the industry and unleashed competition in all segments of the service market. Start-ups in telecom services and technology sprouted like mushrooms, and venture capitalists were confident that investment would pay significant dividends. It should not be surprising that, in this climate, there were many mistakes.

We have spoken to a number of people who were players in the telecom technology industry, and many of them feel that the industry will revive. In fact, what is clear to us is that the Internet has become a part and parcel of everyday life all over the world. Traffic on the Internet includes music and movies, and the demand for high-speed, efficient, cost-effective technology will return to the heady expectations of the 1990s, albeit more slowly. Companies and investors planning to be active in producing and marketing innovations in communications technology need to follow some guidelines in order to not repeat the mistakes of the past.

Avoid euphoria about technology

Technology by itself cannot be the end result. At the end of the day, what is important is whether or not one can build a business around a technology. In the communications industry, it is easy to get carried away by bigger, better, and faster technology. Indeed, many of the companies we analyzed and described in this chapter tried to build what are labeled *god boxes*, state-of-the-art switches that can do everything. The content switches that we described had much more functionality than ordinary add-drop multiplexers, and they were considered god boxes. In many instances, this state-of-the-art technology was much more expensive than other technology that would do the job.

Pushing technology to its limit may be exciting to innovators and engineers, but may not be profitable in the end. Also, getting too excited about technology and downplaying its business implications could lead investors to back the wrong company. Companies and investors should try and develop *hot boxes*, technology without which a significant number of enterprises and service providers cannot live. For example, although IBM was pushing a technology called *token rings* for use in local area networks (LANs), Xerox's Ethernet was a much easier technology to adopt. Thus Ethernets quickly became a hot box technology that all enterprises wanted because of its simple architecture and the ease with which one could create LANs with it. The business implications of developing and investing in hot box technology rather than getting excited about god box technology are significant.

Understand what the market really needs

Cisco used to listen to its customers to understand the bottlenecks in their communications needs, and the company would then either develop technology to fill the gap or acquire companies that had the appropriate technology. Even today, equipment providers should use their experience in implementing networking solutions for enterprises and carriers to get a good sense of the next generation of technology needs. "Disruptive" technology, by definition, is what excites the marketplace.[5] Companies should try to integrate their marketing teams with their engineering teams so that market intelligence will influence innovations to produce technology that can be profitable in tomorrow's communications industry.

There is nothing as important as doing extensive market simulations in order to assess the potential size of the market and therefore what a technology acquisition is really worth. Equipment vendors should perform *scenario analyses* to also assess the different futures, from optimistic to pessimistic, that are in store for the technology that they are planning to acquire. This scenario planning exercise will also allow them to understand what factors need to come together to establish the market potential for the technology and what needs to be done to be successful in this industry segment. It may also show that the market for a particular technology is limited at best, or that the factors that need to converge for success are extremely difficult to control. In the latter case, it may be more prudent to walk away from a technology acquisition.

Perform systematic due diligence on every technology acquisition

Although doing due diligence might seem obvious, it is important, especially in the case of seemingly revolutionary technology, not to get car-

---

5. Clayton Christensen, *The Innovator's Dilemma* (Cambridge, Mass.: Harvard Business School, 1997).

ried away by the hype created by the founders of a company, its venture capitalists, or other boosters. In almost every case we highlighted in this chapter, the large telecom vendors were carried away by the potential size of the future market, the best-of-breed nature of the technology, and in many cases, by the personalities of those trying to make the deal. In Silicon Valley, where a number of the start-ups were founded, many people consider Lucent and Nortel to be "bad acquirers." It is not that the senior management teams at these companies were inexperienced or unaware of what is good and what is bad. In the rough-and-tumble climate of the 1990s, they failed to do thorough due diligence of the companies they pursued.

Part of the due diligence should be to determine whether or not the founders and boosters of the start-up technology companies have track records. Folklore at the time was that being at the helm of a failed start-up was a "badge of honor" that suggested a penchant for innovation and deep technological know-how. From today's perspective, the lesson to be learned is that there were multiple reasons for failure at these technology start-ups, and some of them should be of real concern.

The due diligence should also be extended to venture capital firms. Some venture firms like to roll companies out quickly and recover a multiple of their investment as soon as possible. They are quite willing to put a façade of success on a start-up by dressing it up with an impressive management team and a spectacular office space in order to sell it to the next suitor. If one makes a deal with such a venture capitalist, then one may well be getting more hype than a potentially successful company. The *long-term* record of the companies that the venture capitalists have offered should also be a consideration in making deals with them.

Steer clear of hubris

There was a significant amount of arrogance in the communications technology world in the 1990s. Many of those in both start-ups and established firms were extremely bright people with deep knowledge of technology. As the stock market went through the roof, many of the engineers and executives in the technology firms became wealthy from shares they had in their companies and their stock options. A large number of venture capitalists were top-notch individuals with MBAs from the best universities. Many of the senior people in the communications technology industry felt that they could do no wrong.

Additionally, becoming first-to-market in any particular industry segment became a macho thing. If one company had a particular technology—say, content switches—then a competitor wanted to make sure that it got an even better one in the same segment. If one did a $5 billion deal, then the other wanted to do a $6 billion deal. Sometimes the competition even became personal.

The main point to remember is that one needs to steer away from hubris. The financial success or failure of a company affects tens of thousands of shareholders and employees. Making decisions under hubris will affect the lives of all of these people. Further, hubris colors one's judgment about the real facts underlying a particular technology acquisition. One tends to ignore the negative and get overly excited about the positive. Also, if a person thinks he is infallible, it is easy for a deal maker to focus on massaging his ego and getting the deal done, whether or not it is good for the company. To paraphrase Shakespeare, "Hubris makes a mockery of us all."

6 • Dot-coms: On top of the world for a while

The Internet was supposed to open up new avenues for creating value, and companies with great ideas would create a "new economy." The main driver was the possibility for business and household consumers to be able to buy anything at anytime from anywhere. Dot-coms, companies that rushed to be pioneers in the use of the new networking technology, were the poster children of the Internet era. They had a meteoric rise, especially in their valuations by Wall Street, and they had a spectacular fall, taking with them the savings and retirement accounts of millions of investors. During the heyday of what is called the dot-com era, the mantras were "first-to-market" and "it's now or never." The notion was that these start-ups (we will call them dot-coms) would use the Internet to wipe out traditional companies operating in the same space. Consider the following:

> The battlefield is uneven. Start-ups, with their Internet birthright, have the advantage. Being small, newer companies can move quickly, and their entire business revolves around a single focus. In addition, start-ups have an easy access to venture funding and more risk-tolerant investors than the traditional companies. But most important, the

dotcoms have nothing to lose if the old ways of doing business fade away.[1]

In 1996, Mary Meeker, whom *Barrons* eventually anointed "Queen of the Net," wrote an influential 300-page research document called simply *The Internet Report*, which argued the case for the business success of start-ups on the Internet. Crammed with charts, tables, glossaries, and a listing of public and private companies with recommendations about each, it quickly became the bible for investors interested in the Web. Mary Meeker used this fame to become the arbiter for deciding whether or not a company had a future. Although her official role was as an analyst, she quickly became indistinguishable from an investment banker. Her remuneration was affected in a significant way by the number of companies she was able to attract for Morgan Stanley to underwrite. She was able to arrange for Morgan Stanley to be the primary investment banker for companies like Amazon, Priceline, FreeMarkets, Broadcast, and so on. In 1999, Meeker earned an eye-popping $15 million, an unprecedented amount for a Wall Street analyst.

These start-up companies were supposed to revolutionize the world by bringing consumers of all types closer to the producers, cutting out the traditional middlemen and reducing transaction costs. Ronald Coase, the British Nobel Laureate economist, developed the transaction cost approach to the theory of the firm. *Transaction cost* refers to the cost of obtaining a good or service through the market rather than having it provided from within the firm. Coase describes in his article "The Problem of Social Cost" the transaction costs with which he is concerned:

> In order to carry out a market transaction it is necessary to discover who it is that one wishes to deal with, to conduct negotiations leading up to a bargain, to draw up the contract, to undertake the inspection needed to make sure that the terms of the contract are being observed, and so on.[2]

The transaction costs of doing business are search and information costs, bargaining and decision costs, and policing and enforcement costs. In the beginning, the value proposition of the dot-com companies was primarily

---

1. Mary Modahl, *Now or Never* (New York: Harper Business, 2000), xvii; she is the "other Mary" of the Internet bubble.
2. R. Coase, "The Problem of Social Cost," *Journal of Law and Economics* 3, no. 1 (October 1960): 1–44.

the reduction of all of the different transaction costs by doing business on the Internet. Thus, the dot-com companies became the new intermediaries, or sometimes "infomediaries." Eventually this value proposition turned out to be a mirage, and the dot-coms had to scramble to come up with new value propositions.

The dot-com business model

If the main value proposition for the consumer was the reduction of cost, then the question arises as to how these companies were going to make money. There were many revenue-generating models that came from the Internet era; sometimes it seemed as though there was a new business model every day. Revenue generation depended on advertisements, micropayments, memberships and subscriptions, commissions, and so on. Many of them eventually failed.

During the beginning of the Internet explosion, most companies charged their users a subscription fee. The users of the leading online services, such as CompuServe, America OnLine, and Genie, paid a monthly membership fee that allowed them five to ten hours of use per month with additional fees for additional use. Prodigy, a service started by Sears and IBM, was the only one to provide unlimited access for a monthly subscription fee. Prodigy generated revenue by having advertising banners on each Web page. Eventually all companies started following the model of unlimited use and advertisements. New companies, especially if they were simply passive providers of content and shopping (such as Slate, TheStreet, and Microsoft Investor) rather than Internet service providers (ISPs), even did away with subscription fees. They generated revenue through advertisements along with whatever payments they could gather from enabling a buy-sell transaction. Given the free and open history of the Internet, customers balked at paying a subscription fee for obtaining information, whether it was news or details on purchases.

Yahoo followed the pure advertising model very successfully. During the late 1990s, Yahoo's market capitalization grew so rapidly that in January 2000, its shares were worth $200 billion, which was higher than the market capitalization of NBC, ABC, and CBS combined. However, none of the other dot-com companies was as successful in generating revenue using a pure advertising model.

There was severe competition for advertisement dollars, not only among the dot-com companies, but also from traditional avenues as well. When marketing executives decide where to spend their budgets, they have a choice of television, radio, daily newspapers, magazines, and so on. In 2000, an average American spent 1,633 hours watching television, 961 hours listening to music on the radio, 151 hours reading daily newspapers, but only 124 hours on the Internet.[3] Even if the hours on the Internet doubled every year for three years, it would be no more than one-half the time people spend watching TV. Further, television is a passive form of entertainment, and most viewers do not walk away from advertising messages. To compound it all, for most marketing executives the Internet was a very new medium, and there was insufficient experience and information on how effective it was. Thus, the incentive for companies to spend a lot of money on Internet advertisement was quite low. Advertisers were only comfortable with spending their dollars on companies with Internet sites that were highly viewed. Thus, if one were using advertisements as the primary vehicle for generating revenue, it was imperative to drive as many users to one's site as possible.

Subscriptions and memberships had limited success in generating revenues, and advertising revenue was hammered down by competition and a sense of low effectiveness. Dot-com companies were forced to pursue other sources of revenue. The most popular one was commissions, which were paid by vendors whenever a good or service was bought through the dot-com. Another mechanism used by companies like Priceline.com was to actually buy goods in bulk from vendors with volume discounts and then sell them at a higher price, making money on the difference. Vendors really liked these new arrangements enabled by the net. It provided them with numerous channels through which to market their goods and services. The vendors also contributed to the channel explosion by starting their own online sites to sell their products and services. More important, and to the chagrin of the dot-com intermediaries, competition among the dot-coms allowed the vendors to only pay very small commissions, and thus the concept of micropayments became the vogue in the industry. For companies selling online that depended on volume discounts and differential pricing as their revenue model, vendors did not provide sufficiently deep discounts to allow large margins. Given the extremely small amount of money to be made on the sale of any good, the name of the game for those who depended on this revenue model was also to drive as many users to their sites as possible

3. Veronis Suhler Stevenson Media Merchant Bank report.

in the hope that enough of them would make a purchase to enable the dot-coms to stay in business.

Winning was everything

Thus, "winning" in the dot-com world meant that one had to capture as much market share as possible as quickly as possible. Mary Meeker, the Morgan Stanley analyst/banker, was quick to realize the concept of winning and helped to popularize the notion that the Internet was a land grab. Thus, many companies were focused on rapid growth and the mantra of market share and not on profits. The notion was that once they were large, both economies of scale and network economies would kick in, and the companies would start making money.

Although, traditionally, the stock market was impatient with companies that were losing money, especially with companies that did not seem to have a clear path to profits, analysts surrounding the dot-com companies scoffed at the shortsightedness of those who questioned the fundamentals. In response, Meeker was instrumental in coming up with new metrics to measure the performance of the dot-com companies. For example, Meeker came up with a measure called *discounted terminal valuation*, an esoteric way of calculating the value of a company based on anticipated margins and growth rates five years down the road. As the Internet exploded, nonfinancial metrics, such as "eyeballs" and "page views," permeated the discussion. Analysts used these measures to argue that because those who surfed the Internet would click through pages, the fact that they went to Web pages was an indicator of interest and hence an indicator of the value of the company. For example, in a 1998 report on Yahoo, Meeker said, "Forty million unique sets of eyeballs and growing in time should be worth nicely more than Yahoo's current market value of $10 billion."[4]

The notion that success was equivalent to winning market share was so prevalent that whenever a question was raised about profitability, everyone connected with the industry defended growth as though it were the Holy Grail. Because the stock market was on a wild upward ride, the other way of responding to the critics was to ask the difficult question of why on earth anyone would slow down in a bull market. In the exuberance of the bull market, many highly questionable private companies went public with

4. Quoted in "Where Mary Meeker Went Wrong," *Fortune*, May 2001.

large initial valuations. Companies like Priceline.com, HomeGrocer.com, iVillage.com, Women.com, Tickets.com, Lastminute.com, and so on eventually became an embarrassment to Morgan Stanley, Goldman Sachs, and others.

Winning with network economics

What would it cost to win market share? Due to the enthusiasm of the era, all those selling the dot-com business model spouted the concept of network economics to make their case. *Network economics,*[5] in its fundamental form, is based on the premise that if a company could get a network of users to buy into a product or service, then that product or service would have a higher value to each additional user. Additional users would also reduce the average cost of production. This phenomenon is also known as the *network effect.* The best example of network effects was the telephone network of old. The value of the Bell telephone system to each user increased as more and more of their friends and family acquired phones and joined the network. There are many other examples of network effects, including fax machines, which are only useful if others have fax machines to communicate with you; word processing and spreadsheet software, which are only useful to individuals in a team if others use it as well; and so on. Clearly, those providing telephone services, fax machines, and specific software really like these network effects, especially if the marginal cost of including the new consumer is low. In this case, it is a win-win situation. Network effects provide a strong incentive for more and more people to join a group, and as more and more people join, the average cost of servicing customers gets lower and lower.

Network effects were similar to economies of scale, which is a well-known concept in economics. The fixed cost of producing a car, say, is high due to the investment in plant and machinery that is needed whether one is producing 100 cars or 100,000. However, the incremental cost of producing a car once the factory has been built is considerably lower and only involves parts and labor. The more cars one produces, the lower the average cost. It is imperative for automobile producers to try and sell as many cars as possible to recoup the fixed costs and make a profit. These

5. The concept of Network Economics is well described in the book by Varian and Shapiro entitled *Information Rules* (Cambridge, Mass.: Harvard Business School Press, 1998).

economies are one reason that automobile companies discontinue models that do not sell more than a minimum quantity. Many production facilities exhibit economies of scale, and having as large a market share as possible is a driving force in manufacturing.

Pitching the business model in terms of network economics resonated with a lot of people who understood the fundamentals of economies of scale. Further, given the fact that it was easy to reach an enormous number of consumers with the click of a mouse suggested that the incremental cost of serving a user was near zero, as posited by Varian and Shapiro in their influential book *Information Rules*. Thus, even though it required a significant amount of initial investment to set up appealing Web sites, build hardware and software tools, and create the supply chain infrastructure, including billing and order fulfillment, the optimists had faith that network effects and economies of scale would kick in, making average costs low enough to produce profitability. It was a matter of speed only, and whoever could scale up fast enough would be able to obtain the lion's share of the market and profits.

Armed with the new dot-com business models, entrepreneurs started a whole host of companies with blue chip investments that did not really satisfy the fundamental concepts of either network economies or economies of scale. In some cases, the companies they created had cost and revenue features that were contrary to network economics.

Search engines and portals

Many of the initial dot-com companies focused their attention on providing as much information as possible at the click of a mouse, reducing the search and information cost to the customer. Scores of companies created search engines; the better known among them were AltaVista, AOL, Deja, Google, Infoseek, Inktomi, AskJeeves, LookSmart, Lycos, MSN, and Yahoo. The business proposition was simple: because customers would not pay for using the search engines, the companies had to generate revenue from other sources. The most popular strategy was to use banner advertisements above, below, and sometimes on the side of the information being displayed. Another method, used mostly by Yahoo and MSN, was to get merchants to pay them for being listed in targeted sites such as finance, cooking, and apparel. Of course, AOL was an Internet service provider (ISP) and also had its own search vehicle, and much of AOL's revenue comes from monthly membership dues.

The amount that advertisers and merchants would be willing to pay the dot-com search company depended on the number of people actually using the site. This is similar to television advertising, which is based on Nielsen ratings. In order to survive as a search engine company, the name of the game was to drive as many customers to use your services as possible, or become the dominant company by purchasing as many competitors as you could. In order to capture as many customers as possible, the companies had to invest heavily in making their search engines as easy to use as possible and also to return results quickly. If the customer were interested in a particular subject, the search engines almost had to have the ability to read her mind and find the correct information instantaneously. For the company that was able to satisfy the customers' curiosity best, the sky was the limit. Many bright computer scientists worked furiously to create fantastic search engines, and investors funded them generously to be the first company to capture the market. A major strategy, helped along by investors, was the acquisition. Google acquired Deja; Yahoo acquired Inktomi; Disney bought Infoseek and turned it into Go.com. Eventually after extensive modifications, Disney contemplated closing the portal it had acquired.

Of course many dot-coms have failed miserably. At the time of this writing, the dominant search dot-com is Google, a late starter which learned from the mistakes of others (see figure 6-1). Companies such as Yahoo, AOL, and MSN have also survived, and they have successfully supplemented their advertising income with significant revenues obtained from services that they offer.

So what other Web sites have disappeared as search dot-coms? There were a number of pioneering search engines that no one probably has even heard of today. Open Text Index was the first search engine to introduce field-searching capabilities. In early 1998, the Open Text Index was replaced by a business-oriented search engine known as Livelink Pinstripe, which then changed names several times before it finally expired for good. Magellan and WebCrawler were well-known search engines in the late 1990s and were bought out by Excite in 1998. Excite is now dead. It not only disappeared, but the portal Excite@Home also took the bankruptcy route.

The next stop in the search engine graveyard is for the portals. Many have died or are undergoing a slow death.[6] Back during the Internet's

---

6. The following couple of paragraphs are taken from "Dead Search Engines" by Greg R. Notes, http://www.onlinemag.net/may02/OnTheNet.htm.

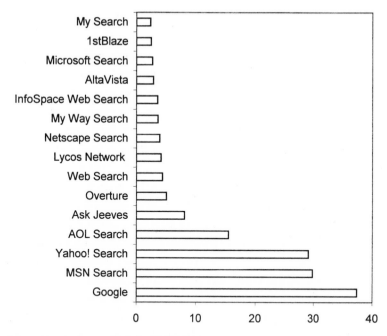

Figure 6-1. Active reach of channels (%)

Source: Nielsen//NetRatings; Active Reach %, Search Destinations, Month of December 2003, US, Home and Work.

heyday, everyone wanted to be a portal—a site that offered search, news, e-mail, and every other common service you could think of. The portals attracted many users and corresponding advertising dollars. Some of the portals had their own search engine databases while others provided some unique search features. Infoseek started as a search engine, but after being bought out by Disney, it became a part of the larger Go portal. Infoseek remained the underlying search engine until Disney gave up on it as a portal.

Another media-sponsored portal went a similar route. Snap, which became NBCi after NBC bought it, used to have its own Web directory, along with a unique treatment of the Inktomi search engine. The directory died outright, and NBC hardly advertises its portal. The site iWon made a name for itself as the portal to use for getting entries into cash giveaway sweepstakes; it advertised this fact heavily on television. Although still alive, one hardly hears of this portal. As the oldest and best known of the portals, Yahoo never had its own search engine. Its core directory remains, although it changed its follow-up search engine from

AltaVista to Inktomi to Google. And although its stock dove for a while, Yahoo is nowhere near death. It is still a hugely popular site for searches and for its many portal offerings. As of this writing, it has been experiencing a strong rebound in revenues and is rolling out its own search engine so that it does not have to depend on Google.

The problem with portals was on both the revenue side and the cost side. Users were not willing to pay a cent for using the search engines. On the revenue side, as we have discussed earlier, the advertisement model did not generate much interest and thus did not create sufficient income for any of the search engines or portals with the exception of Yahoo. Users of a particular search dot-com or portal would instantaneously abandon it if they thought that they were not getting the right information. Few commercial Web sites were willing to pay anything for being listed as a premier site on a search engine, drastically reducing revenue potential. On the cost side, there was a significant amount of cost associated with marketing the Web sites to potential consumers, and in making the search engines as effective as possible. Also, many search engine dot-coms had to pay to be included in the portals of Internet service providers like AOL, MSN, and Netscape. One could even argue that the fixed cost of starting operations as an Internet search engine was not as high as the marginal cost of capturing customers and servicing them, exactly the opposite of the network economics that we examined earlier. It is no wonder that the winners in this venture were cursed and died soon after from a combination of optimism, pressure from stock analysts and investment bankers, and the perils of unrealistic business models.

Selling groceries over the Internet

The Internet era also spawned dot-com companies in industries that, in retrospect, seemed poor candidates for electronic commerce. Electronic retailing was one of the hottest applications on the Internet and one that will undoubtedly survive the recent meltdown. Indeed Dell Computers sells a large portion of its computers electronically. Household and business users can go to the Dell Web site and either buy the models displayed electronically or specify all of the features important to them and have their computers delivered within five business days. Given the efficacy of the Dell direct sales model, most other computer manufacturers have mechanisms for online sales, even providing discounts to consumers who move to the Internet. Clearly, online shopping reduces a significant portion of transaction costs, including search, information, and decision costs, for the consumer. For the producer like Dell, Internet sales reduces a significant amount of overhead costs, including design, order entry, and billing, and also ensures that customers get the exact computer that they want.

Amazon.com was and is the most famous example of electronic retailing. Jeff Bezos talks about how he stumbled onto selling books over the Internet. Amazon now sells a whole variety of products, including CDs, electronics, toys, apparel, home and garden supplies, and so on. Selling books over the Internet has appeal because every copy of a book is identical, and it is not necessary to examine and experience the book before purchasing it. Also books are nonperishable so that delivery can occur in a few days or even weeks. What Amazon provided was the convenience of buying books from one's house or office and the possibility of being able to access thousands of titles instantaneously.

Fundamental questions remain as to how much consumers are willing to pay for these conveniences. If recent history is any indication, consumers will balk at paying $3–5 for shipping and handling, which is 7.5–12.5% of the average purchase of $40. The only way for Amazon to make money is to ensure that its margins on books and other products are high enough to cover the costs of enabling consumers to shop conveniently on the Internet, the costs of both the inbound and outbound logistics systems to deliver the books, and the costs of an accounts receivable system. This has not been the case, and Amazon lost money during the time it was only selling books. Since Amazon diversified, it has been able to show a positive net income. Because Amazon revolutionized the way in which electronic retailing was done and because it went into a variety of other goods that seemed to fit into the Internet marketplace, investors have kept Amazon going.

Books and groceries differ substantially in their suitability to Internet retailing. The grocery dot-coms were propelled by the knowledge that the industry had sales of $450 billion in 1998, not including the over-the-counter drug market and sales of prepared meals, which together were another $100 billion. In addition, the gross margin for groceries, provided one did not have to display them in a brick-and-mortar store, is around 30–35%, which is among the highest in any industry. As in much of the dot-com era, those most excited by the potential of Internet grocers were high-income individuals who could see the value proposition for themselves. These individuals encouraged the start-up of online grocers and invested in them.

In the beginning, the first movers such as Peapod, Webvan, and HomeGrocer did fantastically well in the stock market. In late 1999, Webvan and HomeGrocer each had a market capitalization of more than $5 billion, while the entire dot-com grocery industry had sales of $100 million and negative profits. Compared to these valuations, the brick-and-mortar grocery store Winn-Dixie had a market cap of $3 billion on sales of $14 billion, and Albertsons had a market cap of $11 billion on sales of $31 billion. Such an irrational response of Wall Street to this new industry also set the tone for the hubris of dot-com grocers.

One of the craziest things that happened was that in October 1999 George Shaheen, the CEO of Anderson Consulting (now Accenture) left to join Webvan as its CEO for a paltry $500,000 a year, much less than the $4 million he was earning. The main attraction of the Webvan offer was the $123 million of stock options that Shaheen received. Shaheen was the person who in 1989 helped to separate the $1.1 billion Anderson Consulting from Arthur Anderson, the accounting firm, and built it into the largest global consulting firm with revenues of $8.3 billion. At Webvan, Shaheen's ambitions were no less grand: to build an online grocer from the ground up that would operate in 26 cities within three years. After the brief delay caused by a Securities and Exchange Commission investigation, the Webvan IPO was launched in November 1999, with Webvan selling 25 million shares at $15 each, raising $375 million. The stock opened for public trading at $26, giving the company a market value of $8.45 billion, and the shares climbed to $34 on the first day.

However, things unraveled quickly. Selling groceries over the Internet is a completely different story from selling books or electronics. To begin with, one needs to understand the value proposition pursued by the dot-com grocers. Consumers would shop for groceries using a Web site, and the dot-com grocer would deliver the purchases to the customers' homes. The only electronic part of the experience was shopping on the Internet. Once the order was in, the dot-com company had to behave like a sophisticated, specialized logistics company. Many of the groceries bought by American households are frozen and perishable items, and the dot-com either had to deliver the goods when the consumer was at home, or else have a freezer and a refrigerator available to them where these items could be stored. Because most consumers were unwilling to take on these extra costs themselves, the first few dot-coms that got into the grocery business actually invested in home refrigerators for clients. Further, the bulkiest grocery products like rice, sugar, and flour tend to be among the cheapest and have the lowest margins. They also tend to take up the most space in a logistics system and cost the most to deliver. Thus, the entire logistics chain was fraught with very high cost and very low value attached to the costliest services. Not exactly what the doctor had in mind in terms of the economics of a business model.

Additionally, consumers are generally unwilling to let strangers buy some products such as fruit and meat because they like to examine these products personally. The quality of fruit and meat can indeed be judged by visual examination. For example, the weight of the meat one buys can be easily bumped up by the amount of fat, and that is visible. Bruises on the outside of fruits can make them unappetizing and can be an indication of spoilage inside. If consumers were only going to use the Internet grocers for selected items, then the issue was whether these dot-com companies could really take advantage of economies of scale.

To make matters worse, most consumers were not willing to pay much of a premium for home delivery. The only consumers who bought into the concept were dual career couples who had a high premium for the time spent shopping. However, the dot-com grocers knew that they needed to win as much market share as possible. The hubris surrounding the new age brought on by the Internet made the dot-com grocers believe that they could take advantage of "the inefficiencies that bogged down brick-and-mortar competitors,"[7] and this colored their judgment. Instead of simply focusing on the segment that could generate a profitable business, the dot-com grocers tried in the beginning to become ubiquitous in grocery retailing.

Consumers did not rush to online grocery stores as fast as the dot-com grocers expected. The logistics systems proved to be much more expensive than previously anticipated. The brick-and-mortar grocery chains, while seemingly inefficient, proved to be much more resilient than high-tech executives and entrepreneurs had assumed. The only way for the dot-com grocers to win market share was to change the underlying economics by improving services, enhancing the online experience, and simultaneously reducing costs. Not surprisingly, these imperatives proved elusive.

In order to gain market share, the online grocers rapidly increased their investment. Webvan and HomeGrocer, which eventually merged, tried to reduce logistics costs by automating their warehouses, improving their

---

7. C. Guglielmo and E. Cone, "Will Online Groceries Deliver Profits?" *Inter@ctive Week*, September 24, 1999.

distribution system, and purchasing specialty trucks. They tried using sophisticated tools for fulfilling orders and dispatching delivery vehicles and changed the computer interfaces for the customer. They increased the ability of customers to get information on special deals easily through e-mails. Webvan did win some market share and became the top dog in the online grocery business. Winning came at a significant cost. Webvan had almost $700 million at the end of 1999, $405 million raised in the IPO together with $286 million of proceeds from an earlier sale of pre-ferred stock. By January 1, 2001, a little more than a year later, 70% of this amount, nearly $500 million, was gone.

Webvan filed for Chapter 11 bankruptcy protection on July 16, 2001, just 18 months after its IPO. HomeRuns.com, a privately held online grocer based in Boston, Massachusetts, and Washington, D.C., shut down the same month. By the end of 2002, almost all of the online grocers were out of business. The only Internet grocer that is still standing is one of the pioneers, Peapod, which the giant Dutch supermarket chain Ahold purchased. Ahold also owns Giant Food and Stop 'n' Shop stores. Peapod has become an online extension of the supermarket brick-and-mortar experience and caters to both those who have little time to shop and those who are disabled, infirm, or too old to go to grocery stores.

Online exchanges for chemicals

In the summer of 1997, David Perry and Jeff Leane founded a company called Chemdex as an online marketplace for specialty chemicals, bio-chemicals, and reagents in the life sciences industry. It was among the first business-to-business (B2B) marketplaces. The business model was simple enough and was conceived for the First Annual Business Plan Contest at the Harvard Business School. Chemdex was going to dis-intermediate the market for specialty chemicals and reagents by creat-ing an online marketplace where suppliers and buyers would list products, locate detailed product information, compare prices, and order products. Chemdex would carry no inventory but would arrange direct shipments from manufacturers and distributors to customers.

Chemdex's main value propositions included a central electronic market-place where buyers and suppliers could interact, the use of Internet and database technology to resolve information-related inefficiencies, rapid order fulfillment for customers, and rapid payment for suppliers in an industry where it could take months to clear the market. Chemdex would help reduce overhead for delivery chain activities. The company expected the exchange to be particularly attractive for small and medium suppliers with less than $50 million in sales because it allowed them brand exposure relative to large competitors, an inexpensive distribution channel, and the elimination of paper-based catalogs, which alone had cost $5 million per year for these companies.

Chemdex hoped to make money in four different ways. The largest portion of the revenue (about 80%) was to come from the 5% transaction fees the exchange would charge the suppliers for each order placed through it. Chemdex also hoped to generate revenues by providing customized Web sites for customer orders, thus streamlining their purchasing systems. The company would help the suppliers by using push technology to directly market new products. Finally, Chemdex was hoping to package and sell customer data to suppliers. The last three sources of revenue depended heavily on the ability to take advantage of economies of scale. Chemdex projected revenues in excess of $50 million by the end of 2002 on a transaction volume of $575 million and a net income margin by then to exceed 50%.[8]

In November 1998, Chemdex opened its Web site for business after raising $750,000, half from Bob Swanson, the late founder of Genentech, and the other half from the Internet holding company CMGI. Now the main challenge was to start moving an enormous number of suppliers and users to the dot-com. Using the initial investment and by selling equity in the company to different companies and trade groups, Perry managed to woo 30,000 registered users and 140 buying organizations, including heavy hitters such as Biogen, Dupont, and Schering-Plough, into the Chemdex exchange. Infused with this initial success, the company obtained a second round of funding of $30 million in April 1999 and held a successful initial public offering in July that raised another $112 million.

After the success of the IPO in July 1999, Chemdex decided to enter other vertical dot-com marketplace businesses. In September 1999, the company started Promedix, an e-market for medical supplies. By January 2000, Chemdex had started another company, Broadlane, a joint venture with Tenet Healthcare, an e-market serving the low-end, high-volume medical supply industry. Continuing this trend, Chemdex created Industria Solutions as a joint venture with Dupont to deal with fluid-processing

8. Chemdex Business Plan, June 10, 1997.

equipment. The initial moniker for the company, Chemdex, seemed by this time to be out of place and to not reflect its new strategy of building and operating multiple online marketplace companies. Thus in March 2001, the company officially changed its name to Ventro. Martha Greer, the vice president of marketing, said that the name Ventro was selected because it represented several images, including a new venture, different verticals, and "what we would call an empty vessel that you could do lots with and put lots of equity into."[9]

Ventro operated six B2B e-markets from its Silicon Valley headquarters. From its start in specialty chemicals, it focused on a more wide-ranging strategy. It would "build a powerful transaction engine, outfit it with customer-support and other broad-based services, connect buyers and suppliers efficiently over the Internet, and then leverage the entire operation across multiple industries."[10] The end goal was to create a network of branded e-markets, including Ventro Life Sciences, Ventro Healthcare, Ventro Food Distribution, and so forth.

By October 2000, Ventro was burning $7.5 million each month and operating on razor-thin net margins, 2.5%. Although many thought that Dave Perry, the CEO, would slow down and take stock of his existing operations, because of the thin margins, the only game in town was to get bigger and bigger and to win global market share. Ventro aggressively expanded into Europe.

Initially, the capital markets responded favorably to Ventro's strategy of operating in multiple vertical markets. On February 25, 2000, just three days after Chemdex changed its name to Ventro, the company's stock closed at its high of a shade less than $240. The company valuation skyrocketed to $10 billion on only $30 million in annual revenues. Most financial analysts and writers were excited about Ventro's business model. A *Red Herring* columnist wrote:

> Chemdex/Ventro [has] gone from [a single] vertical [marketplace] to [multiple vertical marketplaces]. . . . What the market seems to be telling us—and it is not often wrong—is that the concept of multiple-upon-multiple vertical exchanges is genius. It represents the possibility for Internet investors [to see] even higher valuations on these stocks.

9. Quoted in J. Soat, "IT Confidential," *Information Week*, February 28, 2000.
10. Tom Kaneshige, "Ventro's Mad Dash," *Line 56*, October 15, 2000.

The stock fell even faster than its original meteoric rise. By the summer of 2000, most investors had lost confidence in dot-com companies and started dumping the shares. Ventro did not go unpunished. By late August, the stock price was down to $16 per share, and the market cap was $735 million. Perry lost $500 million on paper.

However, the response of Wall Street did not stop Ventro. In fact, the company kept moving fast and furiously to be the winner in a number of online markets. By the end of the summer of 2000, Ventro had a total of seven marketplace businesses. It also had plans to launch three more by the end of the year. One of these was MarketMile, launched in a joint venture with American Express, which was supposed to enable businesses to purchase online a wide variety of products, including office supplies and computer hardware, and services such as temporary labor. Another was Amphire Solutions, a joint venture with the Web developer Entangibles, which created a marketplace for the food services industry. An analyst at the Yankee Group, Lisa Williams, applauded this strategy, "Creating an exchange as a joint venture with a brick-and-mortar partner is one of the fastest ways to get product liquidity."[11] However, events did not prove this view to be correct.

First, it turned out to be difficult to get a sufficient number of companies to participate in these exchanges and, even when there was some initial success, to keep them in a buying mood. For a successful implementation of the type of exchanges that Ventro tried to create, classic network economics was important. Unless the suppliers and the buyers thought that they would gain positive externalities by networking with others in a centralized electronic marketplace, it would be difficult for the exchange to become profitable.

Network externalities proved elusive. Suppliers tended to be reticent about exposing too much information for potential buyers and reluctant to participate in an environment where the buyers seemingly had more bargaining power and the ability to drive down prices. Further, many companies and industry groups started their own independent electronic marketplaces rather than trust a third-party vendor. For example, the automobile industry, which was heavily targeted by Ventro and VerticalNet (another exchange), started its own exchange called Covisint. While everyone knew that the fixed costs to create e-markets were high, it turned out the variable

11. Quoted in Tom Kaneshige, "Ventro's Mad Dash," *Line 56*, October 15, 2000.

costs were high as well. As Carl Lenz, research director of the Gartner Group said, "The operating costs to run an exchange are insurmountable. You think about $2 to $3 million per month in operating costs that will eat right through any operating budget you have."[12] Also, the larger the target, the greater is the need to win market share, and the greater is the cost of doing business.

On December 6, 2000, Ventro Corporation closed the vertical e-markets Chemdex and Promedix, laid off 235 workers, and incurred between $380 and $410 million in restructuring charges. This news was not altogether unexpected because in October Ventro had announced that it was changing its business focus from operating wholly owned vertical marketplaces to providing expertise, technology, and catalog services for any marketplace. For a few months, Ventro lived off the interest on its capital. Then in July 2001, for $27 million and assumption of debt, it acquired the privately held NexPrise, a Santa Clara–based software firm with 110 employees and $2.3 million in revenue.

The latest incarnation of Ventro continues to have Dave Perry on the board of directors. In January 2002, it changed its name to NexPrise, Inc.; the business model has changed so completely that it could hardly be called an exchange or even a dot-com company. NexPrise considers itself a "process automation expert." It builds software tools for process applications, product design and engineering, procurement, strategic sourcing, and program and project management. It also licenses its platform to corporations and systems integrators who prefer to develop their own process applications. The company's entire exchange idea in industrial goods, which needed to grow large very quickly, seems to have crashed and burned.

Who really won in the dot-com era?

Of course, not everyone lost when the dot-com bubble burst. Many dot-com managers and investment bankers made a lot of money. Excitement about many of the industries we've discussed in this chapter led investors to speculate in the dot-com market. During the initial stages, many were cautious. However, as the hype of the mid- to late 1990s became stronger and stronger, and the valuations of the dot-com companies grew larger and larger, it was difficult for fund managers, individual investors,

12. Quoted in Jin Ericson, "Ventro Shuts Down Chemdex, Promedix," *Line 56*, December 6, 2000.

and even the customarily cautious institutional investors to stay on the sidelines. After selling the dot-com ideas and the companies to the later investors who entered the picture, the early investors frequently cashed out. The trick was to know when to exit the market before the bubble burst.

As the late MIT professor Charles Kindleberger put it: "Speculation tends to detach itself from valuable objects and turns to delusive ones. A larger and larger group of people seeks to become rich without a real understanding of the processes involved. Not surprisingly, swindlers and catchpenny schemes flourish."[13] The *greater fool theory* is used to explain why bubbles tend to sustain themselves longer than the underlying value of companies. Even when people buy the shares of companies which have doubtful business models and which do not appear likely to become profitable soon, they persuade themselves that there will always be someone, a greater fool, who will be willing to take a larger risk and buy their shares. The greater fool willing to buy shares in unprofitable dot-coms could also be someone who received suspect information from those whose advice was an important ingredient in the investment decision. In his confessional essay, "Diary of a Financial Pornographer,"[14] Nelson Schwartz talks about how people in the media contributed to this bubble madness.

Analysts in investment banking firms certainly helped to create great fools in the dot-com era and made significant amounts of money for their employers. As we pointed out earlier, the reward structure for analysts became intimately tied to the number and size of the deals that they could direct to their investment banks. It was only natural for companies that obtained optimistic write-ups with "buy" ratings to be more willing to be the clients of investment banks than ones that received critical reports. So a whole host of analysts led by Mary Meeker of Morgan Stanley, Henry Blodget of Merrill Lynch, and Jack Grubman of Goldman Sachs gave good reviews of companies that were clearly dogs, and their respective investment banks cleaned up.

Meeker rarely gave a "sell" rating to any company. Even after the dot-com bubble burst, Meeker had either a "buy" or "outperform" rating on more than 85% of the companies she covered.[15] Henry Blodget, Meeker's counterpart at Merrill Lynch, also advised investors to keep buying at a

13. Charles Kindleberger, *Manias, Panics and Crashes: A History of Financial Crises* (New York: Wiley, 1996), p. 112.

14. *Fortune*, April 30, 2001.

15. "Where Mary Meeker Went Wrong," *Fortune*, May 2001.

time when he had written an internal report that conceded that there was a speculative bubble in Internet stocks. Blodget wrote:

> The overall Internet stock phenomenon may well be a "bubble," but at least in one respect it is very different from other bubbles: there are great fundamental reasons to own these stocks. The companies underneath them are (1) growing amazingly quickly, and (2) threatening the status quo in multiple sectors of the economy.[16]

The question is whether this view of a paradigm shift was a core belief or something that was colored by a conflict of interest. There is certainly anecdotal evidence that a negative view by an analyst would have cost the investment bank where he or she was employed millions if not billions. In 1999, Meeker decided not to write a favorable report on Internet grocer Webvan because she did not have faith in its business model. She also passed on the women's content site iVillage. Both companies had spectacular IPOs, and the bankers at Morgan Stanley were livid that they were not part of it. Meeker's reaction was to lower her standards, abandon her "only the best" dictum, and start writing good things about second-tier companies such as HomeGrocer.com, Women.com, Tickets.com, and LastMinute.com, which eventually became an embarrassment to Morgan Stanley.[17]

Investment bankers on the whole did well and were the real winners of the dot-com era. Investment bankers are like real estate brokers. The only difference is the size of the commissions for the properties they sell, and these properties, if handled right, can fetch hundreds of millions of dollars. Managing an IPO is lucrative business. The blue chip Wall Street firms have a cartel-like fee structure. When an investment bank issues $100 million in stock for a new company, usually (in about 90% of the cases) the bank keeps in the neighborhood of $7 million. This underwriting fee is much higher than the 3.4% charged by banks in Japan and the 5% in Europe. One could ask why the start-up companies failed to choose boutique investment banks with lower fee structures. The dot-coms with dubious business models needed the endorsement of the blue chip investment banks and their superstar analysts. During the period 1999–2000 at the height of the dot-com boom, companies collected $121 billion from IPOs, and investment banks collected more than $8 billion in underwriting fees. As we have highlighted using a few cases, most of the dot-com companies seem to have squandered their money pursuing elusive customers and profits.

There are many other ways for investment banks to generate money from the companies they take public. If the company is happy with the way the investment bank and its analysts marketed it, then the same bank is often chosen as the lead in any follow-on financing, stock offerings, and bond issues, which generates more commissions. Investment bankers are also in the middle when two fledgling dot-com companies decide to merge or when one acquires the other. Mergers and acquisitions generate revenue for the investment banks in a variety of ways. The most egregious way in which investment bankers abused the system was to underprice IPOs so that their preferred customers, institutional investors, could get better deals.[18]

Evidence of this underpricing phenomenon is the height to which prices increased on the first day of trading after the IPO. It has been estimated that in 1999 and 2000, companies that went through an IPO left no less than $62 million "on the table."[19] This number was more than twice the amount left on the table from IPOs for the previous 19 years combined. In 1999, the average IPO stock price jumped 71% on the first day, and in 2000, it jumped 57% while the average for the period 1980–1998 was only 11%. The original institutional investors that helped raise the money had few incentives to stick around. In 1999 and 2000, of the 125 funds that bought IPOs, only 10–15 were holding their stocks after a week. Almost all of those that flipped the shares sold them through the underwriting investment bank. Investment banks made $40–60 billion in spreads and commissions in these transactions, dwarfing the underwriting fees of $8 billion. Bill Burnham, the former Credit Suisse First Boston analyst, has been quoted as saying, "It's like shooting fish in a barrel."[20]

Where is the Winner's Curse?

The dot-com phenomenon illustrates the Winner's Curse in a number of ways. The dot-coms, themselves, sought to be winners by being first

18. Shawn Tully, "Betrayal on Wall Street," *Business 2.0*, May 2001.
19. Shawn Tully, "Betrayal on Wall Street," *Business 2.0*, May 2001.
20. *Burnham's Beat* (online magazine) 1/1/2004. http://billburnham.blogs.com/burnhamsbeat/wall-street

in the marketplace and first in market share. The top company in a new business was able to raise the most capital and create a "buzz" to help it attract customers. While some of the dot-coms succeeded for a short period of time, they had deeply flawed business models.

Investors felt they had winning companies and investments. As the market bid up the prices of stock beyond any rational value, investors joined in to buy more and more shares at unrealistic prices. These investors paid far too much for their stock, and those who did not sell quickly experienced the Winner's Curse when the dot-coms' overvalued stocks plummeted.

Investors were caught in a buying and bidding frenzy as stock values rose dramatically. Everyone wanted to be a winner in the tech stock bonanza. During a bull market, everyone (almost) is optimistic and feels invulnerable. Stock analysts and investment bankers, as noted above, were more than happy to fuel the increase in stock prices. No one took a good look at unrealistic business models and investors' irrational exuberance, until it was too late. The Winner's Curse created misery for many individuals, and we believe it contributed to a downturn in the stock market and the economy.

Conclusions

Although we have documented many instances in which dynamic, aggressive dot-com companies crashed and burned by trying to win everything, the dot-com era is not over yet. In fact, what is clear is that more and more companies are going to be doing business over the Internet. The best way to buy a Dell computer is through the Internet. Dell also manages its entire supply chain electronically. The Dell procurement system makes use of the Internet, and the company buys components through auctions that they call *Internet negotiations*. Networked business-to-business transactions continue to grow and were around $2.4 trillion in the first quarter of 2003 according to Forrester Research. Consumer e-commerce, which was the mainstay of a number of dot-com companies, also grew to just over $95 billion. In a recent *Business Week* article,[21] Meg Whitman of eBay, probably the most successful dot-com company to date, observes that "more consumers are coming online every day."

21. *Business Week*, May 12, 2003.

What to do?

The question is not whether e-commerce will grow and become a way of doing business all over the world, but rather how companies that join the fray, the new dot-com companies, can avoid the Winner's Curse and flourish in such a dynamic environment. Academics and intellectuals in think tanks have written extensively on the subject of Internet strategy. We have also talked to a number of people who have been responsible for starting Internet companies, including venture capitalists, investment bankers, and senior management teams, some of which have succeeded, but many of which have failed. A brief synthesis of potentially successful dot-com strategies follows.

The post position is not the end of the race

Winning the post position is only the beginning of the race, not an end in itself. Bettors have always tried to play the odds in races by taking into account the post position of the horse. Yet, it has been noted, for example in the Preakness, that since 1971, every position in a race with 12 horses or fewer has produced a winner. Horses win from the inside, horses win from the outside, and horses win from the middle.[22] The horses that succeed have the stamina, strategy, and speed to win over the entire 13/16-mile of the race. Companies intent on creating an online business have to appreciate that being first is inadequate; they need to understand what it takes to sustain a business over the long haul.

Managers should undertake what is called *scenario analysis* (elaborated in detail in chapter 10) to know what it takes to get to the finish line under uncertain and potentially adverse conditions. At one extreme scenario, a dot-com company could have an easy time obtaining a critical mass of customers quickly and become the front-runner in an industry or market segment. In this case, what is important may not be to run hard, but to conserve energy and resources to be able to outmaneuver potential threats as they emerge. The success of eBay could be attributed to a strategy of not running helter-skelter. After establishing its front-runner status in Internet auctions, eBay has had a very controlled expansion plan. The Internet auction company only moved into new areas when it saw competitors trying to outflank it.

22. Jeff Zillgitt, "Speaking of Sports," *USA Today*, May 14, 2003.

For the dot-com that is not out front, it can be a struggle to keep going. In this case, the company's strategy will involve trying to enhance its finances, get partners, and share costs in the hope that a group effort will enable it to emerge a winner in the long run. Google has followed this strategy in the crowded Web search market. The important thing though is to spend weeks, if not months, getting together experts and all potential stakeholders to perform a scenario analysis to look at all potential futures and to have contingency plans for each.

Avoid the Earl Weaver syndrome

Earl Weaver, the Hall of Fame manager of the Baltimore Orioles who skippered the team to a World Series victory in 1970 and six American League crowns, used to say that games were won by three-run homers and not by singles. Fans have always been excited by the great home-run hitters, like Babe Ruth. In recent years, home-run races have created some summer excitement; Barry Bonds and Sammy Sosa are household names. It is not surprising that in the dot-com era, investors and management alike became so excited about the "big idea" that they spent time and resources trying to hit a home run rather than putting together a rally. This "Earl Weaver syndrome" should be avoided.

In the dot-com world, as in any traditional business, success comes in small steps. There are few "hail Mary" touchdowns, if any. Vinod Khosla of the well-known Silicon Valley venture capital firm Kleiner Perkins Caufield and Byers was quoted in *Business Week* as saying, "Runaway tech projects don't work. You need the revolution by 1,000 small cuts, not one big dramatic change."[23] It is important to break down the big-picture e-business strategy into smaller manageable pieces, each of which can be successful with a reasonable infusion of resources and within a reasonable amount of time. These small victories, or a rally in baseball parlance, improve the chances of the dot-com company becoming profitable in the long run. Small steps will keep revenue and cash flow in the black. Small successes provide morale boosts for employees, improving their productivity and loyalty. Most important, these small victories will improve the company's credibility with investors and creditors, making it much easier to raise capital that will allow the company to pursue victory more vigorously. Going for broke in winning market share will surely

23. *Business Week*, May 12, 2003.

result in actually going broke as many dot-com companies found out. Market share is better won in small profitable steps.

Learn that winning in Internet business costs big bucks

Facts are stubborn things. In the bestseller *Information Rules*, Varian and Shapiro showed that information goods are characterized by large fixed costs and very low variable costs. Most people in dot-com companies focused on the fact that the marginal cost to reach and sell to new customers was low; they seem to have ignored the fact that it takes an enormous amount of investment to be a player in Internet businesses. The ten-year experience (1992–2002) of most dot-com companies is quite telling.

Even after investing in a Web site and setting up an electronic supply chain to fulfill orders, it takes another $300 million or so to build a strong brand. Most dot-com companies ended up spending 65% of their revenues on marketing. While traditional retailers spend, on the average, $5 per head for customer acquisition, online retailers spend $40–50. Although Amazon.com started with the premise that it would be the intermediary between book publishers and customers, it ended up having to set up a sophisticated warehousing system; the cost was $300 million. Webvan spent $40 million on a distribution center. In fact, even to set up a transaction-capable Web site, the cost was between $5 and $15 million. Thus, those with a new idea in the dot-com world should realize that winning customers and market share is a costly business. Finding investors and setting up the initial company may turn into a Pyrrhic victory unless costs are accounted for correctly.

Consider using the second-mover advantage

In many of the cases of dot-com failures, the first mover spent so much money and energy that it ran out of financial resources and the energy to stay the course. With the exception of Amazon, most of the successful companies today entered the e-marketplace in the second wave. Google was not a pioneering search company. Expedia and Travelocity were not the pioneering online travel agencies. Yahoo was not the first portal. Despite the hype about the first movers cleaning up in the dynamic Internet world, exactly the opposite happened.

What the second movers had was both an enlightened market and knowledge from the experience of the first movers. They could enter markets that were primed to interact with them electronically and were able to avoid mistakes made by the pioneers. Further, the cost of being an Internet company continued to fall rapidly, providing later movers with significant technological advantages. For example, computer and communications technologies improved in speed and cost, and it also became quite acceptable to outsource software developments to much cheaper countries. The questions, of course, are: how does one know which industry to enter in the second wave, and how can one ensure a sustainable strategy?

Use the West Coast Offense in the dot-com business

For many years, the National Football League was dominated by quarterbacks with strong arms like Roger Staubach (Dallas Cowboys), Terry Bradshaw (Pittsburgh Steelers), Kenny Stabler (Oakland Raiders), Dan Fouts (San Diego Chargers), and Dan Marino (Miami Dolphins). In order to counter this, defenses would have four to five players in the backfield to try to stop the long throws and prevent touchdowns. The legendary coach Bill Walsh invented the West Coast Offense, which tried to avoid the crowded backfield and move the offense into places vacated by the defensive players. It was so successful that it won the San Francisco 49ers five Super Bowl titles between 1982 and 1995, and it has been copied by almost every team. The point is that Internet companies, like NFL teams, should have a strategy that avoids crowded fields and markets.

In the beginning of the dot-com era, the growth of Internet traffic was exponential, and it seemed like the market could accommodate many different companies in the same line of business. History has shown that markets in almost all new industries grow rapidly in the beginning, but soon start to plateau. When the growth slows down, competition among firms intensifies, especially if more and more companies are entering the business. Those wanting to start netcentric companies should assess whether or not a particular business space is getting crowded and not get into it if there are too many players. Provided that one has financial and human resources and a seasoned management team, there may be many other Internet-based businesses that one can enter and generate revenue and profitability. Using a West Coast Offense in business will allow companies to stick to first principles and not get caught up in the herd mentality that prevailed in the boom-and-bust dot-com era.

Make sure you follow fundamentals

Whether in sports or in business, one needs to follow fundamentals. Authors like Michael Porter think that while there are some important nuances, Internet companies have to strategize the same way as any other company.[24] Success as an Internet company is based on being able to compete on cost leadership, product or service differentiation, and focus. Obtaining a position in the industry landscape that leverages a company's resources and neutralizes the competition is paramount. All of these are fundamentals of sustainable competitive strategy.

In the Internet world, industry profitability is often weak because of the changing expectations of customers and the difficulty of controlling suppliers. While, in some instances, the Internet increases a company's bargaining power over suppliers, in other cases it allows the suppliers easy access to end customers. Because the barriers for a company to become an online retailer are low in a number of industries like travel, electronics, and entertainment, competition is intense. Thus, not paying attention to fundamentals can make the perceived winner in the dot-com world unprofitable quickly.

Investors should not pay Spurrier-like money

The owner of the Washington Redskins, Dan Snyder, is an extremely passionate man. He has been a lifelong fan of the Redskins and wants to win the Super Bowl in a hurry. When he likes a player or a coach, he goes after them, no matter what. In the first three years of owning the Redskins, he paid big money to bring a number of famous players to Washington. In 2002, Snyder gave Steve Spurrier, with no NFL experience, $25 million over five years to lure him from the University of Florida to coach the Washington Redskins. This salary was multiples higher than what anyone had ever paid a professional football coach. As described in chapter 4, the team did worse than in the previous three years and had a 7–9 record in 2002.

Investors in the dot-com era also exhibited Dan Snyder's syndrome and paid more than the going rate for Internet companies' stock. If the

---

24. Michael Porter, "Strategy and the Internet," *Harvard Business Review* (March 2001): 63–78.

stock value and market capitalization exceed credibility, you want to avoid investing. You do not want to become the greater fool and be stuck with expensive but valueless equity in a company. Giving executives incredibly high compensation packages like Shaheen's at Webvan does not make them better executives. Winning an equity stake or a superstar executive may be necessary conditions for ultimate success, but paying too much is not.

The founders of many of the dot-com companies were mostly interested in setting up the business and then making money by going public ("doing" an IPO) quickly rather than building a sustainable business. In a number of instances, when founders saw that they could not become rich quickly, they simply walked away. It is important for small investors, as well as institutional investors that have been entrusted with people's retirement savings, to ensure that founders, senior executives, and investment bankers do not have the most to gain by leaving. Financial compensation for these people should be connected to the long-term success of the company. Rather than paying Spurrier-like money, executives, managers, and investment bankers should be paid for performance. The ultimate victory is in making sure that one's investment in a company pays off over the long run.

7 • Winners and losers in the securities industry

In this chapter, we extend the Winner's Curse analysis to focus on organizations that are winners over an extended period of time. The problem here is not one of overvaluing an acquisition but of allowing a long time in the winner's circle to create powerful forces to maintain the status quo. It turns out that many of the factors that encourage the Winner's Curse lead a company on top into a dangerous state of complacency. A long-term winning company encounters opportunities where it could make investments, but it decides not to. Instead of overvaluing the return from the investment, this long-term winner plays it safe and underinvests in new business models and technology.

Managers are lulled into a belief that they are winners and will always stay on top. They are optimistic about the firm's future performance based on its past and exhibit the same hubris seen in earlier examples. Managers belittle the competition, and the organization develops a culture of avoiding risks and maintaining the status quo. Because the firm has been successful, the board of directors rewards managers with lavish compensation and perks. All of this convinces senior management that it is invulnerable. Often these firms are large, so a small percentage increase in sales is a large dollar amount. Analysts and investment bankers applaud this performance, and the company enjoys a healthy stock price and market cap. The manager has an unrealistic belief that her business model will continue unchanged for years to come.

The Winner's Curse occurs at a discrete point in time when you are trying to value something you wish to acquire, and when there is no agreed-upon market value. Winners over a long period of time are also cursed by being an acknowledged winner, ahead of all the competition. In these situations a new market factor comes into play: the Heisman Syndrome, in which competitors put a great deal of energy into knocking off number one. Pro line backers take particular pleasure in humbling a college Heisman Trophy winner. The undefeated football team faces opponents who get up for the game; they are highly motivated to hand the team its first defeat. PC manufacturers talk about Dell as their primary competitor, and securities firms aim at Merrill Lynch.

We have seen instances where the classic Winner's Curse has threatened the financial viability of a company; the major telecom firms are in serious financial difficulty partially due to the extraordinarily high bids they put in at government spectrum auctions. What is the downside of being a long-term winner? The winners in an industry become conservative and inbred, and they undervalue opportunities to innovate. Their competitors, however, are likely to take advantages of such opportunities as they search for a way to dethrone the industry leaders.[1] Holding to the status quo will not result in a sudden dramatic blow to the company the way the spectrum auctions affected the telecommunications providers, but it will eventually move the company out of the winner's column.

Why was Compaq ready for a merger with Hewlett Packard? Compaq began by specializing in the manufacture of personal computers; it rose to be the number one vendor in the industry, selling high-quality and innovative machines through a network of dealers. Over time, PCs have become a commodity item; the chips that run them are incredibly powerful, and their price continues to decline. Compaq tried to broaden its business by purchasing Tandem Computers and Digital Equipment

---

1. This concept is similar to Christensen's innovator's dilemma. However, Christensen deals primarily with disruptive technologies that lead to a major change in an industry. The Winner's Curse of inertia includes the myriad of small and large opportunities that present themselves to firms. See Clayton Christensen, *The Innovator's Dilemma* (Cambridge, Mass.: Harvard Business School Press, 1997).

Corporation, but Compaq had a difficult time integrating them into its existing organization. What was the major threat to Compaq? The answer is Dell; its direct sales and lean supply chain allow Dell to be profitable while the company relentlessly reduces the price of its products.

Dell's business model has been well publicized, yet Compaq never tried to adopt it or a variation on Dell's approach. Compaq continued to sell through dealers and ended up with a lot of computers in the supply chain and in inventory. PCs are a rapidly depreciating commodity, and Dell has a tremendous advantage by not building a computer until a customer orders it. Undoubtedly, efforts to integrate Tandem and DEC distracted Compaq, but we believe that it enjoyed being number one in sales and failed to pay attention to its business model so Dell took over first place in PC sales.

Most of the winners in this chapter finally recognized their problem and are taking steps to retain or regain their top rankings. Their stories are powerful examples of the problems that affect the long-term winner.

New kinds of securities markets

The NASDAQ opened for business in 1971 as the world's first electronic securities market. There is no physical trading floor; participants in the market use computers and a telecommunications network to interact with the market. The market trades both NASDAQ-listed stocks and certain NYSE securities. There can be a number of professional traders who are market makers on the system; these individuals post bids and ask prices for securities. A broker can see all of the bid-ask prices and choose to buy or sell with a particular market maker. There can be more than one market maker per NASDAQ stock, and actively traded stocks such as Microsoft and Intel have more than 50 dealers' quotes and prices from five to ten electronic communications networks displayed. NASDAQ has been the traditional exchange for smaller-cap companies and for technology firms. Often firms migrate to the New York Stock Exchange from the NASDAQ as they grow. NASDAQ has worked to retain these companies.

For many years, the NASDAQ was unique as an online market for stocks. When the Internet became available for profit-making use in 1995, it provided a relatively low-cost worldwide network infrastructure that could be used by anyone. While the NASDAQ had to build and maintain a proprietary telecommunications network, someone wishing to start an electronic market post-1995 could take advantage of the Internet. Several start-up markets developed for trading securities and became known as electronic communications networks, or ECNs. NASDAQ has managed to increase the share of NASDAQ-listed stocks that it trades, but it trades only about 30% of the total shares changing hands. The ECNs' share of NASDAQ trading has surged to 45%. Brokerage firms have seen the biggest drop in market share as they match only about 25% of NASDAQ orders inhouse.[2]

For years, the NASDAQ watched the ECNs take a larger and larger market share of trades in NASDAQ-listed securities and had no response. Besides the ECNs, a number of exchanges around the world were abandoning their physical floors and moving to electronic markets. NASDAQ suffered from inertia as these new initiatives developed. Finally, the exchange decided to update its original system, and the price tag turned out to be $107 million and three years of work. This investment led NASDAQ to its SuperMontage system. NASDAQ is contemplating a public offering of its own stock and needs a modern system to make itself attractive to investors.

The new system provides more information and easier access to price information in the market. Though called a cosmetic change, it is important because it is the front end through which traders see the entire marketplace. The system is said to resemble some of those used for several years by the ECNs. Users of the NASDAQ system include hundreds of institutions, like mutual funds, and about 830,000 individual investors. With the old system, a trader saw a list of symbols for brokerage firms and ECNs for a security on the left of the screen and their best bids and offers on the right, organized chronologically in the order of posting. SuperMontage has an order book that is organized to display more information. The system shows actual offers to buy and sell from investors, not just the quotes (see figure 7-1). The five best offers are shown; for example, there are five offers to buy Applied Materials (AMAT) at 20.15, each purchase being for a different number of shares ranging from 2200 to 4000. Two investors are offering to sell 2000 and 1900 shares of AMAT respectively at 20.16. The screen shows a number of different bids and asks for the stock. The system allows investors with large orders to be anonymous or to keep their offers invisible from other investors to prevent influencing the stock price with their order. This listing provides more information about the depth of the market: how many buy and sell orders at what price and volume are in the order book. The SuperMontage

2. *Wall Street Journal*, August 29, 2002.

SYMBOL	**AMAT**	Applied Materials (NNM)	
LAST SALE	20.15 q	NASDAQ Bid Tick (+)	
NATIONAL BBO	20.15 q	20.16 q	8900 x 2000

BID	Price	Total Depth	ASK	Price	Total Depth
	20.15	10700		20.16	3900
	20.14	59000		20.17	11100
	20.13	26300		20.18	15900
	20.12	12500		20.19	11200
	20.11	1600		20.20	14500

MPID	Bid	Size	MPID	Ask	Size
BTRD	20.15	2500	SIZE	20.16	2000
NITE	20.15	2400	ARCX	20.16	1900
SIZE	20.15	4000	SIZE	20.17	6000
CINN	20.15	2200	CINN	20.17	3100
ARCX	20.15	3600	BTRD	20.17	2000
BTRD	20.14	28500	SIZE	20.18	5000
SIZE	20.14	12500	SCHB	20.18	3500
NITE	20.14	7500	AMEX	20.18	5000
SCHB	20.14	1000	NITE	20.18	1100
GVRC	20.14	1000	BTRD	20.18	1000
AMEX	20.14	5000	DAIN	20.18	100
LEHM	20.14	2000	NOCI	20.18	100
SNDV	20.14	1500	GVRC	20.18	100
SIZE	20.13	10000	SIZE	20.19	5500
GVRC	20.13	8800	NOCI	20.19	3000
SCHB	20.13	7500	MONT	20.19	1500
RAMS	20.12	4000	BTRD	20.19	1000
TDCM	20.12	3000	JPHQ	20.19	100
SIZE	20.12	2000	SCHB	20.19	100
LEHM	20.12	1000	BEST	20.20	5000
MONT	20.12	1000	GVRC	20.20	4000
SWST	20.12	1000	NFSC	20.20	3000
NOCI	20.12	400	TDCM	20.20	1800
JPHQ	20.12	100	SCHB	20.20	500
PERT	20.11	800	NITE	20.20	100
GVRC	20.11	500	SNDV	20.20	100
LEHM	20.11	100	UBSW	20.21	5000
SIZE	20.11	100	GSCO	20.21	1100
PIPR	20.11	100	NITE	20.21	1000
SIZE	20.10	13500	TDCM	20.21	100
SCHB	20.10	3500	FBCO	20.21	100
TDCM	20.10	2000	LEHM	20.21	100
PRUS	20.10	500	RHCO	20.21	100
NOCI	20.10	100	WCHV	20.22	10000
SIZE	20.09	2500	GKMC	20.22	1000
FBCO	20.09	2400	LEHM	20.22	5000
BTRD	20.09	2200	BWNC	20.22	500
COWN	20.09	1800	GMST	20.22	500
NITE	20.09	1000	ADVS	20.22	200
SCHB	20.09	400	NOCI	20.22	100
UBSW	20.09	400	BTRD	20.22	100

Figure 7-1. The NASDAQ level 2 display, courtesy of the NASDAQ

system is regarded as critical to the future of the NASDAQ, which must stop the loss of business to ECNs for the market to remain viable.

It appears that the first online market made only incremental improvements in its system for 28 years. Was this a sign of managerial optimism and a belief that the NASDAQ was invulnerable? Did NASDAQ management misread the ECNs' business model? Has NASDAQ reacted in time to stabilize and increase its market share in trading its own securities and those from the NYSE? To increase its volume, the NASDAQ has tried to woo firms from the NYSE to list on both exchanges; in early 2004 it had succeeded in attracting a few well-known NYSE companies to list with it, too. The next few years should tell whether the NASDAQ has thrown off its devotion to the status quo, and done so in time.

The NYSE: Fighting for the floor

The NYSE is a not-for-profit corporation and self-regulating organization that is overseen by the Securities and Exchange Commission (SEC). The 353 members of the exchange control it; they are the broker-dealer and specialist firms that own the NYSE's 1,366 "seats." The role of the exchange is to provide a fair and cost-effective market, which in turn encourages liquidity and attracts issuers (companies) to list their stocks on the NYSE and become a "Big Board," or NYSE-listed company. As of March 28, 2002, there were 2,784 listed companies with 343 billion shares and $16.3 trillion in total market capitalization listed on the NYSE. On the 37,000-square-foot floor, there are about 3,000 traders, 481 of whom are specialists using their own capital to trade. The rest are floor brokers, handling orders for clients, clerks, or exchange officials.

Unlike the London or Toronto exchanges, the NYSE has remained committed to its specialist system and a physical floor. It has been and still is the world's premier stock exchange. The New York Stock Exchange regards itself as innovative and has used information technology to try and retain its position and to maintain a physical trading floor. One of its most recent systems allows online trading, which represents the NYSE's first concession to an electronic market bypassing the floor.

During the past 50 years, the NYSE has faced competition for trading and company listings from a variety of sources. First, it competes with the regional exchanges for trade executions of NYSE-listed stocks. A broker may see a better price on a regional exchange and route an order there for execution. The other market for companies to list their stock is the

NASDAQ stock market, and the NYSE competes for listings with the NASDAQ. In the mid-1990s, the exchange also faced competition from ECNs, such as Instinet, and electronic markets that the SEC is allowing to become stock exchanges in their own right. While ECNs handled 45% of all NASDAQ trades and 36% of NASDAQ share volume in July 2002, just 1.5% of the trading of NYSE-listed shares went through ECNs in the fourth quarter of 2001.[3]

During its long history, the NYSE has developed a number of important tangible and intangible resources, including

Listings. The NYSE has the world's leading roster of listed firms, including most of the largest and most successful U.S. corporations.

Market capacity. The NYSE has the capacity to process large volumes of trading messages, hence to transact a substantial number of trades.

Trading infrastructure. The exchange has built a smoothly functioning trading infrastructure consisting of specialists, brokers, computer systems, communications networks, and market data reporting systems.

Market quality and fairness. The NYSE is generally regarded as providing a high-quality market with liquidity. However, it is possible for other exchanges to offer quality marketplaces, although they need to convince users of their benefits to attract trading volume away from the NYSE.

Technological innovations. The introduction of the stock ticker in 1867 marked the beginning of an increasingly important role for information technology (IT) in the NYSE markets. Since the late 1980s, the NYSE has focused on technological innovations that include automatic order routing and processing, online order comparisons, wireless order management, off-hours trading facilities, and, lately, Internet delivery initiatives.

The New York Stock Exchange offers a convenient, efficient, and liquid market to trade the stocks of the firms in which a large number of individuals and institutions want to invest. The NYSE has long had a critical mass of buyers and sellers, and its trading infrastructure makes it easy to execute transactions on the exchange. The established liquidity and the inertia in industry practices help sustain the exchange, but his-

3. www.nasdaq.com; and "Equity Trading Market Share Quarterly," Salomon Smith Barney, February 8, 2002.

tory shows that markets will shift to new locations when the established market becomes unattractive.

The components of the exchange's IT strategy for the last 18 years include investment to

1. enhance and extend strategic resources by providing sufficient capacity for processing trade transactions;
2. enable efficient trade execution;
3. provide a high-quality market for securities;
4. reduce labor expenses and demands for costly physical space; and
5. compete effectively with new types of electronic markets.

IT at the exchange provides for efficient trade execution and adequate trading capacity. IT has also helped to ensure a high-quality securities market and has reduced labor expenses and the demand for physical space. All of the exchange's resources have enabled it to compete successfully with other exchanges, especially ECNs like Island and Instinet, which announced a $508 million merger in mid-2002.

The U.S. securities industry's back-office crisis in 1969 accelerated the NYSE's computerization plans. Increased trading volumes and a paper-based settlement system forced the NYSE and other U.S. stock markets to close for trading on Wednesdays for six months through mid-1970. On these days, brokers and traders helped back-office clerks process trades and sort out unsettled transactions. The continuing growth of trading volumes and additional listings in the 1970s led the NYSE to consider its alternatives for expanding its trading capacity. Rather than undertake costly expansion of its physical floor, the NYSE chose to invest in IT to increase the capacity of the market. The systems introduced between 1977 and 1987 enabled the exchange to remain open for trading and to process record volumes during the October 1987 market crash.

During the 1983–1987 period, the exchange developed a number of systems to speed transactions processing and to provide adequate capacity to handle the growth in volumes and new listings. Its IT strategy was to provide enough processing capacity and systems to assure that the market could function properly with volumes three time those of an average day.

The early projects to develop new capabilities at the NYSE's included the common message switch (CMS, 1977), the designated order turn-around system (DOT, 1976), which became SuperDot (November 1984), the display book, and the broker booth support system (both in 1993). These four systems are described in table 7-1.

Table 7-1. NYSE major IT investments

	System	Description	Specific Functionality
Order Processing	Common Message Switch (1977)	Message-forwarding device that links member firms to exchange systems	Receives and forwards messages
	DOT (1976) and SuperDot (1984)	Order-processing system that receives incoming orders from member firms and routes them directly to specialist post or broker booth	Processes incoming orders, assigns an order reference number Routes orders to trading posts Matches buys and sells for the opening and reports imbalances to specialists Provides a "circuit-breaker"
Broker support	Broker Booth Support System (1993)	Order management system that enhances brokers' processing capability on the trading floor	Integrates many different applications, services, and functions into a single unit Handles booth- routed orders Monitors, reports, and researches orders
	e-Broker (1997)	Wireless handheld device that connects floor brokers to their booths and off-floor locations	Improves communication between floor brokers and booths
Specialist support	Display Book (1993)	Electronic workstation that displays all limit orders and incoming market orders	Sorts the limit orders and displays them in price/ time priority Improves the speed and efficiency of reporting executed orders
Specialists and market professionsals	OpenBook (2002)	Real-time view of aggregate limit-order volume at every bid and offer price for each NYSE-listed stock	Used by market professionals to assess liquidity in a stock
All investors	NYSE Direct+ (2001)	Electronic market bypassing specialists	Currently used for 1099 share limit-orders Proposed no size limit and market orders, too

Source: NYSE FactBook, 1997 and NYSE Web site www.nyse.com.

The exchange's IT strategy from about 1988 to 1994 was to maintain the status quo with its major initiative being broker booth support. After 1994, the NYSE invested more heavily in IT as trading volume accelerated and it faced competition from the NASDAQ, which was becoming known for the IPOs of attractive new technology listings, and the ECNs. The exchange also saw transactions rising dramatically in the buoyant capital markets and the expanding economy of the 1990s. From that time until the present, the NYSE's IT strategy has been to use technology aggressively to meet competition from a number of sources as well as demands for trading capacity.

The cycle time for completing a trade has decreased dramatically since 1984. SuperDot routes orders directly to the floor specialist, bypassing the floor broker and eliminating the need to communicate an order to a person who must walk to the specialist's booth. The broker booth support system electronically routes complex orders to floor traders. The display book reduces the time a specialist requires to complete a trade. In addition, the exchange's overall IT infrastructure makes possible online trading via the Internet by providing real-time quotes, instant trade confirmations, and a short trade cycle.

Openbook, implemented in 2002, provides a real-time view of the aggregate limit-order volume at every bid and offer price for every NYSE-listed security (www.nyse.com). This proprietary data product is used by market professionals as they try to assess liquidity in a particular stock. Some 950 firms and 26 vendors that sell data currently subscribe to the system. Openbook provides important information to market participants and by doing so encourages them to trade on the NYSE rather than on an alternative market.

In 2001, the NYSE began NYSE Direct+, which offered automatic execution of limit orders up to 1,099 shares at the best bid or offer, with an average execution time of 1 second. By 2004, Direct+ was executing 7% of consolidated volume in NYSE-listed equities, which the exchange said was more than all ECNs combined. The exchange has filed with the SEC to expand Direct+ to compete with other electronic markets. First it proposes to let customers enter orders more quickly than 30 seconds, providing faster execution for customers. Second, it wants to eliminate the 1099 share limit for Direct+ orders, making the system more attractive for institutional investors. Finally, the exchange will add market orders to NYSE Direct+. It is very likely that these changes will remove a substantial number of trades from the physical exchange floor and from intermediation by specialists; they are a response to those who criticize the historic business model of the exchange as being behind the times.

The exchange's investments in IT since 1984 prepared it to deliver on many of the promises of electronic commerce, including direct access, real-time quotes, market information, and the new automatic execution system. Reduced trade cycle times facilitate e-commerce, while all of the exchange's technology helps it to meet the challenges of electronic markets. The *Wall Street Journal* compared the NYSE and the troubled London Stock Exchange:

> The New York Exchange is one of the few international markets to survive . . . combining new technology with an old-time trading floor. The others, including London in 1987, have shut their trading floors in favor of computers. Since then, London has been unable to stay ahead of rivals in technology.[4]

So far, NYSE investments in information technology have allowed it to remain a leading exchange by facilitating electronic trading and continually enhancing its strategic resources to compete with regionals, the NASDAQ, and electronic exchanges.

In late 2003, Richard Grasso, the chairperson of the NYSE, was forced to resign over the huge size of his compensation package and pension. The fallout from this unwanted publicity painted Grasso as an autocratic leader who worked to keep the physical trading floor and specialist system in position. The exchange is being forced to adopt a new governance structure, and it remains to be seen if it will be able to maintain its old ways of doing business. Is the NYSE with its floor trading a viable business model for a twenty-first-century stock exchange? Despite the success of the NYSE's technology initiatives, is it fighting a losing battle to keep a physical exchange?[5] Will it be able to avoid being dethroned as the world's leading stock exchange?

New competition in the brokerage industry

The full-service stock brokerage firm has had two challenges to its business model, and it has chosen to ignore them and to rely on past successes.

---

4. *Wall Street Journal*, November 2, 2000, p. C1.

5. H. C. Lucas, Jr., et al., "Information Technology and the New York Stock Exchange's Strategic Resources from 1982–1999" (College Park, Md.: Smith School of Business Working Paper, September 2002).

The first threat was discount brokerage firms, which arose after the SEC abolished fixed commissions. The discounters, however, did not have the impact on full-service brokers like Merrill Lynch that online trading did. Possibly because of their earlier experience with discounters, the full-service brokers at first ignored the online brokers like e-Trade.

One of the industries most affected by e-commerce has been retail stock brokerage, the part of the securities market that serves individuals as opposed to institutions. By June 2000, a *Wall Street Journal* article indicated, 175 firms offered online trading. Electronic commerce has enjoyed some of its greatest success in retail brokerage; the number of online accounts grew from 7 million in 1998 to more than 21 million in April 2001 and represented 28% of all individual investor trades in the first quarter of 2002 in the United States.[6]

Since 1975, the retail brokerage industry has been characterized by full-service and discount brokers. Both types of brokers charged a commission on stock trades, but each included a different set of services with the trade. For instance, while the discount brokers offered bare-bones trade execution, the full-service brokers bundled the trade execution with research, stock recommendations, tax advice, asset and portfolio management, and other services, and they charged a higher commission than the discount brokers. Typical commission charges in the mid-1990s were $100 for a full-service broker and about $50 for a discount broker for trades of 100 shares. These pricing strategies were stable as the different prices corresponded to different products, and no rapid shifts in market share occurred until the late 1990s. While the core retail brokerage product—order processing and trade execution—was a commodity, full-service brokers differentiated themselves by offering proprietary bundles with many components, each of which would have been difficult to price and value separately, as they were not available outside the bundles.

Despite higher commissions, full-service brokers were able to attract customers for several reasons. For instance, a customer interacted with the same broker for each transaction and developed a personal relationship, often relying on the broker for advice and customized financial recommendations. Furthermore, full-service brokers provided timely financial information and high-quality research, among other services, which allowed them to sustain high commissions without a significant loss of accounts and market share to the lower-commission discounters.

6. "Special Report: Online Investing," *Wall Street Journal*, June 11, 2001.

However, the advent of the Internet facilitated the creation of new, low-cost online brokerage firms that offered online trades to customers using the Web. Online brokers did not require costly branch offices and could take advantage of the electronic infrastructure of the Internet to reach and offer service to millions of potential customers. The rapid rise in the popularity of online brokerages such as e-Trade encouraged established discount brokers like Charles Schwab and Fidelity to offer online trading. The Internet also furthered the "third market" for trading NYSE-listed securities, which in turn provided a way for the electronic broker to execute trades online after receiving an order from an online customer. Publicity about the Internet revolution, the "new economy," and electronic brokers in general encouraged the growth of this industry. The percentage of individual investor trades done online reached 41% in the first quarter of 2000, but slipped back to 28% in the first quarter of 2002.

The full-service brokers had led the industry for many years and held out as long as they could. They ignored the threat for years, but eventually realized that they had to compete. They were not just losing current customers; they worried in particular that a new generation of investors coming out of college would expect to use the Internet to buy and sell stocks. The full-service brokers risked losing future generations of investors.

Merrill Lynch strikes back

Before the rise of online stock trading, Merrill Lynch occupied a comfortable position as the largest brokerage firm in the world, which created substantial inertia. At the time, Merrill had more than 60,000 employees in 40 countries and relationships with more than 5 million households. As a full-service firm, Merrill offers far more than retail brokerage services; it provides institutional trading and investment banking services, among others. The company has more than $1.5 trillion in assets under management, and institutional trading amounts to more than $30 billion a day. The company is the world's leading underwriter of debt and securities and is first in mergers and acquisitions. Merrill has an extremely large research group of nearly 800 analysts in 26 countries.

Merrill's business model defined the full-service brokerage industry: a research department produces research products for the brokerage workforce; brokers provide clients with research and encourage them to place trades with Merrill Lynch; the firm earns revenues from commissions, underwriting, fee-based account management, and a number of other sources. Online brokers on the Internet threatened this business model.

Merrill executives saw the publicity and interest in e-brokers, but they did not understand the Internet as Schwab did. On September 23, 1998, the *Wall Street Journal* printed an article quoting John "Launny" Steffens, Merrill vice chairperson in charge of the firm's 17,000 retail stock brokers. According to the journal:

> Steffens . . . has waged an unusually public campaign over the last few months to dramatize what he calls the dangers of buying and selling stocks unassisted over the Internet. . . . Mr. Steffens has badmouthed low-priced cyber-trading, saying it encourages people to trade too much at the expense of long-term returns. . . . "The do-it-yourself model of investing, centered on Internet trading, should be regarded as a serious threat to Americans' financial lives. This approach to financial decision-making does not serve clients well and it is a business model that won't deliver lasting value."

For a trade of 100 shares of IBM at that time, Charles Schwab would charge $29.95, and it would charge the same for 1,000 shares. Merrill would have charged about $100 for 100 shares and nearly $1,000 for buying 1,000 shares.

Merrill's first response to electronic trading was to offer the public free access to its stock research over the Web for a four-month trial period. Steffens announced this initiative on October 15, 1998. Merrill had provided access to research for its clients on the Internet earlier; this effort was intended to generate new leads by making research available to the public.

Why did Merrill hesitate so long? One view is that 17,000 brokers have a lot of influence in the company; these individuals are used to six- and, sometimes, seven-figure incomes. Trading on the Internet has the potential to drastically reduce commissions and incomes. However, the *Wall Street Journal* estimated that in 1998, only about $2 billion of Merrill's $17.5 billion in revenues came from commissions paid by individual investors.

On June 1, 1999, Merrill announced that it would offer online trading at fees of $29.95, matching Schwab and worrying its 17,000 brokers. The Web service allowed individuals to set up online accounts to trade stocks, bonds, mutual funds, and eventually stock options. Customers can obtain complete reports of their holdings and transactions, pay bills, and handle other financial tasks through Merrill.

While Merrill's assets have been increasing 15% annually, this amount pales in comparison to Schwab's growth rate of almost 40% a year. Merrill Lynch will trade for a fixed commission, but the firm wants to convert customers to a new account called "Unlimited Advantage." For a percentage of the assets in the account, starting at a minimum $1,500 fee per year, Unlimited Advantage account holders can access all of Merrill's online services and are able to make as many trades as they want, electronically or through a broker. At the time of the announcement, less than 10% of Merrill's retail customers had fee-based accounts.[7]

What motivated the change? How did Merrill overcome the resistance of its brokers? A cover story in the November 15, 1999, *Business Week* offers a behind-the-scenes analysis of Merrill's conversion to an e-broker. The first indication that there was a problem was when in late 1998 Schwab's market value exceeded Merrill's. By every other metric, Merrill was considerably larger than Schwab. But investors feared Merrill did not understand the Internet. As customers flocked to e-brokers, the firm faced an 85% compression in its margins, much more than retailers of toys and books. Not only did this change concern the retail brokerage division, the huge corporate division began to panic as well. This one event, the change in position based on the market capitalization of Merrill and Schwab, woke up Merrill and those who had stifled efforts at innovation.

Several key executives and strategists at Merrill (including Steffens) became convinced that Merrill had to embrace the Internet and change its business model accordingly. Bringing about such change is difficult in a firm that is on top of its industry and extremely successful. The change in Schwab's business model to embrace the Web was relatively small; for Merrill, the changes were gigantic. It expected to lose $1 billion in equity commissions, but hoped to make it up in fees and assets under management. Merrill also feared the loss of key brokers to rival firms, but this fear may be misplaced as others adopt Merrill's or e-Trades model. In a few years, there will be few customers left for the full-commission broker; the stockbroker will have to adapt to low-commission trades or fee-based services if he is to survive.

7. *New York Times*, October 8, 1999.

What has been the result of this transformation on the retail side? Merrill regained its edge over Schwab in absolute dollars; its inflow in the first quarter of 2000 topped Schwab's at $48.1 billion to $44 billion.[8] However, there are still more Merrill customers transferring to Schwab than vice versa.

The impact of e-commerce on the brokerage industry and the repercussions of Merrill's change in strategy will be difficult to assess given the decline in the stock markets in 2001–2002. The competition became obvious as did the market's reaction to it. While maintaining and defending the status quo, finally Merrill received a shock that broke through its inertia. Not all firms and industries can count on receiving such a wake-up call, and they must be alert to competitors that are intent on moving them out of the winner's column.

Conclusions

The organizations in this chapter were considered winners. Their cultures reflected their optimism, feelings of invulnerability, and hubris. Merrill Lynch employees were highly compensated and were likely to resist changes that could have an uncertain impact on their incomes. Merrill faced pressures for growth and saw its conventional approach to business as the way to achieve this objective. Until its stock price fell to the point that Schwab briefly had a higher market capitalization, everything seemed fine. What happened in these cases is that an ongoing, previously successful business model suddenly became vulnerable to a new model developed by a competitor.

What to do?

When you are on top, watch out

There is always a competitor out there trying to figure out how to invade your market and capture some of your share. That is the beauty of free enterprise, which is designed for the benefit of consumers, not managers trying to protect a franchise. Being the number one stock exchange, brokerage firm, or any other business makes you a target for everyone else in the industry.

---

8. *Wall Street Journal*, July 17, 2000.

Being paranoid is all right; competitors are out to get you!

Andy Grove of Intel wrote a book about only the paranoid surviving. His point is well taken; there are competitors out to get you as Merrill Lynch found out. The NASDAQ thought it had a nice monopoly, and then the Internet came along and made it easy for new entrants, which were happy to savage its market share. ECNs would be happy to overtake the NYSE so that it is no longer on top.

Keep a close eye on your business model and the new business models your competitors are developing

The full-service brokers ignored online brokers and derided their services. Retail investors did not see things that way; they liked the new business models, which let them trade stocks for low commissions and gave them free or low-cost research on the Internet. You can always learn something from a competitor's actions. The full-service brokers began to offer competitive products and appear to have stopped some of the erosion in their customer bases. Merrill's response to Schwab was to learn from its success to offer a competitive product.

Don't be afraid to cannibalize a business or channel

A common argument about adopting a new model is that it will cannibalize the existing business. The flaw in this argument is that someone else out there will develop the model if you do not. Manheim Auctions, the large wholesale used-car auction company, started an online division as soon as the Internet permitted profit-making activities. Manheim's reasoning was that some other company would start this business if it did not. The company took care to provide incentives for the managers of physical auctions to cooperate, even though they would be losing business to the online auction subsidiary.

Staying on top as a winner is hard to do; you are a clear target for everyone else in the industry and for new entrants as well. You need to keep a lookout for what is coming, both in your industry and in new technologies like the Internet that can cause a major discontinuity.

8 • Complacency in the computer industry

Two companies, one survivor

Being a long-term winner lulls one into maintaining an untenable position, staying with a business model that produced a stunning victory but that is no longer viable. In a services industry, like retail brokerage, it is relatively easy to invoke a new business model. The basic infrastructure for a trade is the same whether a broker enters the data or the customer enters the information over the Internet. Customers quickly adapt to this kind of change. It is much more difficult to make a dramatic change in the nature of one's products in a high-tech manufacturing environment, given investments in plant, equipment, support personnel, and employee knowledge. Sudden shifts in product lines are especially difficult when customers have spent years building a technological infrastructure based on your products.

In the two examples in this chapter, IBM and DEC, early victories over competitors, high market share, and a steady stream of profits led to complacency. IBM became the target of the computer industry given its almost monopoly position in the 1960s and 1970s. But the Heisman

Trophy syndrome did not affect the company; no challenger was strong enough to knock it out of first place, though many, including the government, tried. It took major changes in the technology, including the PC technology that IBM helped to create (and then gave away), and a sustained attack on IBM by companies like DEC to push IBM to the brink of insolvency. DEC, on the other hand, became a victim of its own success when personal computers did to the minicomputer what the mini had done to mainframes.

At both IBM and DEC, the boards of directors found a new CEO. At IBM, Lou Gerstner was an outsider who had experience as a customer, and he was able to implement a new strategy that revitalized the company. Robert Palmer, a DEC employee for a relatively short time, succeeded Ken Olsen, DEC's founder. However, by that time, the complacency that had caused Olsen to miss the PC and microcomputer revolution had caused too much damage, and eventually the only solution was to merge DEC with another company. One merger later, DEC pretty much disappeared.

What is the relevance of these stories in the twenty-first century? They offer a powerful lesson that winning is not everything, and that being number one is highly overrated. We are reminded of the old Avis ads that said, "We are number 2 and we try harder!" If you are on top of your industry, be aware that the same forces that lead to the Winner's Curse can lead to your demise, as they did at DEC. Beware of developing an organizational culture that belittles your competitors and their products. You want to be optimistic and realistic at the same time. You have to control the managerial hubris that leads to the kind of attitudes that said PCs were a toy. No firm is invulnerable, regardless of the level of a senior manager's compensation or the company's stock price. A business model that is wildly successful may, after major technological advances, become totally unrealistic. Think of these lessons as you read about how IBM had a near-death experience and how DEC did not survive being a winner.

IBM: A national treasure

Early in 1993, Louis Gerstner, at that time CEO of RJR Nabisco, was considering the position of CEO of IBM, a company that was in a great deal of trouble. Two of the people trying to convince Gerstner to take the position described the company as a "national treasure" that was worth saving. Why was IBM such an icon? To many, the company exemplified U.S. technological leadership. From the mid-1950s through the mid-

1980s, IBM led the computer industry, an industry quite unlike any other in economic history.

Computer and telecommunications technology transformed business. In the 1950s, IBM had estimated that 20 of its first computers, the 650, would satisfy the computing needs of the world. Despite occasional downturns, computer and communications technology has expanded dramatically across business and government, and the technology is embedded in a huge number of products as well. Part of the reason for this success is the continuing, dramatic reduction in the cost of components combined with huge improvements in their performance.

For many years, IBM symbolized America's high-tech economy, and in 1993 it was in danger of being broken up or worse. We argue that IBM got itself into this position as a result of complacency, the major danger for the long-term winner. The company had a tremendous win with its 360 line of computers, beginning in 1964, and this success cemented the role of the mainframe as the company's primary engine for profits, contributing greatly to an inertia that almost doomed IBM.

The huge system 360 win

Complacency can set in after a company has a large victory or when it is at the top of its industry for some time. IBM has both of these distinctions; it won big with its 360 computer system in 1964, and that solidified its position at the top of the computer industry for more than a decade. The computer industry was fragmented in the 1950s, with mainframe computers being the only option for customers. Different computers from the same manufacturer were unable to run each other's programs, so the customer was locked into a particular computer line, not just a computer vendor. The industry was sometimes referred to as "IBM and the seven dwarfs," for the other companies that made mainframes at the time: RCA, GE, Burroughs, Univac, Control Data, Honeywell, and NCR.

In its April 7, 1964, announcement, IBM truly revolutionized the computer industry. The 360 was to provide a full circle (360 degrees?) of computers that were capable of running the same programs. If a company outgrew a system 360 model 30, in theory it could move to a model 40 without having to change any of its programs. Later, this goal had to be modified because IBM found that it could not afford to have the same set of machine instructions in its smallest computer as in its largest, given the technology of the time. So total compatibility among computers changed to upward compatibility. The programs for a 360 model 20 would run on larger machines, but the programs for a 360 model 50 would not run on a model 20.

Anyone who has used a computer recently is aware of the piece of software called the operating system, of which Microsoft Windows is a prime example. The 360 line of computers was the first where one had to have an operating system to run the machine. Earlier generations of computers could, and often did, run program after program that an operator loaded and then started executing. The 360 line ended up with two major operating systems, DOS and OS/360, the former for smaller computers and the latter for larger models. The midrange model 40 usually ran with DOS while larger models worked with OS/360. Now the operating system is an integral part of any computer system.

The 360 was a major advance beyond its ability to have upward compatibility for programs and an operating system. Reports on the government antitrust case against IBM brought at the end of the Johnson administration describe this major event in the computer field:[1]

1. The price-performance ratio of the system 360 was a major leap forward compared to existing systems, largely due to the substitution of solid logic technology or partially integrated circuits for the discrete circuits of the prior generation. Experts agreed that IBM set the price-performance standard for the industry with the 360.

2. The 360 represented a dramatic new computer architecture, one that rendered obsolete all IBM computers from previous generations. The new 360 could not execute the programs of second-generation computers until a customer rewrote them in a different computer language. To ease this transition, certain models of the 360 could "emulate" a prior generation computer, for example, the 360 model 40 could run programs for the popular second-generation IBM 1400 series of computer. This emulation involved a combination of hardware and software to buy time for customers to convert. IBM developed emulation as a stopgap measure so that customers would not reject the new 360 because of the cost and effort required for conversion. Emulation, however, meant that programs ran more slowly than they would when converted to the 360. IBM ran the very real risk with

1. F. Fisher, J. McGowan, and J. Greenwood, *Folded, Spindled and Mutilated: Economic Analysis and U.S. v. IBM* (Cambridge, Mass.: MIT Press, 1983).

the 360 that customers would not flock to the new machines because of the conversion effort required.

3. IBM wanted the 360 to be equally suitable for business or scientific applications, something that had not been the case to date. At the time of the 360, certain lines at IBM were for business (the 1400 series), and others were for scientific use (the 7000 series).

4. The 360 line provided a standardized interface so the user could configure a machine with a variety of different peripherals that operated across the line. The user was no longer restricted to certain peripherals that came with a specific machine.

5. The 360, as mentioned earlier, required the use of an operating system to manage the resources of the computer. Original estimates were that IBM would spend more than $100 million for programming for the new line, and these turned out to be too low. IBM underestimated the effort required to produce OS/360; the project was late and over budget. IBM invested the equivalent of about 5,000 years of labor in OS/360 between 1963 and 1966. Eventually this product turned into IBM's high-end operating system, and its basic structure continues today as a part of IBM's mainframe offerings.

Two different estimates agree that IBM invested $5 billion in developing the 360, truly a "bet the company" decision. We all know in retrospect that this decision paid off for IBM for many years. The demand for the new computers was much larger than the company had forecasted, and by October 1966 IBM had a tremendous backlog of orders. In response, IBM undertook a major expansion of plant facilities and its labor force.

A little history of Big Blue

To understand how IBM experienced the Winner's Curse, we need to review its history, which shows how easy it was for the company to rely on mainframe sales and to ignore changes in the industry. IBM was an office products company well before the time of computers. The first totally electronic computers came out of World War II, and IBM had to make its first major decision about this new technology: should it continue to build office products like typewriters, or take a chance on these new devices? Thomas Watson, Jr., argued strongly for going into computers against surprising opposition.

The first generation

The first generation of computers was made of vacuum tubes; primary input was via punched cards, and secondary storage was on magnetic tapes. Core memory was an innovation in this generation, developed at MIT's Lincoln laboratories. Prior to electronic computers, companies used punched-card equipment for quite elaborate processing tasks, generally involving accounting applications and tasks like preparing the payroll. One of the authors remembers working in a factory that prepared a weekly payroll for 5,000 workers using only electronic accounting machines to process cards. Firms often used their first-generation computers to automate some of the applications previously run using punched cards.

All programming at this time was done in something called assembly language, which was very close to the actual native language of the computer hardware. There were no operating systems; a human operator loaded cards and tapes and ran programs. A good operator made better use of a machine than a poor one. The total investment in software applications at most companies was relatively small.

The second generation

The second generation of computers took advantage of transistors to dramatically increase the power and reduce the cost of computers. The disk drive became the dominant form of secondary storage, and we saw the first online systems made possible by the ability to access data relatively quickly from anyplace on a disk. Operating systems were developed during this period, and many firms had adopted them by the late 1950s. Most programmers still worked in assembly languages, which were incompatible across mainframe vendors and often incompatible within the computer lines of the same vendor.

It was during this second generation that IBM really solidified its lead in the computer industry. Most observers at the time felt that IBM's technology was not necessarily superior to its competitors. However, IBM had unparalleled service and support and won the hearts and minds of information services (IS) managers, who were responsible for providing technology services for their employers. There were industry truisms that said, "No IS manager has ever been fired for buying IBM." And any company getting started in computing was smart to buy at least its first computer from Big Blue.

One of the authors had a summer job in college at a Western Electric plant in Omaha, Nebraska. The plant had a new IBM 1410 computer, a popular midrange, second-generation machine. The computer had a large disk drive, standing about five feet high and three or four feet in diameter. The IBM customer engineer used a small crane to lift the disk itself out of the drive when repairs were needed.

One day, the drive stopped working. The onsite IBM customer engineer tried his usual diagnostics, and they did not find the problem. He called in experts from the branch office downtown. After the drive was down for a certain number of hours, IBM rules required the local staff to notify the IBM manufacturing facility in Poughkeepsie, New York, of the problem. When the repairs ran past another deadline, engineers from Poughkeepsie got on a plane to come to the plant in Omaha. It turned out that the local engineers fixed the problem, and the Poughkeepsie engineers turned around and went home. It is easy to see why IS managers felt comfortable with IBM.

The third generation

IBM changed the world of technology with its third-generation 360 series of computers. IBM intended to make a great leap forward and succeeded in setting the mainframe standard for more than twenty years. The 360 was a step on the way to fully integrated circuits, and it removed all doubts about the viability of operating systems. The 360 also introduced solid state memory, leading eventually to the phase-out of core memories. The 360 had a new character set that contained enough characters that computers could stop printing in all capital letters.

While the 360 is often thought of as a hardware innovation, the software for this line of computers created another sort of revolution. IBM encouraged customers to use higher-level problem-oriented languages rather than assembly language for programming the 360 series of computers. For business, this approach generally meant COBOL, or common business-oriented language. Proponents of higher-level languages felt that programmers were more productive using them and that they were easier to modify later than assembly language programs.

This strategy had one serious problem, however. While companies did not have a lot of programs to convert going from the first generation to the second generation, by 1964 a lot of firms had extensive software libraries. These programs would not run on the 360, and that is why IBM developed emulators for second-generation computers that ran on the 360. This way a customer could replace a second-generation computer with a new 360 and run existing programs until they could be rewritten. And, of course, the programmers would not just rewrite the code but would look at the entire application and see how to improve it.

Neither IBM nor its customers realized just how big a task it would be to convert all of these second-generation programs to the 360; it was an enormous undertaking that lasted far longer than anyone in the industry had predicted. People who went through this conversion said "never again." IBM had probably not foreseen the magnitude of this problem, but in the end it turned out to be a huge benefit for the company because now customers were really locked into IBM. Higher-level languages never achieved their promise of compatibility across computers for two reasons. First, vendors created enhancements to their versions of the languages that were unique to them; and second, the languages all had their own interfaces to the computer manufacturers' operating systems.

As a result, customers became locked into IBM's proprietary hardware and software systems. They remembered the pains of conversion and looked at multimillion-dollar investments in existing programs; the idea of switching to a different vendor or a new paradigm of computing was not very attractive. Today, the term *legacy system* generally refers to an older IBM mainframe application, probably programmed in COBOL and running a successor of OS/360. Companies might adopt a different model of computing for new applications, but there are many applications that still run on IBM mainframes and will continue to do so for the foreseeable future.

The dominance of the mainframe, an engine for profits

The huge victory represented by the 360 had a dramatic impact on IBM: it turned into a one-product company. Lou Gerstner described IBM as a mainframe company "with an array of multibillion-dollar businesses attached to that single franchise."[2] Many of IBM's mainframe competitors disappeared in the years after the introduction of the 360, including GE and Xerox, which both exited the computer business. IBM's revenues grew at 14% compounded from 1965 to 1985 and gross margins were about 60%.

2. L. Gerstner, *Who Says Elephants Can't Dance?* (New York: HarperCollins, 2002), 117.

Complacency rears its head

Given this kind of performance, it was easy for IBM to become complacent. As Gerstner points out, what was happening in the marketplace was "essentially irrelevant to the success of the company."[3] IBM, with the triumph of the 360, created an annuity from customers who were trapped by its proprietary systems and the huge investments they had in applications for these systems.

In 1981, IBM sold its first personal computers, and in doing so told the world that it was all right to have a small computer on your desk. However, the company was so dominated by its mainframe mentality that it gave away the personal computer to its competitors and has never been able to recover. IBM set up its PC group in Boca Raton, Florida, to keep it away from the company culture at headquarters. IBM did not buy the PC operating system DOS when Bill Gates offered it to the company, and IBM used a processor chip for the PC from Intel that anyone could buy. IBM decided to have open, published standards for the PC so that other companies could make add-on equipment. As a result, competitors like Compaq created lower-cost PCs, and IBM has been able to hold its own in PCs only with its portable notebook systems. In essence, IBM gave away the operating system and the processor chip for the PC, losing a huge potential source of revenue. Could this have happened because IBM saw itself first and foremost as a mainframe company?

Winning big encourages big bureaucracies

Observers of IBM suggest that it goes through repeated cycles of innovation followed by the creation of large bureaucracies, which is a pattern that contributes to inertia. Having won big with the 360, the natural inclination was to play it safe and protect the victory. An IBM manager might easily have come to the conclusion that milking the mainframe franchise was the best (and safest) course of action. Bureaucracies are a great structure for playing it safe; you develop layers of management to review decisions so that no one makes a mistake. At one time in the late 1980s there were 17 layers of management from the CEO to a supervisor on a factory floor at IBM.[4]

3. Gerstner, *Who Says Elephants Can't Dance?* 117.
4. Q. Mills and G. Friesen, *Broken Promises: An Unconventional View of What Went Wrong at IBM* (Cambridge, Mass.: Harvard Business School Press, 1996).

The nonconcurrence system

When an IBMer disagreed with a position taken by one of his colleagues, he could announce that he was "nonconcurring." Nonconcurrence could happen at any level of the organization, and it resulted in tremendous delays in making decisions and much duplicate effort. In addition, nonconcurrence led to some bitter feuds among individuals and departments. Gerstner said that he heard this system described as producing a culture in which no one would say yes, but everyone could say no.[5] It is easy to see the nonconcurrence system contributing to complacency as the keepers of the mainframe nonconcurred with ideas for innovations that might threaten their franchise.

Gerstner includes a 1994 memo in his book about IBM that describes how nonconcurrence works. The memo is the official kick-off for the nonconcurrence process for the year. The author of the memo asks who will be the nonconcur coordinator for the remainder of the year. The author of the memo is expecting a large number of nonconcurs that year and talks about entering them in the Nonconcur Management System (NCMS).[6] Imagine having a system to memorialize nonconcurring roadblocks to new ideas.

Losing sight of the customer

It is easy to see how a company with a winning product line, a huge bureaucracy, and the wonderful nonconcurrence system could lose sight of its customers and the rest of the industry. Lou Gerstner, while not a technologist, may have been the best possible CEO for IBM in 1993 because he had been a customer of the company for most of his career, first at American Express and then at RJR Nabisco. It was possible that only an outsider could have saved IBM given how inbred the company had become. John Akers, Gerstner's predecessor, had planned to save IBM by breaking it into 13 smaller companies. This plan showed a lack of awareness of customer needs, as we shall see.

The rest of the world changes

One of the problems with being a winner is that the rest of the world makes you a target. In addition, companies that set standards that bene-

5. Gerstner, *Who Says Elephants Can't Dance?* 193.
6. Gerstner, *Who Says Elephants Can't Dance?* 193.

fit them often incur the wrath of their customers as well as industry pundits. In the days of IBM's dominance of the industry, it received the same kind of criticism that one finds directed at Microsoft today. Customers and competitors wondered, "How can we break IBM's control over computing and our dependence on the company?"

Open standards, Unix and PCs, and client-server

One answer to this question is the *open standards movement*, which can be contrasted with the proprietary standards of IBM. *Open* is often a code word for Unix, an operating system that is supposed to offer compatibility across vendors. Sun Microsystems, Hewlett Packard, DEC, and eventually IBM have embraced Unix. Of course, they each have their own variation so in fact there is not 100% compatibility across computers, but the situation is far better than with IBM's mainframe operating system.

Changes in hardware that occurred around the time of the 360 made open standards viable by lowering the cost of computing. Ken Olsen of DEC was one of the first to realize that integrated circuits made it possible for a small computer to have a lower cost and better price-performance ratio than a mainframe. A department could afford to buy a minicomputer that was quite powerful, and it no longer depended on a centralized IS group with its mainframe. Minicomputers were the first attack on the mainframe, and they were very successful. Due to IBM's inertia, they remained off its radar screen for many years.

The PC joined the minicomputer to provide a wide array of choices to the systems designer. A critical design question became: "what processing should be done locally and what processing should be done on a larger system?" Gradually, a new computing paradigm evolved called *client-server*, which is the model of computing on the Internet as well. The client is a PC on your desktop, which is connected to a more powerful server containing applications programs and data. The client sends requests to the server, which responds to satisfy the request. Debates have raged over "fat" and "thin" clients, which are actually codes for pro- and anti-Microsoft and Intel (Wintel). A fat client runs Windows and does a lot of local processing while a thin client does minimal processing and relies almost entirely on servers. Not surprisingly, server companies like Sun and HP favor thin client configurations. The thin client model with a powerful server looks a lot like a mainframe with terminals, so in essence we have come full circle.

IBM eventually decided that it had to offer minicomputers and came up with the series 1 and system 38, both of which were incompatible with its mainframes. But the company still derived most of its profits from mainframes, and these other products were there to protect that franchise. It was clear that IBM was not committed to this new model of computing; some would say it was in a state of denial. IBM had become so focused internally that it had lost touch with its customers, particularly with the end users of its technology.

The CIO's alliance with IBM

In the early days of computing, IBM sales representatives sold to managers in the firm, often the chief financial officer. As technology became a larger part of a firm's expenses, companies created a new position called the chief information officer, or CIO. A lot of IBM's contacts with a customer shifted to this person, who was responsible for computing in the firm.

The CIO controls a resource that people in the organization want. In many organizations the CIO charges back services to users based on some accounting rules. The trouble here is that the people getting charged rarely understand the basis for the numbers. If you are charged something for a corporate car or truck, you can relate to the components of the charge and have some idea, based on your own car, whether the charges are reasonable. A user with a $1,500 PC looks at her computer charges for the mainframe and cannot understand why they are so high. In fact, her $1,500 PC costs the firm a lot more than that in support, software, and networking, but that cost is not obvious to the user.

The CIO may be unpopular because she is responsible for implementing new technology and applications. There are always more requests for these services than financial resources available to supply them. Too often, the CIO is seen as a gatekeeper who allows or disallows requests for service. The reason an organization invests in the technology is to change something, and change is not easy. Technology does not always work right, especially when it is first introduced. The IT staff is in the business of being a change agent, which does nothing to increase its popularity.

Users are especially frustrated with mainframe technology, which often appears outdated when compared with the great graphical interface on their PCs. Because of the lack of compatibility between a mainframe and a client-server system running Unix, these legacy mainframe systems are difficult and expensive to replace. Companies make an economic decision not to bring in new technology for mainframe systems that still are working well, especially large, complex applications like an airline reservations system.

So IBM worked with the CIO, a person already unpopular in the organization with some because of the CIO's historic association with IBM and legacy systems. As a result, IBM moved further and further away from senior executives in the firm and from the ultimate users of its technology. Eventually, IBM's inward focus led it to ignore even the CIO's problems, and the company kept sending the same message that the right computing model was the mainframe.

One of Lou Gerstner's first meetings as CEO of IBM was with a group of CIOs. These executives were all angry with IBM, saying that its inaction had let "PC bigots" convince the world that the mainframe was dead. This view ignored the world's huge IT infrastructure, which ran the back offices of manufacturing firms, banks, airlines, utilities, and governments; worse than that, somehow users had the idea that all of this infrastructure could be moved to a desktop PC. The CIOs also were unhappy about IBM's pricing for mainframe hardware and software, its huge bureaucracy, and how hard it was to get integration for a problem's solution or across geographic regions.[7]

The pleas of the user

Users like minicomputers and PCs; they have always had a more friendly interface and been easier to use than mainframes. The response to client-server computing has been positive, and it took a long time for IBM to accept this paradigm.

SAP is one of the most successful enterprise resource planning (ERP) system vendors, and its system first ran on mainframes. Because of customer demand, SAP developed a version called R3, for a client-server environment, which became a very successful product. Given these signs, IBM still denied that the client-server model was anything to be taken seriously. And it did, after all, offer some minis and PCs, which one could use to create a client-server environment. Early on, however, IBM's solution involved its proprietary software and operating systems on a mainframe server, not Unix, which did nothing to enhance sales.

7. Gerstner, *Who Says Elephants Can't Dance?* 47.

Notice the huge disconnect between CIOs and end users. Who is right? The truth lies someplace between these positions. It is naïve to think that the world's IT infrastructure could or should be replaced overnight, or that such a replacement with PCs makes any sense. On the other hand, mainframes have long been associated with unresponsive technology that takes a long time to implement and that costs a lot. One of the most difficult tasks in managing IT in an organization today is dealing with a heterogeneous computing environment that has developed from years of investments in the technology.

The problem statement

Gerstner's observations summarize nicely the position IBM had gotten itself into because of its mainframe focus:

> [The] more imminent threat to the mainframe model started with the rise of Unix, an "open" operating environment [which] offered customers the first viable, economically attractive alternative to IBM's mainframe products and pricing. In the open . . . world of Unix, many companies could make parts of an overall solution—shattering IBM's hold on architectural control. . . . After Unix cracked the foundation, the PC makers came along swinging wrecking balls. . . . it's clear that the company failed to understand fully two things about personal computing:
> - PCs would eventually be used by businesses and enterprises, not just by hobbyists and students. . . .
> - Because we did not think PCs would ever challenge IBM's core enterprise computing franchise, we surrendered control of the PC's highest-value components: the operating system to Microsoft and the microprocessor to Intel.[8]

We contend that the complacency of the long-term winner struck IBM with the success of its 360 line of mainframe computers in 1964, and that victory influenced the company for 29 years until it reached a crisis in 1993. The dominance of the mainframe led to IBM giving up something of tremendous value: the control of the hardware and operating system for the personal computer.

8. Gerstner, *Who Says Elephants Can't Dance?* 119–120.

What's a company to do?

The end almost comes in 1993

IBM's revenues peaked in 1990 at $68.2 billion and then dropped steadily to $62.7 billion in 1993. Worse, its consolidated profits hit $5.9 billion in 1990 and turned into losses of $5.01 a share in 1991, $8.70 in 1992, and a huge $14.22 in 1993.[9] Gerstner described the condition of IBM when he was first approached about taking the job of CEO. Not only were sales and profits dropping at an alarming rate, but IBM's "cash position was getting scary." Mainframe revenue had dropped from $13 billion in 1990 to a projection of less than $7 billion in 1993. On the basis of this first review, Gerstner felt the odds were no better than one in five that IBM could be saved.[10]

Breaking up IBM

Industry analysts were saying that IBM should break itself into smaller units, and CEO John Akers was preparing such a plan. Some customers liked the idea, as did many vendors, which saw it as a way to break IBM's remaining monopoly on computing. Other vendors were not sure that they wanted to compete with six or seven small IBMs. When Gerstner arrived, he had the fresh view of a customer. His own experience and what he heard from other customers was that everyone needed a company that could deliver complete solutions. Sure, having a lot of different vendors for different parts of your system helps with competition and may keep prices down, but someone has to integrate all of the parts to make a system work. IBM could do that, but not if it were broken into smaller pieces. One of Gerstner's first decisions, which he characterizes as the most important he made, was to keep IBM together as one company.

How to stop hemorrhaging money

It was clear to just about everybody that IBM had been milking mainframes, yet the managers at IBM seemed blissfully unaware of the negative impact this strategy was having on their market. One of the first things

9. Mills and Friesen, *Broken Promises*, 85.
10. Gerstner, *Who Says Elephants Can't Dance?* 15.

Gerstner did was to meet with the mainframe team at IBM and ask why they were losing so much market share. The answer was that Hitachi, Fujitsu, and Amdahl were pricing 30–40% below IBM. The team argued that to cut prices was folly because IBM would lose revenue and profits when it was in dire need of both. Gerstner felt that to continue the milking strategy was a path that would lead to the eventual death of the company, and he instructed the team to come up with dramatic price reductions that he could announce in two weeks at a customer conference. Note that, at a time when IBM was losing money, the CEO was betting the company on a dramatic price reduction for the products that produced most of its profits.

The new CEO reaffirmed an earlier decision, which turns out to have dovetailed nicely with the mainframe price reductions. The technical staff at IBM had proposed changing from a hardware technology called *bipolar* to one known as *CMOS* in the company's mainframes, which would permit substantial price reductions in the coming years. IBM invested a billion dollars on this conversion during the next four years and managed to save its mainframes by improving their cost-performance ratio dramatically. Mainframes became "high-end servers" and generated $19 billion in revenue from 1997 to 2001.

The price of a unit of mainframe processing moved from $63,000 in 1993 to less than $2,500 seven years later, and mainframe price-performance improved 20% a year on average for the next six years. By 1994, IBM mainframe shipments had reversed their decline to grow by 41%. In 1995, the growth rate was 60%, with 47% growth in 1996, 29% in 1997, 63% in 1998, 6% in 1999, 25% in 2000, and 34% in 2001.[11] By changing the positioning of the mainframe and its perception within IBM and the outside world, the company had finally begun to shake off the complacency that had set in with the launch of the system 360 in 1964.

IBM as a services company

The mainframe curse resulted in a business model that said to everyone inside and outside the company that IBM was a hardware company that also sold software and some services. Consistent with keeping the company together, Gerstner wanted to change its direction to provide end-to-

11. Gerstner, *Who Says Elephants Can't Dance?* 48.

end services for the customer. IBM would help its customers to solve problems. He founded a nascent services organization that would be the vehicle for changing IBM's business model and finally broke free of the mainframe straitjacket. Because the emphasis was on solving the customer's problems, the new IBM services unit would recommend and help install equipment from other vendors, even competitors like Microsoft, Sun, and HP.

There was much resistance within IBM to these changes, and many executives wanted to continue following the existing business model. Gerstner persevered, and in 1996 he broke out the services unit in the form of IBM Global Services. In 1992, services was a $7.4 billion business at IBM (not counting maintenance). By 2001 it had become a $30 billion-a-year business and accounted for about half of the workforce.

The Internet gave IBM's services business a big boost. The services staff recognized the potential of networking built around the open standards and global reach of the Internet. It also figured out that companies would need a great deal of help adapting to a networked world and, most important, that all business would eventually become electronic or e-business. IBM positioned itself as "the e-business company" with a large advertising campaign backed up by new products like Websphere. IBM recognized correctly that most companies are not dot-com start-ups; they have been in business for a long time. These traditional firms have existing transactions-processing systems. To conduct e-business on the Internet, they needed to integrate Internet client transactions with existing systems that company employees operated, for example, taking orders and entering them online into a company computer. Since this company computer was probably an IBM mainframe, what firm was better prepared than IBM to help link their mainframe to the Web?

How the 360 mainframe victory turned into a threat to IBM

We have seen how the system 360 revolutionized computing in 1964 and how IBM profited from this leap in technology. The flaws of the system, namely, the costly conversion from second-generation software, at first worked in IBM's favor by locking customers into its equipment. Because the machines were so powerful and had such an attractive cost-performance ratio, customers dramatically expanded their use of computers. IBM was on top of the computing business with no serious rivals. It was the clear winner; its managers developed strong feelings of invulnerability and were suffused with optimism. They also displayed significant hubris, especially with regard to new computing models like the minicomputer, PC, and client-server technology.

IBM showed steady growth, satisfying the analysts and shareholders as its stock price rose. Akers, with unbounded optimism, staffed the company for sales of $100 billion a year. When sales went in the other direction, he was forced into large layoffs, which were unusual for IBM. In the early 1990s when IBM's results were so dismal, the company almost succumbed to analyst recommendations to break itself apart. (One wonders what might have happened to the mainframe business under this kind of structure.) The success of the 360 led to IBM developing an unrealistic business model built around the mainframe and encouraged the formation of a huge, unwieldy bureaucracy that could not see the flaws in the model.

It took 29 years for the problems to become so painfully obvious that they could no longer be ignored, and it took a CEO from outside the company to provide new direction. IBM was lucky and smart; it recruited a capable CEO who provided direction to its talented managers and who took advantage of the strong technology capabilities of the firm. What should be apparent from the story of IBM is that the long-term winner's complacency is extremely serious; it has the potential to sink a company, which is what happened with Digital Equipment Corporation.

Digital equipment: $70,000 and some circuits

In the early 1950s, Ken Olsen, a new engineering graduate from MIT, was employed at MIT's Lincoln laboratories on a defense project to build an early warning radar system. As a part of his assignment, Olsen had to work with another contractor on the project, IBM. He was appalled by the bureaucracy and the kind of engineering he saw at IBM.

By 1953, Olsen was convinced that he could build a better computer and computer company than IBM. Olsen and two colleagues secured financing from the famous General Georges Doriot's venture capital firm, American Research and Development (ARD), $70,000 in exchange for 70% ownership of the company, a pretty steep price. Doriot thought that Olsen was premature in wanting to build an interactive computer of the type constructed for the air defense system and urged him to start by selling circuits. So Digital Equipment Company (DEC) began its business selling circuit modules.

The famous PDPs

DEC brought out its first computer and called it the programmed data processor, or PDP-1, to disguise the fact that it was a computer from General Doriot and the board of directors. The tradition in the computer industry at this time was for customers to lease computers from vendors; DEC changed the model by selling the PDP-1 for $120,000. The initial customers were scientists and engineers, who would make up most of DEC's customer list for many years. While not in the league of a mainframe, the PDP-1 gave its users more performance for the price than anyone expected.

Olsen's great insight was that the cost of fabricating the central processing unit (CPU) of a computer was falling dramatically as technology advanced. IBM with its proprietary mainframes had a high-cost, high-price business model. He felt DEC could attract a new kind of customer by providing a small computer with a better price-performance ratio than a mainframe and that such a computer would have wide appeal to scientists, engineers, and academics.

The PDP-1 was soon followed with other models, but the next breakthrough was the PDP-8 in 1960. DEC priced the computer aggressively at $18,000, an extremely low price for a general purpose computer. Over the product's 15-year life, DEC sold 50,000 PDP-8s. A number of manufacturers of other products embedded the PDP-8 in their designs; for example, a typesetting machine might use a PDP-8 for its logic. Sales to these original equipment manufacturers soon reached 50% of DEC's total sales.

Olsen was aiming at a segment of the market that, for the most part, IBM ignored. He did not want to take on Big Blue in head-to-head competition, though he was trying to create a revolution in the industry. Olsen's vision and strategy are important in understanding the rise and fall of DEC. Olsen attacked the mainframe paradigm of computing by producing a smaller computer with a better price-performance ratio, a computer that appealed greatly to customers because it was much easier to use than a mainframe. DEC's success with these minicomputers helped to change the way the world viewed computing, but it also led to the PC fiasco and, ultimately, to the demise of DEC.

Olsen, for most of the company's history, was synonymous with DEC. He structured and restructured the company a number of times, often creating great confusion among employees and customers. For a long period, DEC was organized by product lines in a matrix structure with centralized manufacturing and engineering. DEC paid sales representatives a salary with no commission. Olsen was known for shouting matches with employees, generally with Olsen doing most of the shouting. What emerges is the picture of a strong entrepreneur who was tremendously successful with his original concept of a computer with a better price-performance ratio than IBM and with the concept that individuals wanted local computers that were easy to use.[12] However, Olsen could not accept or understand any other vision of computing or any new computing paradigms. His obsession with a single approach to computing led to DEC's inertia when the marketplace changed, which ultimately doomed the company.

In 1966, DEC went public with only moderate interest from Wall Street; analysts thought that Olsen and DEC were hard to figure out. Shortly thereafter, DEC brought out the PDP-11, which put it back in control of the minicomputer market after having lost its lead to new competitors Varian, Hewlett Packard, and Data General. Eventually DEC sold more than 250,000 PDP-11s. By 1974, DEC hit $1 billion in revenues, had a 41% market share for minicomputers worldwide, and was on the Fortune 500 list for the first time.

In the mid-1980s, IBM woke up and decided that there was a large enough market for minicomputers that it should enter the field. DEC was making inroads in more than minicomputers; its machines helped the industry move toward distributed computing, in which significant processing power resides at the local level rather than only in centralized mainframes. DEC was also working to create networking capabilities so that its customers could tie DEC computers together as well as computers from other vendors. At one time, DEC had a display in which a DEC computer was networked to an IBM computer and told visitors that IBM, itself, could not do that.

The VAX

In 1977 DEC introduced the VAX, a highly advanced machine that was soon labeled a "super-minicomputer." Gordon Bell, DEC's legendary computer designer, developed the strategy that DEC should eliminate all

---

12. G. Rifkin and G. Harrar, *The Ultimate Entrepreneur: The Story of Ken Olsen and Digital Equipment Corporation* (Chicago, Ill.: Contemporary, 1988).

of its other computers and offer just one line, the VAX. It was not easy to convince Olsen or others at DEC, but eventually Bell succeeded. At this time, IBM had several lines of computers, each with a different architecture, and communications among the machines was a challenge. With this strategic move, DEC was providing its customers with the ability to use the same software across its entire line of computers, and furthermore all of the computers could communicate with each other using DECnet, Digital's networking software.

Along came the PC

Despite the constant management chaos and reorganizing at DEC, the company was generally successful. There were downturns, but DEC always managed to recover. It was known in the industry for a high-quality product and for representatives who were "sales engineers," not just salespeople.

In 1981, IBM changed the computing world forever, though it did not recognize what it was doing. The introduction of the IBM personal computer said that it was all right for someone to have a computer that was exclusively hers; the user did not have to share a mainframe with thousands of others.

Ken Olsen opposed the entire concept of personal computers. When Olsen and DEC engineers bought and disassembled their first IBM PC, he was shocked at the poor construction and design. In Olsen's mind, there was no need for an individual to have a private computer. The way to compute was with minicomputers with each user having a terminal to share the resources of the computer with others. At first Olsen only saw personal computers as something for the home, and in his opinion, no one needed a computer at home. PCs were toys that children used to play games.

Others at DEC felt that the personal computer represented an opportunity as well as a threat, but there was little encouragement from Olsen to proceed. Finally, after being goaded by the press, Olsen agreed that DEC should develop some low-end products. The company designed three PC-like products, including the DECmate word processor, the PC Pro, and the Rainbow. Competing divisions were responsible for each of these products, and they came to market late and without adequate software.

Olsen wanted high quality in all DEC products; he failed to realize how quickly technological advances would make PCs obsolete and that customers were not going to keep their machines for five or ten years. They had to last long enough, not forever. It took DEC a full year after IBM's PC to develop its products, and in the meantime, a number of others entered the business. The week DEC announced its PCs, competitors unveiled four others. None of these vendors, including DEC, could compete with IBM on service and support.

In 1983, Olsen reorganized DEC again and dropped its existing product-line structure. Unfortunately administrative systems were not in place, and DEC lost orders and shipments. When it announced earnings, they were down 72% from the previous year. And the analysts had not been warned. DEC's stock plunged 21 points that day and kept dropping. In addition to the snafus with administrative systems, DEC's PC strategy was a failure in the marketplace. The PC Pro was a disaster. DEC had planned to ship 55,000 Pros in 1983 and 215,000 in 1984; the revised estimates were 13,000 and 60,000 with a $78 million loss projected for 1983 and $46 million for 1984. The machine had little in the way of applications software. By 1985, DEC had halted production of the Pro. The Rainbow was exceeding sales expectations, but it still produced losses. The company had a hard time marketing three different machines, especially when they lacked adequate software. DEC ended up selling about 300,000 Rainbows to its existing customers while IBM sold more than a million machines a year. Even though the Rainbow ran MS-DOS, it had some incompatibilities with PC software, which did nothing to enhance its business use. In a 1984 interview, Olsen described personal computers to the *Boston Globe* as "cheap, short-lived and not very accurate machines."[13]

The end of a great company: Compaq takes over

Olsen's and DEC's failure to develop a PC was more serious than not having a low-end product. The rapid technological advances that fed PCs made it possible for companies to develop small systems with price-performance ratios that exceeded that of DEC's minis. These computers competed directly with DEC's machines, but at a fraction of the price. IBM also started to target DEC, recasting its midrange 4300 computer as a "minicomputer" to compete in DEC's markets. Later, IBM's AS/400 helped it retain customers as well. In 1988, DEC agreed to sell Tandy PCs under the DEC label in order to have a product; DEC also began offering

13. Quoted in Rifkin and Harrar, *The Ultimate Entrepreneur*, 242.

a version of Unix for its VAX computers. It began development with MIPS Computer Systems of a RISC (reduced instruction set computer) chip, a new and fundamentally different architecture from the VAX. In 1993, DEC started to deliver systems built around a powerful RISC chip named Alpha.

In 1992, however, the end had come for Ken Olsen. DEC was hemorrhaging cash, and on July 16 the board forced Olsen to resign as CEO. Powerful desktop computers were stealing sales from DEC. The board's solution was to drastically slim down the company and rebuild DEC around Alpha technology.[14] The board felt that Olsen could not undertake the changes and layoffs required to cut costs. DEC's share of the minicomputer market had fallen to 14%, while IBM's AS/400 gave it a 27% share. DEC's model of expensive product development and heavy R&D spending was not competing well against low-margin clients and servers based on PCs.

The new CEO, Robert Palmer, was unable to stop the flow of red ink. In 1994, DEC recorded its fourth losing year in a row, a total of some $4 billion. In January 1998, Compaq announced an agreement to buy DEC for $9 billion, a 20% premium. At the time of the announcement, DEC had twice as many employees as Compaq, and this purchase would turn out to be another example of the original Winner's Curse: paying far too much for a wounded company. In the two years after buying DEC, Compaq lost more money than in all of its previous history, more than $2 billion. It appears that Compaq choked on its purchase.

What was the appeal of DEC? Compaq wanted to move into the profitable market for services and higher-end hardware that would not be heavily affected by each new Intel chip. DEC had a services organization and the powerful Alpha chip on the high end. Twice, Compaq tried to buy DEC's service organization, but was rebuffed. By 1998, DEC was self-destructing, having laid off more than 75,000 employees between 1993 and 1997. Since 1991, DEC's cumulative net losses were nearly $6 billion.

After the purchase, Compaq did little to prepare for the merger, and then it became distracted by problems with PC sales. It may have been a mistake for Compaq to rebrand everything with its name, dropping the name DEC, which had brand loyalty and a positive reputation for its products. Compaq did make money by selling part of DEC's Web search site, AltaVista, to CMGI. Most of DEC's factories were sold, and Compaq

---

14. G. McWilliams, "Did DEC Move Too Late?" *Business Week*, August 3, 1992.

acquired some nice tax loss carry forwards.[15] After the Compaq merger with HP, there is not much of DEC left.

How the minicomputer victory turned into defeat

Ken Olsen was a visionary and leader during his years at DEC. Unfortunately, he was not open to ideas from the outside, and his view of the dominance of the minicomputer created considerable inertia when technology and the industry changed. Two observers suggested that Olsen's view that the PC would "fall flat on its face in business" was one of the biggest misjudgments in American business history.[16] The technology and marketing of the personal computer did to DEC and Olsen what they had done to the mainframe vendors.

Looking at our model of the Winner's Curse, there is no doubt that Ken Olsen displayed considerable hubris during his career, and certainly he felt that DEC and his model of computing were invulnerable. When things started to go bad for DEC, stock analysts and the declining stock price did not help. In the end, Olsen's beliefs defied all evidence to the contrary, and his actions eventually sank the company.

Conclusions

In the long term, no one declares a moment of victory among competing companies; there was no announced victory of IBM's mainframes or DEC's minicomputers. Over time, these companies built up significant market shares and profit streams. The problem is that such good performances too easily lead to inertia; it is easier and safer to go with an older model that works than to try something new. The manufacturing environment encourages this tendency to stay the same; one looks at huge investments in plants, equipment, and staff, and it is easy to argue that change is too disruptive or expensive. Not only is change disruptive for the manufacturer, but its customers may react negatively given their investment in the manufacturer's products. IBM and DEC were also terribly inbred, and this contributed to their inertia. It is significant that Gerstner was able to provide an outsider's objective view. He also got to IBM in time, and the company had the resources he needed to redirect strategy. Olsen and DEC

---

15. "Merger Brief," *Economist*, July 22, 2000.
16. Rifkin and Harrar, *The Ultimate Entrepreneur*, 199.

stuck with their business model and ignored PCs for too long. We had two great manufacturing companies, but only one survivor.

What to do?

When on top, guard constantly against complacency

The euphoria of winning quickly turns to complacency. Just as professional linemen go after Heisman Trophy winners when they get to the pros, competitors like to take business away from number one. They may do so with a new business model or new technology that appeals to customers. They will attack the weak points in your products and services. To remain a winner, you have to look for these threats and be ready to adapt to new technologies.

Your best revenue stream won't last forever

Marketing experts will tell you that all products have a life cycle; at some point they go into decline. You may be able to bring out revised versions and add features, but at some point sales are going to drop. IBM forgot this marketing maxim and evidently thought the mainframe would carry the company forever.

Never belittle a new product that could affect your sales

If IBM and DEC illustrate one concept, it is that one is foolish to deride a new product. The consumer will be the judge of a product, not the producer. Ken Olsen thought PCs were poorly built, but who wants to pay for a machine designed for 20 years when it is obsolete in 3? When new products come out, look carefully at them, understand their appeal and how they affect your product line, and decide whether to compete with them or to develop new products.

Keep scanning the environment for threats and opportunities

This advice may seem obvious, but both IBM and DEC either failed to look at what was coming, or else they chose to ignore it. You want to listen carefully to those who call attention to threats to your business. You may even want to hire a few skeptics and assign them the task of evaluating new products and services that might affect your business.

Don't let your own prejudices get in the way of sound analysis

There is a great tendency for self-attribution, which is thinking that your reaction represents the reaction of customers. How many of your customers are CEOs or senior managers? Maybe people in different positions will not agree with your perceptions of a product. A lot of PC buyers did not see things the way Ken Olsen did. Use market research to find out what buyers think of your products and competitive products.

One of the outcomes of winning for a long time is complacency, which is another type of curse. It is easier to be complacent than to be an activist looking for threats and opportunities. If you start to feel that way, just remember IBM and its mainframes and DEC, Ken Olsen, and the PC.

III • • • How Does One Avoid the Winner's Curse?

9 • Winning is not everything

Vince Lombardi, the famed coach of the Green Bay Packers, once told his team, "Winning isn't everything; it's the only thing." In business as in sports, everything is posed as winning or losing by managers and executives alike. The desire is to win market share, or win the battle for technological leadership, or win the race to deliver a drug for a particular disease, or even beat your opponent to acquire a company. In this book, we have tried to show that the plan of action that this philosophy entails can be detrimental. In a football game, the opponent is on the field with you and the 60-minute game is all that matters. In business, the game goes on much longer. Those who seem to win corporate battles can end up losing the larger, longer-term wars. Winning may entail paying a real cost or an opportunity cost so large that it ends up as a curse on the company.

In this book, we have examined the Winner's Curse in action in different settings. In table 9-1, we summarize the many cases and our analyses of the reasons that there were problems. The most dramatic and classic case of the Winner's Curse happened in the auctions for radio spectrum, which companies needed to provide third-generation wireless services. In many cases, companies bid much more than their own rational initial

Table 9-1. Summary of examples

Force/Example	1994 PCS U.S. Spectrum Auction	Spectrum Auctions: U.K., Germany, Italy	Tyco	MCI-WorldCom
Psychological and Personal Factors				
Buying & bidding psychology	Yes; auction yielded $42 billion with initial estimates of $10 billion	Yes; governments trying to replicate U.S. experience	Large number of acquisitions	Purchase of MCI, attempt to buy Sprint
Competition & winning	Highly competitive	Yes	Win the acquisitions	Win the acquisitions
Organizational culture	Highly structured	Quasi-governmental telecoms	Loose, freewheeling	Loose, freewheeling, fraudulent practices
Managerial optimism		Yes	Become the next GE	Ebbers started from a very small base
Hubris	Not a major factor	Not a major factor	Kozlowski	Ebbers
Compensation	Not a major factor	Not a major factor	CEO one of highest-paid executives in United States	Generous
Invulnerability	Not a major factor	Not a major factor	Likely feelings of invulnerability	Huge accounting scandal
Market Factors				
Pressures for growth	Yes	Yes	Yes	Yes
Investment bankers	Not a major factor	Not a major factor	A serial acquirer	Salomon profited
Stock analysts	Some influence	Some influence	Pressures for results	Jack Grubman's many roles
Stock price	Definite consideration	Yes	Steady growth	Increase value of stock to fund purchases
Unrealistic business models	Yes; winners could not afford to use the licenses fully	Yes; inability to use licenses due to high debt load	What happens when the economy declines?	Are there scale economies in telecom?
Winner's Curse	Yes; dramatic overpayment for spectrums; bidders going bankrupt or merging	U.K. $35 billion, Germany $46 billion, and Italy $10 billion bid	Kozlowski forced out and indicted; Tyco sells CIT Financial for large loss	Bankruptcy following expansion and accounting scandals

Force/Example	AOL Time-Warner	Bank One	First Union	Vivendi/Seagram's/Others
Psychological and Personal Factors				
Buying & bidding psychology	More from inflated stock	More than 100 acquisitions	90 acquisitions	Exhibited by Messier
Competition & winning	Win in digital convergence	Win the acquisitions	Winning the acquisitions	Messier's ambitions to create a huge media firm
Organizational culture	Clash between AOL and Time-Warner	Growth	Growth	Confusing
Managerial optimism	Exhibited by Levin and Case	McCoy	Crutchfield	Extensive
Hubris	Levin and Case	McCoy	Crutchfield	Messier
Compensation	Generous	Generous	Generous	Not a major factor
Invulnerability	World's largest merger to date	Willing to bid high multiples of earnings for acquired banks	Bought CoreStates, Money Store, Wachovia	Provided convoluted financials; who would care if the company grew?
Market Factors				
Pressures for growth	Yes on both companies	Led to unsound practices at First USA	Yes	Vivendi needed cash and earnings
Investment bankers	Happy to help out	Yes	Helpful	Helpful
Stock analysts	Minor role	Minor role	Minor role	Mixed reaction
Stock price	Inflated, allowing merger	The currency for acquisitions	Currency	Eventually plummeted
Unrealistic business models	Inability to gain synergies from merger	Can digest large number of acquisitions, unable to integrate systems	Financial conglomerate?	Can you manage movies, beverages, and utilities?
Winner's Curse	Sharp decline in value of combined firms; Time-Warner takes control; Levin out	Purchase of First USA for premium and subsequent performance; McCoy out	Problems with CoreStates; huge loss on closing the Money Store	Shareholders took a beating, especially the Bronfman family

(continued)

Table 9-1. (continued)

Force	Bristol-Meyers Squibb	United Artists/Transamerica	Walt Disney	Washington Redskins
Psychological and Personal Factors				
Buying & bidding psychology	BMS needed new drugs; buying is one option	The hunt for new movies	Used to bidding for scripts and movies	Bidding for coaches esp Spurner
Competition & winning	Need for new drugs to be competitive	Winning at the box office	The nature of Hollywood	The NFL
Organizational culture	Very loose at ImClone	Hollywood	Hard to describe	Winning is everything
Managerial optimism	Dolan at BMS?	For each new project	On the part of both Eisner and Ovitz	You can buy victories
Hubris	Waksal and Dolan	A hollywood trait?	Eisner and Ovitz	Extensive
Compensation	Generous for Waksal	Huge sums at risk with a movie	Extremely high for both men	High for a coach at the time
Invulnerability	Waksal's actions in the stock market	Cimino had won an Oscar with *The Deer Hunter*	Eisner and Ovitz	Not a factor
Market Factors				
Pressures for growth	On both companies	Constant on studios	Not a major factor	Not applicable
Investment bankers	Lehman Brothers, Morgan Stanley, and the $2 billion agreement	Not applicable	Not applicable	Not applicable
Stock analysts	Minor role	Not a major factor	Need for second in command	Not applicable
Stock price	Not a factor	Not a factor	Not a factor	Not applicable
Unrealistic business models	Failure to conduct due diligence on Erbitux trial	Not applicable	Each man had unrealistic expectations of how Disney would work	Can a coach turn a team around?
Winner's Curse	BMS paid 40% premium for ImClone shares; value dropped on FDA rejection of Erbitux	Huge overpayment for *Heaven's Gate*, which failed at the box office, forcing Transamerica to close United Artists	Huge payments to Ovitz on his termination	Successful record in college did not predict success in the pros

196

Force/Example	Lucent	Nortel	Cisco	Search Engines and Portals
Psychological and Personal Factors				
Buying & bidding psychology	Yes; a scramble to acquire companies	Yes	To some extent	The dot-com frenzy
Competition & winning	Yes	Yes	An acquiring firm	Be first-to-market
Organizational culture	Left over from AT&T	Structured	Aggressive	Very loose
Managerial optimism	Yes	Yes	Yes	Extremely high
Hubris	Yes	Yes	Yes	Yes
Compensation	Yes; stock value and options	Not a major factor	Yes, especially stock options	Promised
Invulnerability	Yes	Yes	Yes; the leading network firm	Probably not
Market Factors				
Pressures for growth	Yes	Yes	Definitely	Extreme
Investment bankers	Yes	Yes	Yes	Yes
Stock analysts	Yes	Yes	Yes	Definitely
Stock price	Yes	Yes	Yes	Yes
Unrealistic business models	Especially for certain acquisitions whose products Lucent abandoned	Yes for some of the acquisitions and their products	Does optical fit with Cisco's core competencies?	Totally
Winner's Curse	38 acquisitions for more than $46 billion, many of which failed	5 acquisitions for more than $11 billion; several resulting in write-downs and abandoned products	3 optical companies for nearly $10 billion	Company might win market share for a while, but revenue model was fatally flawed

(continued)

Table 9-1. (continued)

Force/Example	Webvan	Chemdex/Ventro	NASDAQ	New York Stock Exchange
Psychological and Personal Factors				
Buying & bidding psychology	The dot-com frenzy	The dot-com frenzy	Not applicable	Not applicable
Competition & winning	Capture market share	Build market share	Ignored the competition	Responded to competition
Organizational culture	Loose	Loose	Complacency	Many vested interests compete
Managerial optimism	Very high	Very high	Optimistic that current model was just fine	Not a major factor
Hubris	Yes	Yes	Overconfidence in existing market	Not a major factor
Compensation	Incredible stock options	Yes	Not applicable	In general not major, except for specialist firms on the floor
Invulnerability	Probably not	Probably not	Of current market	Of current market
Market Factors				
Pressures for growth	Extreme	Extreme	Yes; losing market share	Yes; slight loss in market share
Investment bankers	Yes	Yes	Not applicable	Not applicalbe
Stock analysts	Definitely	Definitely	Not applicable	Not applicable
Stock price	Yes	Yes	Not applicable	Not applicable
Unrealistic business models	Totally, especially for logistics	Yes; much industrial purchasing is by yearly contract	Yes; existing business model threatened by ECNs	Is a physical floor and specialist system a viable model in the twenty-first century?
Winner's Curse	Seen as a winner at IPO; went through $700 million in 18 months and entered bankruptcy	A winner in the capital markets until revenue problems and the dot-com market meltdown	Status quo too long; trying to revive market share with SuperMontage	Trying initiatives with technology and procedures to protect current business model

Force/Example	Merrill Lynch	IBM	DEC
Psychological and Personal Factors			
Buying & bidding psychology	Not applicable	Not applicable	Not applicable
Competition & winning	Highly competitive firm	Highly competitive	Highly competitive
Organizational culture	Culture of success	Bureaucracy	Autocracy
Managerial optimism	Extensive	Yes	Yes, especially from Ken Olsen
Hubris	Extensive	Occasional	Olsen
Compensation	Generous	Not a major factor	Not a major factor
Invulnerability	General sense of being number one in the industry	Yes; the most successful computer firm to date; reliance on the mainframe	Feeling that minis were invulnerable to PCs
Market Factors			
Pressures for growth	Yes	Yes	Yes
Investment bankers	Not a major factor	Not a major factor	Not a major factor
Stock analysts	Not a major factor	Not a major factor	Not a major factor
Stock price	Yes; wake-up call when Schwab's valuation exceeded Merrill's	Collapse of stock price awakened the board	Collapse of stock price encouraged DEC to sell out to Compaq
Unrealistic business models	Yes; lack of online trading a major drawback	Technology changed; a business model based only on the mainframe was not viable	Technology changed; a business model based only on minis was not viable
Winner's Curse	Complacency; Merrill changed its strategy and business model to respond to online trading	Complacency; Gerstner brought a new strategy, successful so far	Complacency and hubris; DEC merged with Compaq and disappeared in HP-Compaq merger

assessment of the value of the spectrum. It happened in the rollercoaster 1990s, when everyone was excited about technology and the dramatic changes that the Internet could deliver.

Around the same time, companies that wanted to become major players in optical communications went shopping aggressively for start-ups with potential, though frequently unproven, technology. The biggest companies, like Lucent and Nortel, despite their histories of conservatism became like kids in a candy store, outbidding each other and paying huge amounts of money for optical technology. In a number of cases, the products they paid for never came to market and the companies they bought had to be shut down.

Mergers and acquisitions (M&As), which are considered essential for implementing certain strategies, provide a nice stage for the Winner's Curse to play itself out. When a company is thinking of acquiring another company or merging with it, besides the strategic fit, the question is always: what should be paid for the transaction? Most chief executives use a combination of analysis by well-trained and experienced financial analysts and gut feel to determine the final price to be paid. The chief financial officers then have to determine the financial instruments to be used—cash, stocks, debentures, and so on—to execute the deal. While pricing M&As is not an exact science and mistakes can easily be made, in many instances, we saw a flawed analysis or no analysis at all, leading to a huge overpayment and the Winner's Curse. The Curse was clearly present for Tyco, MCI-WorldCom, AOL Time-Warner, Vivendi, and especially for the companies known as serial acquirers. Some of these companies ended up cooking their books to make them look better because of the huge financial drains caused by their M&A activities.

Sometimes being a winner in the past tends to disorient future decisions. An organization that is on top continues to see itself as a winner only needing to consolidate its position, and complacency sets in. The NASDAQ and the New York Stock Exchange examples show what happens when you maintain the status quo. These two organizations had to scramble to catch up to electronic markets and other forms of technology-based competition. The Merrill Lynch case also illustrates this problem; it continued to work on improving its traditional channels of customer relationships while Charles Schwab went headlong into the Internet. Merrill was lucky enough and strong enough to be able to turn around its business model and compete with online stock trading.

IBM and DEC are also powerful examples of what can happen to the long-term winner. The former rested on its laurels of being the winner in large mainframe computing, and the latter was the winner in mini-computers. Complacency blinded them to the advent of new computing paradigms. Only IBM has survived, and it has done so by instituting a radically new business strategy and plan.

That being a winner in the past may actually curse future decisions is best known in sports. Time and again, owners and general managers of sports teams pay millions of dollars to acquire or trade for players and coaches who have just completed excellent seasons, only to find that they have a bust on their hands. In fact, among many players, it is a well-known course of action to play their very best during the last year of their contracts so that they land somewhere else with a fatter paycheck. Many articles have been written in *Sports Illustrated* about the acrimony between players and coaches, especially in basketball, over playing time during the last year of a contract. During this last year, players want in whether or not they are injured and whether or not they fit into the offensive or defensive schemes at the time. The new teams that win these players either get players past their primes or with hidden injuries. Getting coaches with excellent winning records is not immune to this curse. Witness the record of the Florida coach Steve Spurrier, who went from virtual domination in college football with 122 victories in 12 seasons, 7 SEC championships, and one national title to complete failure as head coach of the Washington Redskins. Dan Snyder was left holding a completely demoralized franchise.

One of the best publicized examples of the Winner's Curse happened in Hollywood. Michael Cimino made the Oscar-winning movie *The Deer Hunter*, which grossed more than $100 million on a budget of less than $10 million. He was considered a star who could do no wrong and was able to get support for a project which eventually was called *Heaven's Gate*. His original budget of $10 million kept getting bigger and bigger and was justified by the fact that Cimino was a winner. After spending more than $35 million, Cimino produced a dud that was not only a financial flop, but was also ridiculed by the film critics. Hollywood has not learned much. All actors or directors have to do is have one financially successful film, and they can command huge salaries and percentages of their next movie's gross.

Why is the Winner's Curse so prevalent?

We began the book with a simple model in figure 1-1 and with table 1-2, which illustrated two kinds of factors that promote the Winner's Curse, and we have seen how these factors have contributed to the problems encountered in the examples in table 9-1. These drivers of the Curse include the psychological and personal factors of buying and bidding psychology, competition and winning, organizational culture, managerial optimism, hubris, compensation, and invulnerability; and the market factors of pressures for growth, investment bankers, stock analysts, stock price, and unrealistic business models. Although it might seem as though these factors operate independently, as we review the examples, we can see that they interact and reinforce each other.

A history of winning, a competitive nature, and sometimes the culture of the organization encourage managers to overbid for acquisitions, new drugs, movies, star athletes, and senior managers to run their firms. A track record of winning makes the manager more optimistic. High levels of compensation encourage hubris and a lack of humility. All of these factors combine to produce a sense of invulnerability, which in turn leads the manager to take short cuts when confronted with the need to value an acquisition or other potential purchase.

Market factors also motivate the manager, for example, by applying ongoing pressures for growth. Investment bankers are eager for companies to grow through mergers and acquisitions as that is how they earn lucrative fees. Stock analysts produce favorable reports on companies that grow and that helps keep the stock price high so that stock can be used to buy other companies. If stock prices fall too much, senior managers' jobs are in jeopardy, so there is more than one reason to try to keep stock prices up. Unrealistic business models doomed many of the dot-coms, and business models that once worked but are no longer viable contribute to the Winner's Curse.

Some additional factors that lead to the Curse

In addition to the psychological and personal factors and the market factors in our model, we observed other pressures that contribute to the Winner's Curse. The need to win and the way winning ends up creating significant distortions frequently reflect personality effects at play. Equally, the market provides rewards and incentives to win at all cost.

Personality traits

There are many stories about the personalities of leaders in American industry and multinational companies. The results are mixed. In some cases, successful executives tend to focus on transactional issues and in some cases transformational issues. In the latter cases, companies are headed by charismatic leaders who are visionary and able to create consensus around a strategy to reach the goals of the company. In transactional leadership, it is important to have the personality to manage the operational aspects of the firm.

An interesting study by the Hagberg Consulting Group examined the personality traits of executives whose companies were in trouble in 2002, roughly the end of the period that we have examined in this book.[1] From their comprehensive list, all of the executives in the companies we analyzed seem to have exhibited at least some of the following characteristics:

- More intelligent than other executives, often "brilliant" technical experts
- Intellectually arrogant, "know it all"
- Too inspirational, substitute vision for domain knowledge
- Skeptical of others' ideas, stubborn, and unyielding
- Slow to adapt to change, risk-averse about new opportunities
- Circle the wagons, hold on, and defend

All of these are reflective of Type A personality traits. The first three traits are strong enough to launch companies into the unknown successfully or unsuccessfully. The last three traits ensure that there are little or no changes to old winning ways, although being skeptical of others' ideas could work either way.

These personality characteristics of executives in trouble can and did lead their companies to the Winner's Curse. In many cases, once the executive in charge decided on acquiring something, whether it was wireless spectrum or another company, a Type A personality led to the need to compete and win. Executives in large firms acquiring start-ups, the CEOs of the start-ups themselves, and those in the venture capital firms who had private equity investments in the start-ups had extensive technological expertise and knowledge. In the roaring 1990s, these technology experts used

1. Hagberg Consulting Group, *Profiles of Executives in Trouble* White Paper (Foster City, Calif., 2002).

their intellectual superiority to steamroller deals from which they should have walked away.

Many of the managers who brought the Winner's Curse on their firms were arrogant. Arrogance is a real danger because it encourages managers to make decisions themselves and to execute them without due diligence. Gerald Levin reportedly decided over a weekend to merge Time-Warner with AOL, the largest merger in history, without extensive consultation with senior management at Time-Warner. Arrogance and a know-it-all personality make managers complacent about doing the right systems and life-cycle analyses for new acquisitions.

Dennis Kozlowski, the former CEO of Tyco, was legendary in his stubbornness and refusal to listen to others' opinions. He was going to build the company by acquisition, no matter what. He had a sense of invulnerability that affected a number of situations when he confused professional and personal gain. How much analysis did Tyco undertake of its acquisitions before making offers? The strong visionary personality of the CEO might also persuade the other executives and the board of directors to go along with him with only a cursory analysis of financial and operational factors governing the decision. There could be a shared belief that the CEO was good at managing the integration of any company or technology acquired or in ensuring profitability even in a suspect situation.

The boards at companies with stubborn, able, intellectually arrogant, visionary leaders abrogated their responsibilities because doing otherwise could be quite costly. The boards could also be swayed by the charismatic personalities of the chief executives. Were the boards at Tyco fully involved in the purchase of CIT Financial, and what about First Union's board when it bought the Money Store?

Know-it-all managers are also excessively optimistic and feel invulnerable; they tend to consider only their preferred outcome. A thorough analysis looks at multiple scenarios, not just the one everyone is hoping for. In the cases of Tyco and CIT Financial, First Union and the Money Store, the Washington Redskins, and the AOL Time-Warner merger, among others, it looks like those involved did not look beyond the most optimistic scenarios.

Then there are the CEOs of IBM and Digital Equipment Corporation, who were risk-averse about making a change. A closed mind and denial of evidence help a firm get the full benefits of complacency. When it was obvious that there was miniaturization of component parts and that microprocessors were getting faster and faster, the executives at IBM simply circled the wagons and tried to make their mainframes better. Even if IBM and DEC were unaware of the appeal of emerging technologies to their customers, it was no secret from the rest of the world. Industry publications constantly trumpeted the decline of the mainframe and extolled the virtues of personal computers. Articles on client-server computing pointed out for years that it was hard for customers to see a role for the mainframe in this model and that IBM needed to do something to protect its franchise. The explosive sale of personal computers and their myriad applications in industry should have made it apparent to DEC that PCs offer serious computing and that they threatened the market for more expensive minicomputers.

When Steve Jobs and Steve Wozniak came out with the first Apple computer, the executives at IBM started to scramble to get into what was called the microcomputer market. However, they wanted to be in the hardware business and did not think that they could make money on operating systems. The legend goes that at a meeting with Bill Gates, the 20-year-old CEO of a fledgling company, who was introduced to IBM by his mother, Mary, they "let the kid do it." IBM gave up the operating system franchise to Microsoft. The conservative-but-determined personality trait turned out to be a boon to Microsoft, but was a multibillion-dollar opportunity loss for IBM.

Decision-making psychology

Clearly, individual personality traits affect the way decisions are made and could result in the Winner's Curse. However, there are a number of psychological factors that also enter decision making under uncertainty. The relationship of psychology and decision making has a long history of scholarship. The Nobel Prize in economics for 2002 was given to Princeton economist Daniel Kahneman for research that he did jointly with the late Amos Tversky, a professor at Stanford University, on the biases inherent in decision making under uncertainty. In many of the cases we examined, psychological biases also entered the picture, leading to the outcome of the Winner's Curse. The main point is simple: managerial decisions are fraught with uncertainty, and when dealing with these uncertainties one should be careful not to succumb to biased behavior.

We will use the constructs summarized in the Tversky, Slovic, and Kahneman book, *Judgment under Uncertainty: Heuristics and Biases*, to understand the problem.[2]

Representativeness bias.   People rely on the representativeness, the degree to which the thing about which they are trying to make a decision is similar, or *represents*, a previous outcome. The problem is that people are insensitive to the history of prior outcomes.

Even when it was clear that only one in ten technology acquisition investments had succeeded in the past, Lucent and Nortel assumed that the companies they bought would be successful. Why this confidence? The executives could always point to a successful company with similar characteristics and the same technology space to argue their case. The unwarranted confidence created by the representativeness bias is an illusion of validity. Thus, the executives at the large telecommunications equipment companies minimized the risk of optical acquisitions. If Lucent had used better knowledge about the true risk, it would have spent far less on acquisitions.

Availability bias.   Most people succumb to vivid or more recent information than to information that is complex or dated. For example, individuals assume a much larger risk probability of airline accidents than automobile accidents, even though the risk of a car crash is two orders of magnitude higher than the former. Airline crashes are highlighted in television and newspapers because of their rarity and magnitude, and these images stick in people's minds.

Most of the cases we examined occurred during a time when the stock market was booming and the global economy was expanding at a terrific rate. There were few reports of company failures; the airwaves were filled with success stories. Everyone was optimistic, and no one believed that they would fail in any venture. Clearly, company executives should try to stay above this psychology and do the proper analyses before making decisions. In an environment like this, executives overestimated the frequency of success and were resistant to contradictory data in many of the cases we reported. One could say that availability bias was everywhere, and it is not surprising that there were many instances of the Winner's Curse.

2. A. Tversky, P. Slovic, and D. Kahneman, eds., *Judgment under Uncertainty: Heuristics and Biases* (Cambridge: Cambridge University Press, 1982).

Anchoring bias.   In numerous experiments, psychology researchers have found that people make estimates by starting from an initial value, an *anchor*, that is adjusted to yield the final answer. If we have a history of triumph, then our anchor for the probability of success is too high. As a result, we tend to underestimate the probabilities of failure in complex systems.

If executives have a history of winning, they tend to believe that winning will persist. A track record of winning anchors the assessment of executives, makes them more optimistic, and encourages them to overbid for acquisitions, new drugs, and movies, to name a few. This story plays over and over again in the sports arena, where past history, even a single season of winning, anchors decisions about whom to pick for a team and what to pay them.

Another arena in which the anchoring bias leads to the Winner's Curse is overoptimism about integrating new technology into an existing product line. If a chief executive has been successful in completing and implementing an acquisition of a small company, it does not mean the success will translate into the acquisition of a larger, more complex company. The WorldCom case is an illustration of the overestimation of the probability of success for complex ventures. Its executives did not envisage failure because of their previous experience with small, successful mergers.

Tversky and Kahneman also developed *prospect theory*, which is concerned with the differential psychology of winning and losing. They discovered that most people react in a counterintuitive way about winning versus losing a chance event. If you consider a poker table in Las Vegas, it turns out that once people *win* a few hundred dollars (say, $500), they tend to stop and do something else, play another game or attend an entertainment event. Conversely, at the same poker table, if someone is losing, she will tend to stay to see if it is possible to win back her losses. Those who are losing tend to get more and more aggressive in their betting in order to try and recover all their losses in one fell swoop. People are risk-averse about winning, but risk-prone (or risk-seeking) about losing.

In many of the companies we examined, an acquisition or merger that went wrong only increased the determination of the chief executive to do the next deal, and do it right. While this behavior could be caused in part by personal arrogance, we believe that the widespread occurrence of negative outcomes led to a greater tendency to take risks.

Most managers we have met are uncomfortable with business uncertainty and exhibit the psychological effects that we have described when dealing with risky decisions. One does not need an advanced degree in statistics or psychology to evaluate risky decisions and potential outcomes. Managers who recognize the problems of making decisions under uncertainty should be able to avoid the Winner's Curse.

The interaction of market and financial incentives

Market and financial incentives helped to promote the Winner's Curse in our examples. Our model includes a number of market factors, and we cannot stress enough how these different factors interact with some of the psychological factors, like managerial compensation. The compensation of executives in large firms is much greater than the compensation of executives in small firms. So there is a strong incentive to make firms bigger and bigger, usually by acquisitions. Further, the board of directors usually rewards the chief executive for seemingly successful events, such as technology acquisitions or short-term revenue growth. It has become the norm to tie the compensation package of senior management to the company's stock performance.

During the heady 1990s, many companies saw their valuations in the stock market increase at a tremendous rate, and their CEOs' pay increased even faster. As Holly Sklar wrote in *Business Week*, "CEOs aren't shy about claiming all the credit for company success to justify taking a big chunk of the rewards."[3] Tyco CEO Dennis Kozlowski told *Business Week*, "While I gained $139 million [in stock options], I created about $37 billion in wealth for our shareholders." As Sklar states, "thousands of Tyco employees in 80 countries didn't have anything to do with creating that wealth. Many CEOs make more in a year than their employees will make in a lifetime. According to *Business Week*'s 2003 survey of executive pay, average CEO compensation has reached $34,000 a day, including Saturdays and Sundays. In 1980, CEOs made 42 times the pay of average factory workers. In 1990, they made 85 times as much. By 1999, CEOs made 475 times as much as workers."[4]

The short-term growth of companies could have resulted from a merger, even if the acquired company were wildly unprofitable. Investment bankers are eager for companies to grow through mergers and

---

3. Holly Sklar, "Minimum Wage in the Millions," http://www.inequality.org/sklar2.html.
4. The preceding paragraph has parts of Holly Sklar's article "Minimum Wage in the Millions" verbatim.

acquisitions as that is how they earn lucrative fees. Stock analysts produce favorable reports on companies that grow. High levels of compensation also encourage hubris and a lack of humility and produce a sense of invulnerability. Compensation, which is usually tied to winning, leads the manager to take short cuts when confronted with the need to value an acquisition or other potential purchase. So the incentive to grow at all costs contributes to the Winner's Curse both directly and indirectly through the psychology it creates of hubris and invulnerability.

There were some strange compensation packages during this period. Disney made headlines in 2001 when it was discovered that CEO Eisner was given a salary increase, 2 million stock options in the Disney Internet Group valued at $37 million, and an $11.5 million bonus after three years in which Disney's net income fell by more than half, from $1.9 billion to $920 million. As we have chronicled, the board at Disney was infamous for providing an incredible severance package for the failed executive Michael Ovitz. He negotiated a generous severance package at a time when he was considered a winner who could bring Disney out of the doldrums. In fact, the compensation package was so lopsided as to actually distort the incentives for Ovitz to perform well. The behavior of the Disney board was suspect enough that a Delaware judge criticized it severely for not acting in the best interest of the company's shareholders.

Wall Street played its role in quite an insidious way. The boards of companies frequently compensated executives using stock options that were closely tied to the market signals provided by Wall Street. If stock prices fell too much, senior managers' jobs were in jeopardy, and chief executives in companies were cordial to analysts who could talk up their companies and hence their stock prices. It was difficult for any critical Wall Street analyst to get a seat at the table. It was a vicious cycle. Analysts who talked up the stock price were given privileged information and could write reports that were better informed than their peers. These analysts, like Jack Grubman and Mary Meeker, were then considered the stars in the analyst community due to their public reports. The predictions of the star analysts were taken to be the final word. Many junior analysts and analysts in smaller boutique firms simply mimicked the reports of the stars. Analysts' reports helped create a consensus about a firm, and the analysts wrote their reports with information provided by executives who would personally benefit from a positive recommendation about the company. Clearly, incentives to be fair, free, and forthright simply went out the window.

As we have highlighted, investment banks made a lot of money by taking start-up companies in the Internet and technology space public. Investment banks and their analysts also had built-in incentives to be nice to these companies. So all in all, there was little financial incentive to analyze companies honestly and certainly no incentive to be critical. These extremely positive market signals and stock market valuations gave the executives a distorted view of how well they were performing. It is no wonder that while their stocks and stock options were doing well, it was difficult for them to think that their winning strategy was wrong. If anything, they tried to do more of the same.

Why win?

The love of athletics and sporting events is a common denominator around the world, and the assumption is that one always goes for victory. Woody Hayes, the celebrated football coach at Ohio State, is supposed to have said, "Show me a good loser, and I'll show you a loser." While there are some useful analogies between athletics and life, an obsession with winning is not one of them. As we have seen, many companies that have won are now worse off because of the Winner's Curse.

Consider mergers and acquisitions, where the company initiating the merger believes that it will advance its strategy. In a football game, you have to play the opponent that is on the field. In the case of a merger, it is likely that there is another company that is similar enough to fit your strategy should the present target not work out. In business you can, in fact, change the other team on the field. There are CEOs who make a practice of avoiding hostile takeovers for two reasons. In a hostile merger, the price of the company being acquired is usually bid up, and the hostility involved makes it hard to integrate the two firms after the merger. There may well be another less ideal but more amicable target that one can acquire with many fewer problems. The need to win drives CEOs to ignore the latter for the former. The less-than-ideal situation with respect to the latter is used as a justification for the need to win.

The seller at an auction wants to focus the buyers on winning and paying the highest possible price for whatever is being auctioned. How much better off would the European telecom firms be today if they had not succumbed to government efforts to earn as much money as possible from auctioning spectrums? Could telecom managers have dropped out of the bidding and picked up licenses in a secondary market? Could these managers have foreseen the industry's inability to build out 3G networks because they had such huge debt loads from buying licenses? What would be the position today of a telecom company that refused to overpay for spectrum and concentrated instead on improving existing technology?

Can you avoid being seduced by the psychology of winning and the excitement of the auction? The objective bidder looks at not only this auction, but the aftermath of the auction as well. Was anyone in the optical industry looking objectively at the amount of fiber that was being installed? It is estimated that more than 80% of the fiber in the United States is dark, that is, unused right now due to overcapacity. It is easy to understand 10% or 20% unused, but how could an industry install so much capacity that 20% or less is in use? The seller does not want the buyer to be objective, but objectivity is one of the best defenses against experiencing the Winner's Curse.

The point is that there are many possible ways to win and focusing on just one can lead to the Winner's Curse. Sailing offers a better analogy here than football. Sailboats cannot sail directly into the wind. To make progress to windward, a sailboat has to tack back and forth at an angle to the wind. Often, one tack is favored because of the wind direction and the current; you will make more progress toward your destination on that tack, but eventually you will have to go off on the other tack. In a merger or an auction, there is more than one strategy to achieve your objectives, just as there are several different ways a sailboat can achieve its objective. By focusing on winning in the short term, you may end up a loser in the long term.

The argument here is simple: you need to focus not on winning, but on understanding the implications of both winning and losing and especially the alternatives available if you do not win today. In the next chapter, we look at ways to improve the analysis of situations that can lead to the Winner's Curse.

Conclusions

This chapter has summarized the examples in the book that provide evidence for the existence of the Winner's Curse. We find the evidence compelling; the Curse does exist, and it has wreaked havoc on many firms and individuals. There are also many examples, which we did not discuss, of firms that made successful decisions. Why do some firms suffer from the Curse and others manage to escape? We believe that the real winners, the individuals and companies that succeed, do things differently than the companies analyzed in this book, and in the last chapter we explore ways that you can join their ranks. You too can avoid experiencing the Winner's Curse.

10 • Avoiding the Winner's Curse

We hope the examples in this book have convinced you that the Winner's Curse is a serious threat to businesses and managers. There are two main points to take away from our analysis. The Winner's Curse is prevalent to an alarming degree in a variety of industries and occurs from the confluence of a number of factors. Knowing these cultural, personality, and psychological factors and the set of market-based mechanisms that contribute to the Winner's Curse should help organizations guard against it. In addition to moderating the factors that contribute to experiencing the Curse, there are some positive steps that companies can take to improve the quality of their decisions. This chapter offers suggestions to reduce the chance of experiencing the Winner's Curse. (See figure 10-1 and table 10-1 for summaries of our advice.)

We want to make it clear at the outset that we do not believe that every industry is ripe for the problem of the Winner's Curse, nor that every auction winner experiences it. Far from it; in fact, American and global businesses offer numerous examples of success, many in industries that we analyzed. Verizon is a telecommunications company that started out as Bell Atlantic and merged with NYNEX to form an even stronger company.

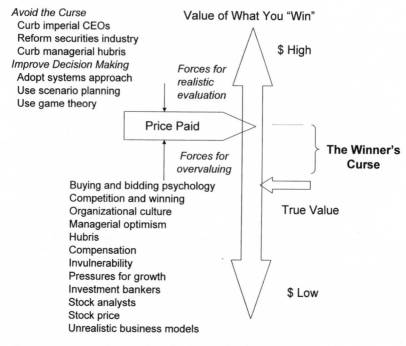

Figure 10-1. Strategies to reduce the chances for the Curse

Verizon has played its cards right in spectrum auctions to emerge as the largest wireless company in the United States. Even in the world of optical equipment and dot-coms, there are success stories, such as Alcatel, which turned away at the last moment from merging with Lucent. Another success is eBay, which has been steadfast in building a sustained business model while winning market share by acquiring the right companies.

The problem of the Winner's Curse has been significant in world business in recent years and in some cases, like telecommunications, has had an adverse impact on the economy as a whole. The complexity of the environment in which business decisions are made is further compounded by built-in incentives to succumb to the Winner's Curse. In addition to acknowledging the factors we highlighted in the previous chapter, what is needed are organizational checks and balances, proper incentive mechanisms, and new business analytics to ensure that managers make proper decisions. Ray Smith, former CEO of Verizon, puts it this way:

Leadership . . . is all about making decisions in the midst of complexity—something that traditional management systems fail woefully to

Table 10-1. Approaches for avoiding the Winner's Curse

Avoiding the Winner's Curse
  Curb the imperial CEO
    Create a truly independent board
    Control CEO compensation and incentives
    Appoint an expert advisory board
  Reduce conflict of interest in the securities industry
  Curb the hubris of CEO and senior management
    Seek a second opinion
    Look for consensus estimates on valuations
    Avoid high-pressure auction settings
    Do not be afraid to lose
    Do not assume past behavior and success are perfect predictors of the future

Improving Valuation Decisions
  Adopt a systems approach for decision making
    Strive for effective problem solving
    Implement more effective corporate planning
    Provide effective leadership
    Avoid the founder's syndrome
  Use scenario planning
  Use game theory
    Analyze decisions through the eyes of competitors
    Reassess assumptions and decisions continually

prepare executives to do. To succeed in this sometimes baffling environment, managers have to devise dynamic new systems to assist them. These systems must do the following:

- They have to give managers a way of analyzing the impact of conflicting, sometimes contradictory market forces.
- They have to eliminate the blind spots that prevent managers from seeing all the consequences of their decisions.
- They have to help managers change direction as the environment changes.
- And they have to do all this in real time, so that the organization remains limber enough to move at exactly the right strategic moment—and not a moment later.[1]

In this chapter, we propose mechanisms through which you can moderate the potential of the Winner's Curse. We divide our recom-

---

1. Taken from "Business as a War Game: A Report from the Battlefront," *Fortune*, September 30, 1996.

mendations into two groups: mechanisms to reduce the impact of factors favoring the Winner's Curse and approaches to evaluating decisions that minimize the chances of experiencing it.

Mechanisms and policies to avoid the Winner's Curse

There are a number of changes in industry and within firms that can help to reduce the factors associated with the Winner's Curse. The approaches in this section are intended to attack and weaken the forces shown in figure 10-1. Many of these steps are needed to reduce the chances of experiencing the Curse, but they are not sufficient. The suggestions in this section need to be combined with some of the techniques in the next section, which will help to improve the quality of the decisions you make when evaluating various options for your business.

Curbing the hubris of the imperial CEO

We have seen several examples of imperial CEOs, managers who provided such strong leadership that they could only be classified as autocrats. Whether they have staked their claim through previous successes or sheer intellectual superiority, the trouble with these CEOs is that they stop listening and begin to believe they know everything. They ridicule dissenting voices within their organizations and easily ignore warning signals in the marketplace. Imperial CEOs want to win at everything they undertake in order to perpetuate their image of being infallible. This behavior produced the costly victories of the serial acquirers. Winning at all costs also undermined many companies in spectrum auctions and in the optical technology industry. Imperial CEOs are so sure that what they and their companies are doing is correct that they develop complacency from sitting on their winning laurels. We saw this behavior play itself out in the computer industry.

How do you replace CEO hubris with organizational humility? In the cases we examined, senior management in addition to the CEO displayed a level of self-confidence out of proportion to their companies' performance. We believe that much of this decision-making arrogance comes from the CEO's and senior management's view of their intellectual superiority and their level of compensation, which puts them in an altogether different financial orbit than the rest of the firm's employees. It is not unusual to hear, "If you are so smart, how come you are not rich?" It may well be common to feel condescension toward those who earn much less. Given that the final line of control over the actions of senior management, especially the CEO, is the board of directors, there are some actions that boards can take to curb the hubris of the imperial CEO. The board should seriously discuss some of the following questions:

How should the CEO be compensated?   How many multiples of the lowest-paid employee's salary should the CEO's salary be? How many multiples of the second highest paid executive should the CEO's salary be? We know of one company where the chairperson's annual salary (without stock options or bonus) was five times the salary of the next highest paid manager. Is the CEO that much more important than the other managers and workers in the company? In a number of cases we examined, the astronomical sums paid seemed to directly contribute to the sense of infallibility and arrogance of the CEO.

Since 1980, the average pay of workers has increased just 74%, while CEO pay grew a whopping 1,884%, according to the AFL-CIO. An article in the *Sacramento Bee* describes a report by the Institute for Policy Studies and United for a Fair Economy: "[T]heir report 'Executive Excess 2001,' . . . details the factors that led to the meteoric rise of CEO salaries, which now average $13.1 million a year, 531 times the pay of the average production worker's salary of $24,668."[2]

How should senior management be compensated?   Balaji Krishnamurthy, president of Planar Systems, has implemented a novel bonus plan that other companies might well consider.[3] Shareholders of the flat panel display manufacturer are the first to receive bonuses after the company has achieved tough operating income goals. After the shareholders are satisfied, then rank-and-file workers receive their quarterly or annual bonuses. Only when these employees receive their bonuses do middle managers receive bonuses. Senior executives come next, and Krishnamurthy, as CEO, is the last person to get a bonus.

What kind of perquisites are appropriate for senior management? Can the board demonstrate shareholder value from corporate aircraft? Should the board provide living quarters in different cities for the CEO? Given

2. http://classic.sacbee.com/ib/news/old/ib_news03_20010924.html.
3. *Wall Street Journal*, April 14, 2003.

different scenarios for the stock, how much are senior executives likely to receive in extra compensation through their options? Should the CEO be rewarded for a general increase in the stock market, or for the relative performance of the company? Consider adopting a scheme often seen in Europe, where stock options are pegged to the performance of a specific industry rather than to general market performance.

It is likely that the SEC accounting board or the FASB (Financial Accounting Standards Board) will require firms to expense stock options when granted, using some kind of options pricing model like Black-Scholes to value them. This requirement may reduce the popularity of options since they have been seen as free compensation. We should encourage the immediate expensing of options in order to help reduce the counterproductive behavior they motivate. As mentioned above, stock options should be based on the relative performance of a firm in its industry in order to control for the effects of general trends in the stock market. Stock options should also be awarded broadly in the company, with much less of a gap between the CEO and other employees. In July 2003, Microsoft announced a dramatic reduction in the use of stock options and a move toward direct stock compensation. If this move catches on, then some of the excesses from options should disappear, though the board will still have to decide what constitutes a reasonable program to award stock to employees.

Creating a truly independent board

To provide more effective oversight and to reduce the power of the CEO, boards need to become truly independent of the CEO. One way to accomplish this is to have a maximum of three insiders as board members and to have no insiders on the nominating committee for new board members. In addition, insiders should not be allowed to suggest new board members. Insiders on the board should be able to review the nominating committee's candidate list and strike individuals to whom they object. But the CEO should not be able to pick board members.

Shareholders also need to verify the performance of the board on an ongoing basis. They need to ask the following questions:

- Is the board willing to disagree with the CEO? Would the board ever say that the company should walk away from a deal?
- Does the board meet regularly without management present (a new requirement of the Sarbanes–Oxley Act of 2002)?

- Should the board consider splitting the COO and CEO functions by having a non-executive chairperson of the board?
- Does management provide the board with periodic presentations on the market and the company's position in that market? Does the board talk about new directions in the industry?

Appointing an advisory board of experts

In most of the cases we examined, one of the reasons for the existence of the Winner's Curse was excitement about the industry in general (for example, optics and wireless), or overoptimism about the revenue potential for a particular product or service (for example, dot-coms). It is important for the CEO and the board to be informed by an outside advisory board of domain experts who may provide a more realistic perspective on the corporate decisions than internal managers. This group should examine major decisions like acquisitions, new product development, trends in the marketplace, and so on. Their role is to see if the "emperor has no clothes," to provide outside perspective. This group, had it existed at Tyco, would have questioned the acquisition process and the prices paid for some acquisitions. Such a group would have given feedback to DEC and IBM about their models of the computing industry and marketplace.

Members of the board serve as devil's advocates for proposals. They also look at emerging business trends and forecasts and try to shock the firm out of complacency and inertia. In addition to being skeptics, when they find that a proposal is worth pursuing, they should become cheerleaders for it. This group is also charged with testing the realism of current and proposed business models. They would have warned IBM, DEC, and Merrill Lynch about their existing models and would have suggested new directions. Questions they should ask include:

- Is there a strategic plan? How viable is it? Does the firm manage according to the plan?
- Have we reviewed the due diligence on every acquisition or merger? Do we understand the rationale for each offer? Have we reviewed the plans for combining the operations of the companies?
- What is the state of R&D in the company? Is anyone looking for disruptive technologies?
- Is the organization structured to accomplish its goals?
- Is the board representing the shareholders?

The board should consist of five independent members and should be well compensated. Members should have a variety of backgrounds so they can help assess business risk; for example, a board might consist of members with experience in accounting, technology, finance, marketing, and general management.

Would a thorough evaluation of the AOL Time-Warner business model have withstood such scrutiny? Would independent reviewers have agreed with the optimistic forecasts of digital convergence? Independent boards of directors and boards of advisors should thoroughly examine proposed business models with a skeptical perspective.

Equally important as looking at new business models is thinking carefully about old models. These boards also need to be alert to the onset of complacency for the long-term winner. The skeptics should encourage management to conduct studies and do research about likely trends in their industry that could prove to be frame breaking or disruptive. This investigation should lead to discussions of significant questions, including: Is the firm's existing business model viable today? Will it succeed tomorrow? Would a truly independent board of directors, aided by a questioning advisory board, have let the mainframe dominate IBM for so long? Would it have accepted Ken Olsen's statements that PCs were just a toy?

Be aware on a personal level

There are a number of things that can be done by individuals to ensure that the Winner's Curse is avoided, or at least minimized. These include:

- Always seek a second opinion. When you are making a major decision, ask for help; important decisions demand multiple views.
- Look for a consensus estimate on value. You and your colleagues must be convinced of the possible range of values for any acquisition.
- Try to avoid high-pressure auction-like settings. We know that people are caught up in the excitement of auctions. Sometimes you cannot avoid them, for example, if you need to purchase a spectrum license and the only way is through a government auction. However, you need to have a firm stopping rule that says that your company will not bid beyond a specified amount.
- Realize that losing is not always a bad thing. Every situation you encounter is not a contest; there is a time to fold up your tent and go home. Wouldn't Tyco's shareholders be better off if it had not

won CIT Financial? Wouldn't the employees of United Artists be better off if the company had not been so impressed with *The Deer Hunter's* Oscar and therefore not invested far too much in *Heaven's Gate*?

- Ask if past behavior is always a good predictor of the future. Is it clear that a coach is always responsible for how a team performs, or is it more likely that a combination of players, management, and the coach determines outcomes? Does an Oscar mean that every subsequent movie will be a hit, or does a bestselling book guarantee the sales of the author's next book?

Improving evaluation decisions

The recommendations above are directed at minimizing the factors that we have seen lead to the Winner's Curse (figure 10-1). Our suggestions have dealt with psychological and personal factors and with market factors that make an individual or organization susceptible to the Curse. In doing research for this book, it became clear that the chances of encountering the Curse would be far less if certain decision-making processes in organizations could be improved. In the rest of this chapter, we present some of these ideas.

Adopting a systems approach to decision making

An important way to reduce the possibility of the Winner's Curse is to use systems thinking when faced with business decisions, especially decisions that involve valuing an asset. In fast-moving bidding situations, using a systems approach is critical to guard against seat-of-the pants judgments. The systems approach includes relationships beyond the decision faced by the CEO or senior management. It attempts to identify all of the variables that influence a decision and describes the likely impact of each possible outcome.

For example, consider a specific decision problem a telecom manager is facing. How much should she bid for a license to provide third-generation wireless services? The telecom company would first decide on how much the spectrum license is worth and would instruct the manager to bid up to this amount. As we saw in chapter 2, caught up in the pressure to win the spectrum auction, managers often bid much more than the value of the licenses. The result has been that telecom companies have taken on a massive debt that they have yet to get out from under.

The reason for this outcome is the narrow focus of the wireless services departments of the telecom companies. Most wireless managers participated in the spectrum auction with the view that if they did not get the licenses, they would be shut out of the new data services that the winners would offer in the future. A systems approach to the same bidding problem would have examined their actions in the light of the company and industry as a whole. Figure 10-2 presents such an analysis; note that it includes outcomes beyond the bid. The systems approach places a decision in a larger context and defines relationships with other variables in the system. It anticipates the outcome of a decision and shows its possible impacts.

Perhaps it was better for the wireless company in this example not to be a player in the most advanced wireless services. In fact, there may have been a number of other options open to the company to provide useful data services using the wireless spectrum it already had. Further, having a systems (or, in this case, companywide) perspective would have made the wireless managers realize that they needed to limit overall debt, otherwise everyone in the company would lose. A complete systems view might have predicted the outcomes from overbidding depicted in figure 10-2: the failure to build new systems, the failure to purchase new equipment, and the impact of all of this on telecom manufacturers and the economy.

Using a systems approach to decision making is difficult in business because of the way companies are organized and the way in which man-

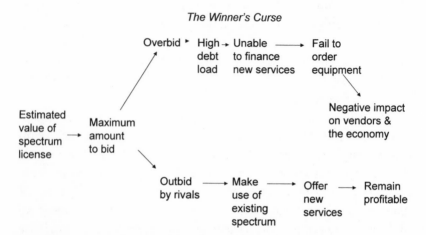

Figure 10-2. A system approach to spectrum auctions

agers are rewarded. Systems thinking is fundamentally different from traditional forms of analysis. Traditional analysis focuses on separating the individual pieces of what is being studied; the word *analysis* actually comes from a root meaning "to break into constituent parts." Systems thinking, in contrast, focuses on how the object being studied interacts with the other constituents of the system—a set of elements that interact to produce behavior—of which it is a part. Instead of isolating smaller and smaller parts of the system being studied, systems thinking works by expanding the company's view to take into account larger and larger numbers of interactions as an issue is analyzed. A systems approach often results in strikingly different conclusions than those generated by traditional forms of analysis, especially when applied to a complex decision that has many implications for the firm.

The character of systems thinking makes it extremely effective for the most difficult types of problems to solve: those involving complex issues, those that depend a great deal on the past or on the actions of others, and those stemming from ineffective coordination among the parties involved. Research on the experiences of companies shows that there are many benefits to be gained by a systems approach to decision making. It turns out that many of these benefits would also go a long way toward mitigating the occurrence of the Winner's Curse.

More effective problem solving

Nobody will disagree with the view that it is better to solve the *correct* problem suboptimally than to solve the *wrong* problem optimally. Without a clear understanding of the big picture, leaders tend to focus only on the behaviors and events associated with specific problems rather than on the reason for trying to solve the problem in the first place. For example, in the case we have already examined, the wireless managers were focused on winning licenses to get into third-generation mobile services, and this may well have been the wrong problem to solve. The correct problem was to ensure that the company provided advanced wireless services, which it could have done in a limited but effective way with the spectrum it already had. An important outcome from the problem of how to approach 3G licensing was to be profitable rather than debt-ridden.

When focusing on the local rather than the global issue, it is likely that decision makers will be affected by psychological effects such as representation bias, availability bias, anchoring, and an asymmetric response to winning versus losing, thus leading them to solve the wrong problem. The systems approach leads to more effective problem solving in cases where the decision involves uncertainty and competition. Take the example of Tyco, which had a reasonable strategy of expanding the company and getting into select technologies by mergers and acquisitions. In the process of expanding, Kozlowski and the senior management lost sight of the big picture and got into the mindset of pursuing all potential acquisition candidates. The psychological impact of focusing on the local chase was devastating.

More effective corporate planning

A corporate planning process includes identifying the desired results (goals and outcomes), what outputs (tangible results) will indicate that those results have been achieved, what processes will produce those outputs, and what resources are required to enable those processes in the system. When corporate planning is done with a systems view, one tries to embed each of these processes in a higher-level context. For example, the processes that can yield a particular result would not only be analyzed from the perspective of the company and its shareholders, they would also be examined from the point of view of the industry. This kind of analysis might tell the company that there are better ways of building an optical switch than the one that it is planning. This realization might prompt the company to either abandon an acquisition that it is contemplating or to change a product under development. Using a systems approach at every step of the corporate planning process will help ensure that you avoid mistakes.

Avoiding founder's syndrome

Founder's syndrome occurs when an organization operates according to the personality of one of its members (usually the founder), rather than according to its mission. When first starting their organizations, founders have to do whatever it takes to get the company off the ground, including making seat-of-the-pants decisions in order to deal with the frequent crises that arise suddenly in the workplace. As a result, founders often cannot see the larger picture and are unable to effectively plan and make proactive decisions. Consequently, the organization gets stuck in a highly reactive mode and deals with one major crisis after another. The best cure for this syndrome is using a systems approach to obtain a broader understanding of the structures and processes of an organization, including an appreciation for the importance of planning.

Systems thinking forces the decision makers, whether they are the CEO, senior management, or the board, to think outside the box. All corporate officers need to buy into the concept of systems thinking to improve the effectiveness of problem solving and corporate planning and to avoid the founder's syndrome. Two important components of a systems approach are scenario planning and game theory (or competitor) analysis, which we will now describe.

Scenario planning

Scenario planning goes hand in hand with a systems approach and is useful in situations that are fraught with uncertainty. Scenarios are specially constructed stories about the future. Each scenario represents a distinct, plausible world. The purpose of scenario planning is not to predict the future but rather to show how different forces can manipulate the future in different directions. It is important to realize this distinction, for this procedure helps to identify these forces if and when they happen. The utility of scenario planning lies in its ability to anticipate the future. When this is accomplished, the ability to better respond to future events is increased. Table 10-2 contains an example of using scenario planning for corporate strategy.[4]

Scenario planning allows users to explore the implications of several alternative futures before making a decision.[5] For example, the development of any prescription drug is fraught with uncertainty. Each potential drug has to go through many different decision points: during the initial lab tests, at the first application with the Food and Drug Administration (FDA), during clinical trials, and so on. At each of these points, drug development could go awry or could show promise. A well-defined process has to be followed in order to get final approval from the FDA, and a scenario analysis would take into account every possible combination of events (good

---

4. This case example is from Meeting Facilitators International, www.facilitators.com/scenario-planning.htm.

5. There are many well-known sources that deal in detail with scenario planning. We recommend Paul J. H. Schoemaker, "Scenario Planning: A Tool for Strategic Thinking," *Sloan Management Review* (Winter 1995): 25–40; and Pierre Wack, "Scenarios: The Uncharted Waters Ahead," *Harvard Business Review* (September–October 1985): 72–89.

Table 10-2. Case study of scenario planning

Situation

This company is a large and successful organization. However, senior management is afraid that many people do not fully comprehend the magnitude of the threats they are facing. Far too many people see the future as business as usual. A scenario planning approach is used to build consensus around the need to change.

Objective

The objective is to help the management team acknowledge and address the threats they are facing and to then come up with a viable strategy to counter these threats.

Process

To accomplish this, three very different future scenarios are developed. In two of these scenarios, the client's business is all but taken over by competition from alternative business approaches. Teams made up of a cross-section of different levels and departments within the organization are assigned to each scenario. They are instructed to gather evidence and to develop arguments as to why their description of what the future holds is the most likely. When the groups all meet, the two most likely descriptions of the future do not present very attractive situations at all. Once people realize that the future could be pretty grim if they do not take action, they are able to move on to the questions of what to change and how to change.

Results

The company is well on its way to successfully countering the threats that it once would not acknowledge.

Source: Meeting Facilitators International. www.facilitators.com/scenario-planning.htm.

or bad) that will affect the final result. By doing a scenario analysis, one avoids the dangers of pursuing an analysis based on a single set of assumptions and forecasts. For example, using a scenario-based approach to problem solving, Bristol-Meyers Squibb might never have pursued the cancer drug Erbitux. By surfacing, challenging, and altering beliefs, managers can test their assumptions in a nonthreatening environment. Having examined the full range of possible futures, the company can more rapidly modify its strategic direction as actual events unfold. There are four environmental factors that affect scenario planning.

Sociopsychological issues. Much of future uncertainty comes from the way humans interact with systems. Even if one comes up with a cost-effective technological marvel, sometimes people just do not adopt it. For example, the technology for videophones, which are telephones that can project images of the calling and called parties, has been around for more than 25 years, but no one has really wanted it. Every 7 years or so, AT&T tries to market services associated with videophones, but has never been successful. For a number of reasons connected to taste, lifestyle, privacy, security, and so on, people either get excited about a new technology or service, or are cold toward it. A scenario planning exercise should take into account different sociopsychological issues.

Economic issues.   Business decisions are affected by economic uncertainty. One might be ready to introduce a dramatic new product or service, but if the economy is in recession, then the launch will be a failure. The future is affected by macroeconomic trends and forces shaping the economy as a whole as well as microeconomic trends, such as competition among small, innovative companies. The different ways in which economic uncertainty can affect a firm should be a factor in scenario planning.

Technological issues.   Technology creates a great deal of uncertainty about the future. The technology infrastructure is changing rapidly, and many business processes are becoming obsolete. Thus, strategic planning in almost any business has to consider different manifestations of future technology. Even those who are trying to compete in technology-based industries cannot say for sure whether their technology will be superior to their competitors' or not. Scenario planning examines different ways in which technology will affect corporate business decisions.

Political issues.   One of the most important impacts on any business decision is political uncertainty. In the domestic market, the focus is largely on regulatory uncertainty. For example, will there be government intervention or a free, competitive market? How will taxation affect decisions? Will participatory government prevail in the upcoming century? In the international market, there are a number of uncertainties, including tariffs and barriers to entry that can change, domestic content laws, political turmoil, and so on. These days, when most enterprises are global in nature, political uncertainty has to be part of a scenario planning exercise.

The key steps in the scenario planning process are to

- clearly state corporate strategy;
- determine the scope and time frame of the decision problem at hand;
- identify the current assumptions about potential futures and the positions of individuals who influence these decisions;

- create divergent, yet plausible, scenarios with underlying assumptions of how the future might evolve after the decision has been made;
- test the impact of key variables in each scenario;
- develop action plans based on solutions that are robust across scenarios; and
- monitor events as they unfold and be prepared to modify the plan as required.

Through the use of the scenario planning methodology, a company can

- examine and challenge both implicit and explicit beliefs and assumptions about the business, its likely future, and the specific decision that it is currently contemplating;
- develop a farsighted view of the future to enable the organization to analyze the life cycle impact of its acquisition decisions;
- establish contingency plans to respond purposefully to changes in the environment, whether the final decision is to try and triumph in the current business situation or to walk away from it.

Game theory

Game theory[6] is another useful mechanism for mitigating the possibility of the Winner's Curse. Game theory was developed on the life-and-death stage of World War II when British navy officers used it in the risky game of trying to outwit German submarine commanders. The officers developed processes for analyzing different scenarios, exploring interdependencies, and changing strategies midcourse—all while the action was unfolding around them. American and British mathematicians working on the war effort further refined this thinking into what was called *game theory*. In the process, they formed the kind of flexible decision-making structure required in the modern corporation.

Saul Gass offers a good description of game theory:

A basic example helps to illustrate the point. After learning how to play the game tick-tack-toe, you probably discovered a strategy of play that

6. For an extensive discussion on the use of game theory in business, the reader is referred to Pankaj Ghemawat, *Games Businesses Play: Cases and Models* (Cambridge, Mass.: MIT Press).

enables you to achieve at least a draw and even win if your opponent makes a mistake and you notice it. Sticking to that strategy ensures that you will not lose. This simple game illustrates the essential aspects of what is now called game theory. In it, a game is the set of rules that describe it. An instance of the game from beginning to end is known as a play of the game. And a pure strategy—such as the one you found for tick-tack-toe—is an overall plan specifying moves to be taken in all eventualities that can arise in a play of the game.[7]

Incorporating game theory as a business analytical tool ensures that the company analyzes the decisions through the eyes of competitors over time, and hence looks for solutions that will be robust no matter how the environment changes. Game theory suggests that it is advantageous for the company to constantly reassess decisions made in the planning process as the situation unfolds.

Analyze the business decision through the eyes of competitors

All analyses of games start just like the cat-and-mouse game of submarine warfare. You have to figure out how your opponent will react to every one of your moves, or how your opponent will preempt you to try to secure a first-mover advantage. The exercise of placing yourself in the shoes of your opponent will help prevent the tunnel vision that plays a critical role in enabling the Winner's Curse. Ray Smith outlines some of the techniques that Verizon used to put itself in the shoes of the competitor:

We've used three in particular:
- *Fishbowl*. This exercise brings everybody with an ax to grind on a given issue together in one room, with advocates of certain points of view in the center of the "fishbowl" and executives accountable for the decision on the outside. The experts present their data and debate one another, while the executives evaluate the quality of the facts at hand, expose weak positions, and analyze the strategic options.
- *Red team/Blue team*. In this variation of the classic war game, we assign managers to teams representing major competitors and have them plan the strategies they would use to beat us. This team research increases our competitive intelligence and

---

7. Saul Gass in *Scientific American*, http://www.sciam.com/askexpert_question.cfm?articleID=000B8A10–F94C-1ECC-8E1C809EC588EF21.

quickens our reflexes by building a competitive awareness into all our actions—rather like a good chess player is always aware of what an opponent will do in response to the next move.

- *Future mapping.* This is a fancy name for a way of looking at different scenarios for the future. We look at several alternative futures, or "end states," for our business, assign a probability to each one, and identify the forces that will determine whether that scenario will happen. The key is to select those actions with the biggest returns, the least risk, or both. Knowing that we can't manage every single variable, we're trying to make sure we're concentrating on those that will give us the most bang for the buck.[8]

Look for robust solutions

When using game theory for structuring business decisions, one always starts with an analysis of different scenarios. These scenarios come about because the present and future environment could change, or because competitors could react in different ways. We have already discussed the use of scenario planning as a vehicle for understanding different worlds in which business decisions are made. Game theory provides a way to analyze these scenarios and come up with a decision that is robust, no matter how the game is played out. In many cases, this kind of analysis might make all the difference between truly winning or winning only if the gods are aligned with you. Cases where such a robust decision cannot be found would also be informative for senior management. In either case, game theory helps to reduce the risks of the Winner's Curse.

We quote Ray Smith on how he used game theory to make a critical robust decision for his company:

> This is the principle we've used at Bell Atlantic in making decisions about modernizing our telephone plant. We know that, like every telephone company, we have to upgrade our old copper plant with fiber optics and other broadband technologies. We also know that interactive applications are driving the market and that the costs of high-speed lines and other digital technologies are dropping dramatically. However, we don't know precisely how digital content will be delivered. We don't know exactly what the product mix will be—PCs? digital TVs? the new Internet appli-

---

8. Ray Smith, quoted in "Business as a War Game: A Report from the Battlefront," *Fortune*, September 30, 1996.

ances?—or what people will pay for them. And we don't know how digital technologies will become an affordable, mass-market phenomenon.

So rather than commit our capital dollars to a limited technology platform that will be correct based on only one reading of the tea leaves, we have opted to deploy a flexible, full-featured digital network that will deliver high-speed interactive content in any form—data, video, or voice. Meanwhile, we're covering all the bases by supplementing our existing network with new digital technologies and by entering new markets quickly with low-cost, easily deployed technologies such as wireless video. With this flexible strategy, we are in a position to win, no matter how the market develops.[9]

Constantly reassess business assumptions and decisions

Game theory examines situations where sequential decisions have to be made. The method suggests how to make the best decisions today in a situation where the environment changes over time and where competitors react. Game theory shows how anticipating the future and constantly reassessing it is the optimal way to make decisions over a longer time horizon. Senior managers want clear yes-or-no answers after a period of study and believe that further analysis will lead to confusion and indecision. Game theory questions this behavior. In order to avoid the Winner's Curse, it is important to recognize the dynamic nature of business and the uncertainty of future events.

One way to take future uncertainty into account is for the board to establish an independent review process that examines all major decisions as the future unfolds, without questioning the initial judgment of the CEO or senior management. Again quoting Ray Smith:

> At Bell Atlantic we call this "performance assurance." A senior-level executive is given the responsibility for monitoring our progress on our top 20 or 30 corporate priorities. This highly respected executive works with the operating units to revisit goals and targets, track progress, analyze problems, and basically keep us from marching resolutely down blind alleys. If this executive is carefully selected and performs the task without regard to politics, the operating managers come to regard him or her as a built-in sanity check who helps keep the organization focused and aligned.[10]

9. Ray Smith, quoted in "Business as a War Game."
10. Ray Smith, quoted in "Business as a War Game."

To make effective use of game theory, organizations must learn to analyze, adjust, and change direction in midflight, without losing the sense of purpose and action required in a competitive world. The organization must be committed to a systematic and constant reassessment of its business decisions. The game theory approach to business strategy also requires a different kind of corporate manager: flexible, intellectually rigorous, and highly tolerant of ambiguity. It takes a special kind of manager to revisit decisions constantly and reverse course, even at the risk of personal embarrassment.

It also takes a special kind of company to nurture a climate of open, frank, and relentlessly objective discussion so that all variables are scrutinized honestly and without political repercussions. The loyalty required in this system differs subtly but crucially from the loyalty that prevails in most hierarchical organizations. This is loyalty not to one's own advancement or one's boss or one's department, but to the truth as it bears on the goals of the organization. In the last analysis, the game theory approach to business strategy challenges corporate leaders to build not only a different kind of system but a different kind of team.

Conclusions

All of us are susceptible to the Winner's Curse; we can overpay for something we passionately want to acquire, or, if we are successful, we rest on our laurels and let complacency carry us along when we really should be taking action. The Winner's Curse does not happen with every decision, but it happens enough that we should be aware of it. This book has presented a general model of the Winner's Curse and examples that illustrate its pernicious effect on individuals, organizations, and industries.[11] We hope that the evidence has been convincing and that you have been warned about the Winner's Curse.

We would like to end this book on a positive note. We believe that the recommendations in this chapter will go a long way toward mitigating the impact of the Winner's Curse. Awareness of its potential is the first step. The second is to take positive action along the lines suggested here.

---

11. We have not discussed the Winner's Curse as it applies to nations because of the controversy that it would raise. However, consider the old saying that a country "has won the battle but lost the war." Equally plausible in today's imbalance in power among countries and with the rise of terrorists is the possibility of winning the war, but losing the peace.

A careful analysis of valuation decisions and likely outcomes has to reduce the incidence of the Curse. An ongoing effort to look for disruptive threats to your business model will help overcome complacency.

The Winner's Curse is not automatic nor is it guaranteed. Those who, for whatever reasons, do not respect the Curse are likely to experience it and some potentially costly consequences. By remaining suitably humble and taking some of the steps suggested here, you can become an observer of the Winner's Curse rather than a victim.

When you are in a situation that involves a purchase, an acquisition, a merger, or a bid, and the price of what you want to acquire keeps going up, the most important questions to take away from this book are: When will someone say, "No, it's time to stop," and who will say it?